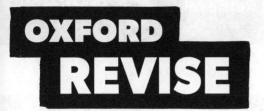

OXFORD REVISE

KEY STAGE 3

SCIENCE

COMPLETE REVISION AND PRACTICE

Series Editor: Primrose Kitten

Jo Locke

Helen Reynolds

Reviewers:

Philippa Gardom Hulme

Lewis Matheson

Alom Shaha

Jessica Walmsley

OXFORD
UNIVERSITY PRESS

Contents

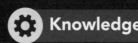 Knowledge  Retrieval 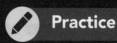 Practice

 Shade in each level of the circle as you feel more confident and ready for your exam.

Physics

How to use this book

This book uses a three-step approach to revision: **Knowledge**, **Retrieval**, and **Practice**.
It is important that you do all three – they work together to make your revision effective.

1 Knowledge

Knowledge comes first. Each chapter starts with a **Knowledge Organiser**. These are clear, easy-to-understand, summaries of the content that you need to know for your exam. The information is organised to show how one idea flows into the next so you can learn how all the science is tied together, instead of lots of disconnected facts.

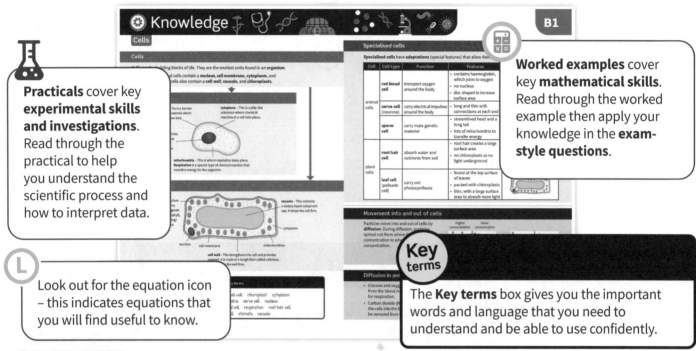

Practicals cover key **experimental skills and investigations**. Read through the practical to help you understand the scientific process and how to interpret data.

Look out for the equation icon – this indicates equations that you will find useful to know.

Worked examples cover key **mathematical skills**. Read through the worked example then apply your knowledge in the **exam-style questions**.

The **Key terms** box gives you the important words and language that you need to understand and be able to use confidently.

2 Retrieval

The **Retrieval questions** help you learn and quickly recall the information you have acquired. These are short questions and answers about the content in the Knowledge Organiser. Cover up the answers with some paper and write down as many answers as you can from memory. Check back to the Knowledge Organiser for any you got wrong, then cover the answers and attempt *all* the questions again until you can answer *all* the questions correctly.

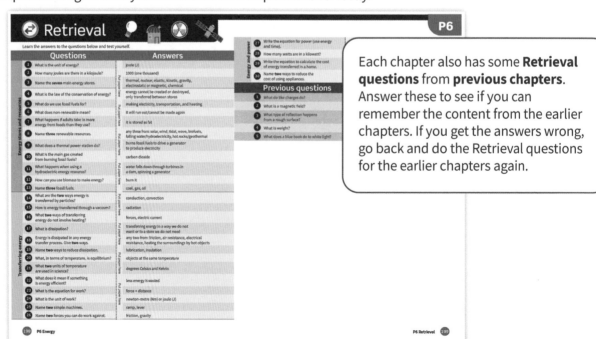

Each chapter also has some **Retrieval questions** from **previous chapters**. Answer these to see if you can remember the content from the earlier chapters. If you get the answers wrong, go back and do the Retrieval questions for the earlier chapters again.

Each chapter also has some **Retrieval questions** from **previous chapters**. Answer these to see if you can remember the content from the previous chapters. If you get the answers wrong, go back and do the Retrieval questions for the previous chapters again.

Make sure you revisit the Retrieval questions on different days to help them stick in your memory. You need to write down the answers each time, or say them out loud, otherwise it will not work.

3 Practice

Once you think you know the Knowledge Organiser and Retrieval answers really well, you can move on to the final stage: **Practice**.

Each chapter has lots of **exam-style questions**, including some questions from previous chapters, to help you apply all the knowledge you have learnt and can retrieve.

Each question has a difficulty icon that shows the level of challenge.

 These questions build your confidence.

 These questions consolidate your knowledge.

 These questions stretch your understanding.

Make sure you attempt all of the questions, no matter what grade you are aiming for.

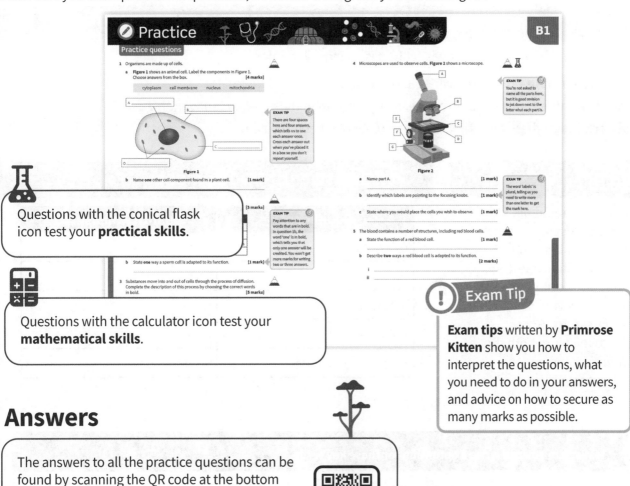

Questions with the conical flask icon test your **practical skills**.

Questions with the calculator icon test your **mathematical skills**.

Answers

The answers to all the practice questions can be found by scanning the QR code at the bottom of every right-hand page, or by visiting the link go.oup.com/OR/KS3/Science. You can also find the glossaries and more revision help there too.

! Exam Tip

Exam tips written by **Primrose Kitten** show you how to interpret the questions, what you need to do in your answers, and advice on how to secure as many marks as possible.

Working scientifically

Planning an investigation

Scientific plan

Scientific investigations are experiments where you collect **data** (**observations** or measurements) to answer a scientific question. A scientific plan includes:

- the scientific question that you are trying to answer
- the *independent* and *dependent* variables
- a prediction or hypothesis
- a list of variables you will control, and how you will do this
- a list of the equipment you will need – this may include a diagram
- a step-by-step method of how you will collect your data
- any safety precautions that you should take.

Prediction and hypothesis

Scientists often have an idea about what they might expect to happen in an investigation. This is called their **prediction**.

Scientists back up their predictions with reasons why they think something will happen, using scientific knowledge. This is known as a **hypothesis**.

Variables

Anything that can change during an investigation is called a variable:

- *independent* **variable** – this is the variable you change
- *dependent* **variable** – this variable changes as you change the *independent* variable
- **control variables** – these are the variables you need to keep the same

Equipment

Your equipment should be able to produce measurements or observations to help you answer your scientific question. For example, you could use a microscope to see very small objects. You need to choose equipment to measure both the *independent* variable and the *dependent* variable.

Common scientific equipment

Equipment	Quantity measured
ruler or tape measure	length
thermometer	temperature
stopwatch	time
balance	mass
measuring cylinder	volume

Key terms

Make sure you can write a definition for these key terms

accurate   control measure   control variable   data   dependent variable   hazard   hypothesis   independent variable   observation   precise   prediction   repeatable   reproducible   risk

Risk assessments

You may need to complete a risk assessment for an investigation before you carry it out. A risk assessment usually consists of three sections: **hazard**, **risk**, and **control measure**.

A risk assessment will help you stay safe.

Something that could hurt you or anybody else	How you could hurt yourself	How you can reduce the risk

Hazard	Risk	Control measure
Broken glass.	Cut yourself when clearing it up.	Use a dustpan and brush, and place glass in a glass bin.

Hazard symbols

Hazard symbols warn people of dangers, and helps them to work safely.

These symbols will help you stay safe in a lab.

Oxidising   Flammable   Corrosive   Compressed gas   Toxic   Irritant

Accurate and precise data

It is important to collect data that is both **accurate** and **precise**:

- Accurate data is close to the true value of what you are trying to measure.
- Precise data means getting similar results if you repeat measurements.

not accurate   accurate   not accurate   accurate
not precise   not precise   precise   precise

Repeatable and reproducible data

Precise data has a very small spread. If you repeat an investigation several times, your data should be similar. The data is then said to be **repeatable**.

Sometimes, the same experiment is repeated by other students, or by using a different method or equipment. If these experiments produce similar data, then the data is said to be **reproducible**.

Working scientifically

Recording and presenting data 1

Simple results table

To answer a scientific question, you should take several observations or measurements to see a pattern or trend. Use a results table to help you to organise your data.

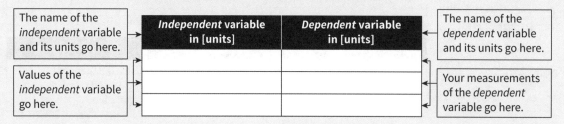

The name of the *independent* variable and its units go here.

Values of the *independent* variable go here.

Independent variable in [units]	*Dependent* variable in [units]

The name of the *dependent* variable and its units go here.

Your measurements of the *dependent* variable go here.

Not all data are numbers. Sometimes, you need to use words to record observations.

Results table for repeat measurements

Repeats will help you to spot anomalous results. An **anomalous result**, or outlier, is a result that is very different to the others when repeating measurements. Anomalous results should not be included when calculating a mean result.

Independent variable in [units]	*Dependent* variable in [units]			
	1st measurement	2nd measurement	3rd measurement	Mean

Values of the *independent* variable go from smallest to largest.

If possible take each measurement three times.

The mean value of the *dependent* variable will be written here.

Mean

$$mean = \frac{result\ 1 + result\ 2 + result\ 3 + ...}{number\ of\ results}$$

For example, a student collects leaf length measurements of 13 cm, 14 cm and 18 cm. The mean leaf length is:

$$mean = \frac{13\,cm + 14\,cm + 18\,cm}{3} = \frac{45\,cm}{3} = 15\,cm$$

Median and mode

Sometimes it is useful to use a different type of average:

- **mode** – the most common value or group in the data
- **median** – the middle value, when the data are placed in numerical order.

Types of data

The data you collect in an investigation can be:

- **continuous** – the data can have any value within a range, such as temperature
- **discrete** – the data can have whole-number values only, such as shoe size
- **categorical** – the value is a word, such as 'blue'.

Choosing a chart type

Different types of data are displayed using different charts:

- **bar chart** – used to plot discrete and categorical data
- **line graph** – used when both the *independent* and *dependent* variables are continuous
- **pie chart** – used to plot discrete and categorical data
- **histogram** – used to plot continuous grouped data

Bar charts

Bar charts are used for discrete and categorical data. Think about what type of data you have when choosing your chart.

Plot the *dependent* variable on the *y*-axis. Choose which numbers the axis should start and finish on, and mark out an equal scale inserted.

Label the *y*-axis with the *dependent* variable, and its units.

The *independent* variable is plotted on the *x*-axis. Each category or value should be equally spaced along the axis.

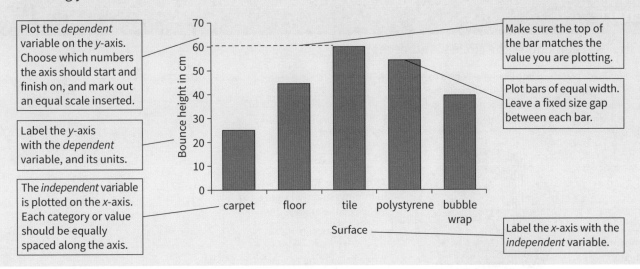

Make sure the top of the bar matches the value you are plotting.

Plot bars of equal width. Leave a fixed size gap between each bar.

Label the *x*-axis with the *independent* variable.

Key terms

Make sure you can write a definition for these key terms

anomalous result   bar chart   categorical   continuous
discrete   histogram   line graph   median   mode   pie chart

Working scientifically

Recording and presenting data 2

Histogram

A histogram is a chart that is used to visualise the shape of a set of data. It presents continuous data in groups.

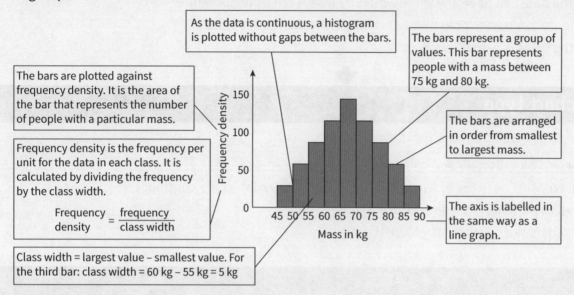

As the data is continuous, a histogram is plotted without gaps between the bars.

The bars represent a group of values. This bar represents people with a mass between 75 kg and 80 kg.

The bars are plotted against frequency density. It is the area of the bar that represents the number of people with a particular mass.

The bars are arranged in order from smallest to largest mass.

Frequency density is the frequency per unit for the data in each class. It is calculated by dividing the frequency by the class width.

$$\text{Frequency density} = \frac{\text{frequency}}{\text{class width}}$$

The axis is labelled in the same way as a line graph.

Class width = largest value – smallest value. For the third bar: class width = 60 kg – 55 kg = 5 kg

Histograms look like bar charts, but they have no gaps between the bars because the data is continuous.

Pie chart

Pie charts use segments of the circle to represent data.

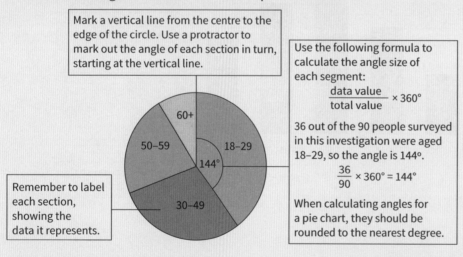

Mark a vertical line from the centre to the edge of the circle. Use a protractor to mark out the angle of each section in turn, starting at the vertical line.

Use the following formula to calculate the angle size of each segment:

$$\frac{\text{data value}}{\text{total value}} \times 360°$$

36 out of the 90 people surveyed in this investigation were aged 18–29, so the angle is 144°.

$$\frac{36}{90} \times 360° = 144°$$

When calculating angles for a pie chart, they should be rounded to the nearest degree.

Remember to label each section, showing the data it represents.

This is the age range of people who wanted to carry out a bungee jump. Pie charts are used to show percentages, or proportions of a total. The whole pie chart represents 100%. It is then divided into sections to represent data values.

Key terms — Make sure you can write a definition for these key terms

line of best fit   pattern (trend)

Line graph

Line graphs are used when both the *independent* and *dependent* variables are continuous.

Values on both axes should increase in equal intervals, for example, 2, 4, 6... or 5, 10, 15.

Plot the *dependent* variable on the *y*-axis. Label the axis, including units.

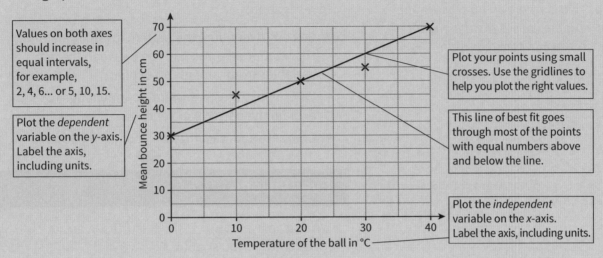

Plot your points using small crosses. Use the gridlines to help you plot the right values.

This line of best fit goes through most of the points with equal numbers above and below the line.

Plot the *independent* variable on the *x*-axis. Label the axis, including units.

Line graphs can show trends in your results.

To make the **pattern** or **trend** easier to see on a graph, you should add a **line of best fit**. This is a straight line or a smooth curve that goes through, or very close to, as many data points as possible.

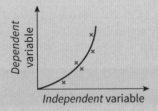

If the *independent* variable increases, then the *dependent* variable increases.

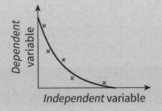

If the *independent* variable increases, then the *dependent* variable decreases.

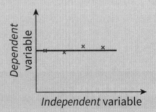

If the *independent* variable increases, the *dependent* variable does not change.

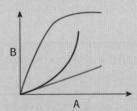

In these graphs, if A increases then B increases.

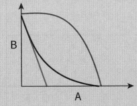

In these graphs, if A increases then B decreases.

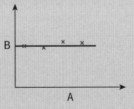

In this graph, if A increases B does not change.

Working scientifically

Analysing and evaluating data

Linear relationships

Straight-line graphs show a **linear relationship**. This is where an increase in the *independent* variable causes the *dependent* variable to increase at a constant rate.

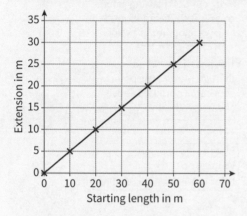

A straight-line graph that passes through the origin (0, 0) is a special type of linear relationship, called a **directly proportional relationship** – doubling the *independent* variable causes a doubling of the *dependent* variable.

Conclusions

A conclusion states what you have found out in an investigation:

- Start by describing the pattern in your data or the relationship you can see between the two variables from your graph or chart.
- Where possible, use scientific knowledge to explain the pattern or trend.
- Compare your results with your prediction.

Evaluations

Writing an evaluation is the final step in an investigation. You should:

1 identify the strengths and weaknesses in your results

2 decide how confident you are in your conclusion

3 suggest and explain improvements to your method, so you can collect data of better quality if you do the investigation again.

Simple equations

Data can be substituted into equations to describe relationships and explain results. When you write an equatio
you can use words or symbols.

Equation in words	Equation in symbols	Units
weight (N) = mass (kg) × gravitational field strength (N/kg)	$W = mg$	newton (N), kilogram (kg), newtons per kilogram (N/kg)
speed (m/s) = $\dfrac{\text{distance (m)}}{\text{time (s)}}$	$v = \dfrac{d}{t}$	metres per second (m/s), metre (m), second (s)
pressure (N/m²) = $\dfrac{\text{force (N)}}{\text{area (m}^2\text{)}}$	$P = \dfrac{F}{A}$	newtons per metres squared (N/m²), newton (N), metres squared (m²)
resistance (Ω) = $\dfrac{\text{potential difference (V)}}{\text{current (A)}}$	$R = \dfrac{V}{I}$	ohm (Ω), volt (V), amp (A)

Key terms **Make sure you can write a definition for these key terms**

bias   directly proportional relationship   linear relationship   peer review
random error   range   repeatable   secondary data   spread   systematic error

Change the subject

You can change the subject of an equation to find a different value in the relationship.

$R = \dfrac{V}{I}$ ⟩ multiply both sides by I

$R \times I = \dfrac{V \times \cancel{I}}{\cancel{I}}$ ⟩ cancel the I

$R \times I = V$ or $V = I R$

Identifying strengths and weaknesses

To identify strengths and weaknesses:

1 identify anomalous results or outliers
2 look at the **spread** of data – the spread is the difference between the highest and the lowest readings in a set of repeat measurements
3 check for errors.

Types of error

Random error is where an unexpected change affects your results, such as the temperature of the room changing because someone opens a door.

Systematic error is where something consistently affects all of your results. These are often caused by faulty equipment, such as a newtonmeter showing a reading without a load attached.

Confidence in conclusion and improvements

You can be confident in your data if:

• there are few anomalies – this means your data is unlikely to contain errors
• there is a small spread in the data – this means your method is **repeatable**.

You could also look at **secondary data** – graphs or data that someone else has collected.

You can improve an investigation in three ways:

1 Use a bigger **range** of results. This means using larger or smaller values of the *independent* variable. The wider the range, the more certain you can be that your conclusion is always true.
2 Complete more repeat readings. You should always take at least three repeat readings for each value of the *independent* variable.
3 Use different equipment. If you had anomalies, or a large spread of data, you could use different equipment to collect your measurements.

Peer review and objectivity

For the results of an investigation to be accepted as scientific evidence, it must be **peer reviewed**. The data and conclusions are checked by other scientists working in the same field.

The method, results, and analysis of an investigation must be objective – that is, without bias. If someone has a **bias**, it means that they have a preference for something, which can be unfair. Bias can include personal opinions, statements with no factual basis, or prejudice against something or someone.

Understanding command words

Tips for answering questions

1 **Underline the verb in the question.** Whilst you are learning, refer to the command word table (below) and the examples to make sure you are doing what you need to do.

2 **Check the number of marks.** These tell you how many points you need to make, stages in your calculation, or reasons you need to give.

3 **Write separate points on separate lines.** This will make it clear that you have answered in full.

Command words

Verb	Meaning	Verb	Meaning
Analyse	Interpret data to arrive at a conclusion	Give	Produce an answer from recall or from given information
Calculate	Work out the value of something	Identify	Name or otherwise specify
Comment	Present an informed opinion	Interpret	Draw conclusions from information provided (which may be on a graph)
Compare	Identify similarities and/or differences	Label	Provide appropriate names on a diagram
Complete	Finish a task by adding to given information	List	List a number of features or points without further elaboration
Define	Specify the meaning of a word or phrase	Name	Identify using a recognised technical term
Describe	Set out characteristics (say what it looks like, or did)	Predict	Give a plausible outcome
Determine	Use given data or information to obtain an answer	Show	Provide structured evidence to reach a conclusion
Draw	Produce a diagram	Sketch	Draw approximately
Estimate	Assign an approximate (rough) value	State	Express in clear terms
Evaluate	Judge from available evidence	Suggest	Present a possible case, solution or reason
Explain	Set out purposes or reasons		

Worked examples

1 A nerve cell is an example of a specialised animal cell. <u>Describe</u> **two** ways the cell is adapted to perform its function. **[4 marks]**

Sample answer

| This gains the first mark for identifying a feature. | This gains the first mark for describing its function. |

Nerve cells are long   so they can carry impulses across long distances.
Nerve cells have connections at each end   so they can join to other nerve cells.

| This gains the second feature mark… | …and the second mark for describing its function. |

EXAM TIP

- Identify **two** features in the cell. (There may be more features you can choose but naming more will gain no further marks.)
- Describe how each feature helps the cell to function.
- Think of the four things you can say to gain four marks.

2 Here is some information about the speed of light in different materials.

Material	Speed of light in the material in million km/s
glass	200
diamond	130

Describe and explain what you would see if you shone beams of light at an angle into blocks made of glass and diamond. **[4 marks]**

Sample answer

This gains the first mark for describing what happens.

The beam of light would change direction (be refracted) as it goes into each block. This is because light slows down as it goes from air into a medium like diamond or glass.

This gains the second mark for explaining why (using 'because').

This gains the third mark for using the data in the table...

The speed of light in diamond is less than the speed of light in glass. The beam of light would change direction more in the diamond than in the glass.

...and the fourth mark for linking the data to the description.

EXAM TIP

- This question asks you to 'describe what you would see'.
- Then it asks you to 'explain' why that is what you saw.
- Next, you need to compare the materials in the table using the data.
- You should refer back to what you would see.
- Four marks means that you need to provide four points or key pieces of information.

3 An astronaut has a mass of 70 kg. <u>Calculate</u> their weight on Mars where $g = 3.7$ N/kg. **[4 marks]**

Sample answer

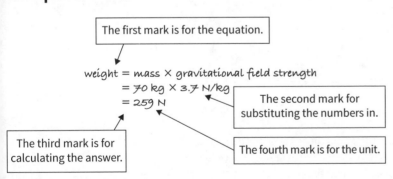

The first mark is for the equation.

weight = mass × gravitational field strength
= 70 kg × 3.7 N/kg
= 259 N

The second mark for substituting the numbers in.

The third mark is for calculating the answer.

The fourth mark is for the unit.

EXAM TIP

- Use the following process – equation, numbers in, answer, unit – each element is worth one mark.
- Write the equals signs underneath each other.

There are more tips and hints of how to answer questions throughout this book – look for the ⊙.

⚙ Knowledge

B1 Cells

Cells

Cells are the building blocks of life. They are the smallest units found in an **organism**.

Both plant and animal cells contain a **nucleus**, **cell membrane**, **cytoplasm**, and **mitochondria**. Plant cells also contain a **cell wall**, **vacuole**, and **chloroplasts**.

Animal cells

cell membrane – This is a barrier around the cell. It controls which substances can move into and out of the cell.

cytoplasm – This is a jelly-like substance where chemical reactions in a cell take place.

nucleus – This controls the cell and contains genetic material. Genetic information is needed to make new cells.

mitochondria – This is where respiration takes place. **Respiration** is a special type of chemical reaction that transfers energy for the organism.

Plant cells

chloroplasts – This is where **photosynthesis** happens. Chloroplasts contain a green substance called chlorophyll, which absorbs light energy transferred from the Sun.

vacuole – This contains a watery liquid called cell sap. It keeps the cell firm.

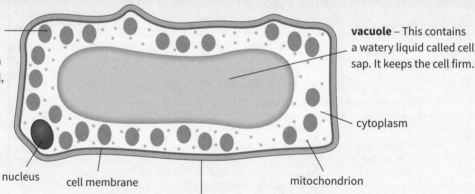

cytoplasm

nucleus   cell membrane   mitochondrion

cell wall – This strengthens the cell and provides support. It is made of a tough fibre called cellulose, which makes the wall firm.

Key terms

Make sure you can write a definition for these key terms

adaptation   cell   cell membrane   cell wall   chloroplast   cytoplasm
diffusion   leaf cell   mitochondria   nerve cell   nucleus
organism   photosynthesis   red blood cell   respiration   root hair cell
specialised cell   sperm cell   stomata   vacuole

Specialised cells

Specialised cells have **adaptations** (special features) that allow them to do a specific job or function.

Cell	Cell type	Function	Features	Diagram
animal cells	**red blood cell**	transport oxygen around the body	• contains haemoglobin, which joins to oxygen • no nucleus • disc shaped to increase surface area	
	nerve cell (neurone)	carry electrical impulses around the body	• long and thin with connections at each end	
	sperm cell	carry male genetic material	• streamlined head and a long tail • lots of mitochondria to transfer energy	
plant cells	**root hair cell**	absorb water and nutrients from soil	• root hair creates a large surface area • no chloroplasts as no light underground	
	leaf cell (palisade cell)	carry out photosynthesis	• found at the top surface of leaves • packed with chloroplasts • thin, with a large surface area to absorb more light	

Movement into and out of cells

Particles move into and out of cells by **diffusion**. During diffusion, particles spread out from where they are in a higher concentration to where they are in a lower concentration.

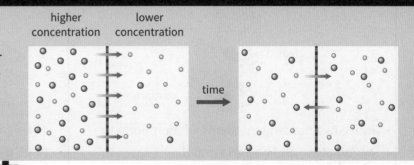

higher concentration   lower concentration

time

Diffusion in animal cells

- Glucose and oxygen diffuse from the blood *into* the cells for respiration.
- Carbon dioxide diffuses *out* of the cells into the blood so it can be removed from the body.

Diffusion in plant cells

- Carbon dioxide and oxygen diffuse into and out of the leaf through **stomata**. These are tiny holes found mainly on the underside of the leaf.
- Water diffuses into the root hair cells from the soil. It then travels to other cells in the plant by diffusion. Inside the cell, it fills up the vacuole. This pushes on the cell wall, making the cell rigid.

B1 Cells continued

Practical: Using microscopes

Microscopes are used to observe (look at) very small objects, like cells. They magnify the image using lenses.

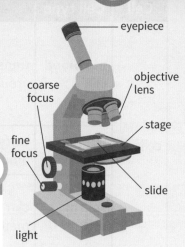

- Samples observed must be very thin.
- Coloured dyes, such as iodine, can be added to make structures easier to see.
- The object being observed is placed on the stage.
- The coarse and fine focus knobs are used to focus the image.

Worked example: Magnification

A microscope has an eyepiece lens with ×10 magnification and an objective lens with ×50 magnification. Calculate the total magnification.

total magnification = eye piece lens magnification × objective lens magnification

$$= \quad ×10 \quad × \quad ×50$$
$$= \quad ×500$$

Ⓛ

Unicellular organisms

A **unicellular** organism is made up of only one cell. Examples include amoebas and euglenas.

To reproduce, they split themselves in two to form two identical cells. This is known as binary fission.

Amoeba	Euglena
nucleus food vacuole cell membrane contractile vacuole	chloroplast eye spot – detects light contractile vacuole nucleus flagellum
• move by changing the shape of their body • engulf algae and bacteria and digest them in their food vacuole	• move using their flagellum • photosynthesise to make food; however, in poor light conditions, they engulf bacteria and algae

Key terms

Make sure you can write a definition for these key terms

microscope   unicellular

Learn the answers to the questions below and test yourself.

	B1 Questions		Answers
Cell structure			
1	What is a cell?		the smallest functional unit in an organism – the building block of life
2	Name the **four** components found in all cells.		nucleus, cytoplasm, cell membrane, mitochondria
3	What is the function of the cell nucleus?	*Put paper here*	controls the cell and contains genetic material
4	What is the cytoplasm?		jelly-like substance found in cells, where all the chemical reactions take place
5	What is the function of the cell membrane?		controls which substances can move into and out of the cell
6	What are mitochondria?	*Put paper here*	cell components where respiration takes place
7	Name the **three** components found in plant cells only.		cell wall, vacuole, chloroplasts
8	What is the function of the cell wall?	*Put paper here*	surrounds the cell, providing support
9	What is the function of the vacuole?		contains cell sap and helps to keep the cell firm
10	What are chloroplasts?		cell structure where photosynthesis takes place
Specialised cells			
11	What types of cell have adaptations that mean they can do a specific job or function?	*Put paper here*	specialised cells
12	Give **three** examples of specialised animal cells.		nerve cell, red blood cell, sperm cell
13	Give **two** examples of specialised plant cells.		leaf cell, root hair cell
14	What is the function of a root hair cell?	*Put paper here*	absorbs water and nutrients from the soil
15	Describe the adaptations of a nerve cell.		long and thin, with connections at either end to join to other nerve cells
Movement in to cells			
16	Name the process where particles move from an area of higher concentration to an area of lower concentration.	*Put paper here*	diffusion
17	Name **four** substances that diffuse into and out of cells.		oxygen, carbon dioxide, water, glucose
Microscopes			
18	What piece of equipment is used to observe cells?	*Put paper here*	a microscope
Unicellular organisms			
19	What is a unicellular organism?		an organism consisting of just one cell
20	Name **two** unicellular organisms.		amoeba, euglena

Practice questions

1 Organisms are made up of cells.

   a **Figure 1** shows an animal cell. Label the components in Figure 1. Choose answers from the box. **[4 marks]**

| cytoplasm | cell membrane | nucleus | mitochondria |

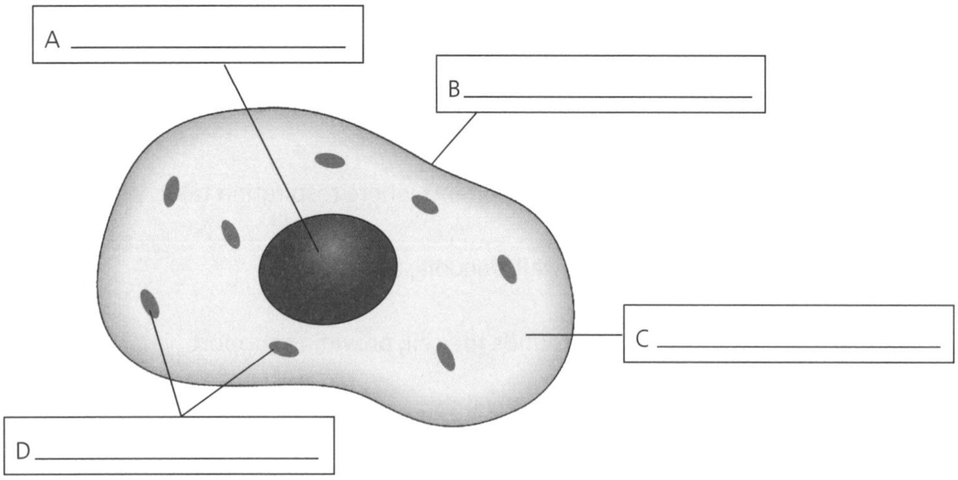

A _____

B _____

C _____

D _____

EXAM TIP

There are four spaces here and four answers, which tells us to use each answer once. Cross each answer out when you've placed it in a box so you don't repeat yourself.

Figure 1

   b Name **one** other cell component found in a plant cell. **[1 mark]**

_____

2 Specialised cells are adapted to perform a particular function.

   a Match each specialised cell to its function by drawing lines. **[3 marks]**

Specialised cell
leaf cell
red blood cell
root hair cell
nerve cell

Function
carry electrical impulses
carry out photosynthesis
absorb water and nutrients
carry oxygen

EXAM TIP

Pay attention to any words that are in bold. In question 1b, the word 'one' is in bold, which tells you that only one answer will be credited. You won't get more marks for writing two or three answers.

   b State **one** way a sperm cell is adapted to its function. **[1 mark]**

_____

3 Substances move into and out of cells through the process of diffusion. Complete the description of this process by choosing the correct words in bold. **[5 marks]**

Substances move into and out of a cell through the **cell membrane / cytoplasm**. Substances move from an area where they are at a **higher / lower** concentration to an area where they are at a **higher / lower** concentration. For example, for respiration to occur, **carbon dioxide / oxygen** diffuses into the cell from the **blood / intestine**.

4   Microscopes are used to observe cells. **Figure 2** shows a microscope.

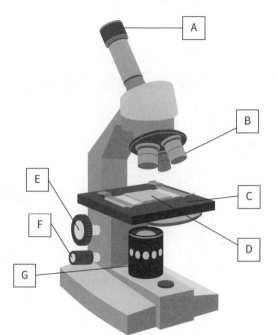

Figure 2

a   Name part A.   [1 mark]

_____

b   Identify which labels are pointing to the focusing knobs.   [1 mark]

_____

c   State where you would place the cells you wish to observe.   [1 mark]

_____

5   The blood contains a number of structures, including red blood cells.

a   State the function of a red blood cell.   [1 mark]

_____

b   Describe **two** ways a red blood cell is adapted to its function.

                                                               [2 marks]

   i   _____

   ii _____

6 **Figure 3** shows a typical plant cell.

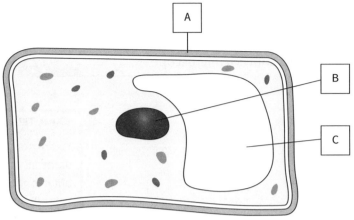

Figure 3

a Name parts A and B. [2 marks]

A _____

B _____

b Describe the function of the nucleus. [1 mark]

_____

_____

c Describe the function of part C. [1 mark]

_____

_____

7 A student wanted to observe the nuclei in the skin cells from the back of their hand. They took a sample of cells by sticking a piece of sticky tape on the back of their hand to remove some dead cells. Describe how they could observe these cells using a microscope. [4 marks]

_____

_____

_____

_____

_____

8 An amoeba is an example of a unicellular organism.

a State what is meant by a unicellular organism. [1 mark]

_____

b Amoeba contain cytoplasm surrounded by a cell membrane. Describe the function of the cell membrane. [1 mark]

_____

_____

c Amoeba divide by binary fission. Describe the main steps in this process. **[2 marks]**

_____

_____

_____

9 A student observed some leaf cells and some root hair cells using a microscope.

a Explain why chloroplasts were only observed in **one** of these cell types. **[3 marks]**

_____

_____

_____

_____

b The student observed the cells using a ×10 eyepiece lens and a ×40 objective lens. Calculate the total magnification used in the observation. **[2 marks]**

> **EXAM TIP**
>
> Look back at the Knowledge section to see a worked example for total magnification.

× _____

10 **Figure 4** shows a cell. Substances move into and out of cells by diffusion.

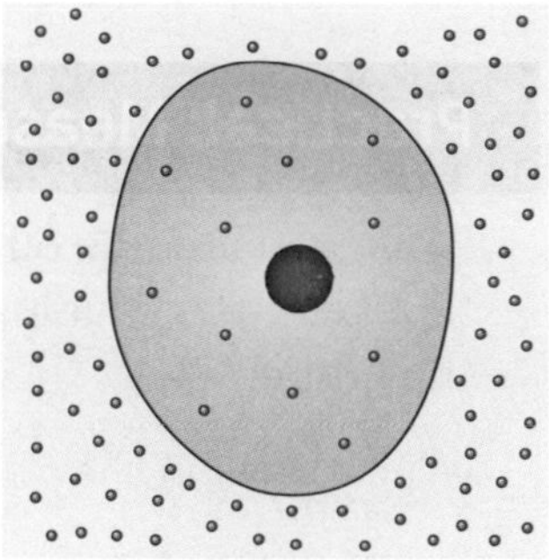

Figure 4

a Add an arrow to Figure 4 to show which way the particles will move. **[1 mark]**

b Give a reason for your choice of direction. **[1 mark]**

_____

_____

c In a plant, water molecules diffuse into the root hair cells and then into other plant cells. Explain how this helps to keep a plant upright. **[3 marks]**

_____

_____

_____

Knowledge

B2 Structure and function of body systems

Levels of organisation

Multicellular organisms are made of many cells. They have five levels of organisation, often referred to as a hierarchy.

Cell	**Tissue**	**Organ**
The smallest building block of an organism – e.g., muscle cell, red blood cell, leaf cell	A group of specialised cells working together – e.g., blood, nervous tissue, xylem vessels	A group of tissues working together – e.g., heart, stomach, leaf

Gas exchange system

The function of the gas exchange system is to *take in* oxygen and *give out* carbon dioxide.

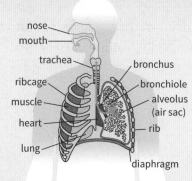

nose
mouth
trachea
ribcage
muscle
heart
lung
bronchus
bronchiole
alveolus (air sac)
rib
diaphragm

Air enters your body through your mouth and nose.
↓
Air moves down the **trachea** (windpipe) – a large tube.
↓
Air moves moves down a bronchus – a smaller tube.
↓
Air moves through a bronchiole – a tiny tube.
↓
Air moves into an **alveolus** – an air sac.
↓
Oxygen then diffuses into the blood.

Alveoli

There are millions of alveoli in the lungs. They help gas exchange occur quickly and easily by having:

- a large surface area
- thin walls (one cell thick)
- a good blood supply.

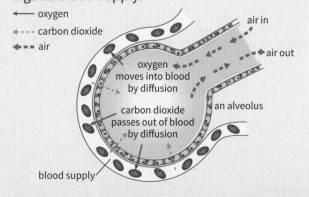

← oxygen
←--- carbon dioxide
←-- air

air in
air out
oxygen moves into blood by diffusion
carbon dioxide passes out of blood by diffusion
an alveolus
blood supply

Practical: Measuring lung volume

When you breathe out fully into the plastic tube, air from your lungs pushes water out of the bottle.

volume of air in the plastic bottle = **lung volume**

Lung volume can be:

↑ increased by exercise

↓ decreased by asthma, old age, and smoking.

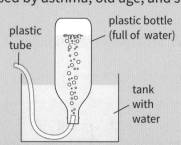

plastic tube
plastic bottle (full of water)
tank with water

Key terms

Make sure you can write a definition for these key terms

alveolus   diaphragm   exhale   inhale   lung volume
multicellular   organ   organ system   tissue   trachea

Organ system	Multicellular organism	
A group of organs working together – e.g., gas exchange system, reproductive system	A group of systems working together – e.g., animal, plant	Increasing complexity →

Inhaling and exhaling

The changes that take place when you **inhale** (breathe in) and **exhale** (breathe out) are shown in the table. They can be modelled using a bell jar.

	Inhaling (breathing in)	Exhaling (breathing out)
Changes that take place inside the chest cavity	1. Muscles between ribs contract. 2. Ribs are pulled up and out. 3. **Diaphragm** contracts and flattens. 4. Volume of the chest increases. 5. Pressure inside the chest decreases. 6. Air is drawn into the lungs. air drawn in · muscle lung · rib · diaphragm	1. Muscles between ribs relax. 2. Ribs are pulled in and down. 3. Diaphragm relaxes and moves up. 4. Volume in the chest decreases. 5. Pressure inside the chest increases. 6. Air is forced out of the lungs. air forced out
The bell jar model	1. Rubber sheet is pulled down. 2. Volume inside the jar increases. 3. Pressure inside the jar decreases. 4. Air rushes into the tube. 5. Balloons inflate.	1. Rubber sheet is pushed up. 2. Volume inside the jar decreases. 3. Pressure inside the jar increases. 4. Air rushes out of the tube. 5. Balloons deflate.
Composition of gases	oxygen (O_2) 20.96% carbon dioxide (CO_2) 0.04% nitrogen (N_2) 79% **inhaled air**	oxygen (O_2) 16% carbon dioxide (CO_2) 5% nitrogen (N_2) 79% **exhaled air** Exhaled air is warmer and contains more water vapour than inhaled air.

Knowledge

B2 Structure and function of body systems continued

Skeleton

The **skeleton** is part of the **muscular skeletal system**. It is made up of all the **bones** in the body. Bone is a living tissue. It has a blood supply and can repair and grow. The skeleton has four main functions:

- Support – it provides a framework for muscles and organs to connect to.
- Protection – it protects vital organs, for example, the ribs protect the lungs.
- To make blood cells – red and white blood cells are produced in the **bone marrow**.
- Movement – muscles pull on bones to move the body.

Joints

Joints occur between two or more bones. They allow the body to bend.

Type of joint	Example (s)	Movement
hinge	knee, elbow	forwards and backwards
ball and socket	shoulder, hip	all directions
fixed	skull	none
pivot	neck	around a point

In a joint:

- the ends of the bones are protected by **cartilage**
- two bones are held together by **ligaments**
- fluid lubricates the bones (makes them slippery) so they slide over each other smoothly.

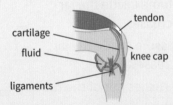

Muscles

Muscles are a type of tissue. Muscles are attached to bone with **tendons**. When a muscle contracts, it shortens and pulls on the bone. If the bone is part of a joint, it will move.

Muscles in the heart pumps blood around the body. Muscles in the gut squeeze food along the digestive system.

Antagonistic muscles

Muscles at a joint work together in pairs. Pairs of muscles are called **antagonistic muscles**. When one muscle contracts, the other relaxes. For example, biceps and triceps work together to bend and straighten the forearm.

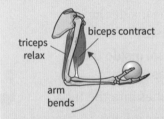 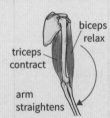

Practical: Investigating muscle strength

The strength of a muscle can be measured by how much force it exerts. Force is measured in **newtons (N)**. Muscle strength can be measured using a newton scale. The stronger the muscle, the harder you can push on the scale.

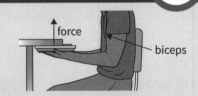

Key terms

Make sure you can write a definition for these key terms

antagonistic muscles   bone   bone marrow   cartilage   joint   ligament
muscle   muscular skeletal system   newton (N)   skeleton   tendon

Learn the answers to the questions below and test yourself.

B2 Questions — Answers

Levels of organisation

#	Question	Answer
1	What is a multicellular organism?	an organism made of many cells
2	What is a tissue?	a group of similar cells working together to perform a function
3	What is an organ?	a group of tissues working together to perform a function
4	What is an organ system?	a group of organs working together to perform a function

Gas exchange system

#	Question	Answer
5	What is gas exchange?	the transfer of gases between an organism and its environment
6	Where does gas exchange take place in humans?	in the lungs
7	What is the function of the ribs?	to protect the lungs

Mechanism of breathing

#	Question	Answer
8	How does inhaled air compare with exhaled air?	it has more oxygen, less carbon dioxide, and the same amount of nitrogen
9	What happens when you inhale?	the muscles between the ribs contract, pulling the ribs up and out; the diaphragm contracts and moves down, so chest volume increases, pressure decreases, and air is drawn into the lungs

Skeleton

#	Question	Answer
10	Name the **four** main functions of the skeleton.	support, movement, protection, make blood cells
11	How does the body move?	muscles pull on bones
12	Name **four** different types of joint.	pivot joint, hinge joint, ball and socket joint, fixed joint
13	What is a ligament?	a tissue that joins two bones together

Muscles

#	Question	Answer
14	What is a tendon?	a tissue that joins a muscle to a bone
15	What are antagonistic muscles?	a pair of muscles that work together to control joint movement

Put paper here

Previous questions — Answers

#	Question	Answer
1	What is the function of the cell nucleus?	controls the cell and contains genetic material
2	What are mitochondria?	cell components where respiration takes place
3	Name the **three** cell components found in plant cells only.	cell wall, vacuole, chloroplasts
4	Name some substances that diffuse into and out of cells.	oxygen, carbon dioxide, water, glucose
5	What is a unicellular organism?	an organism consisting of just one cell

Put paper here

Practice

Practice questions

1 Multicellular organisms have a number of levels of organisation.

   a Complete the missing level. **[1 mark]**

   cell → _____ → organ → organ system → organism

   b Give **one** example of an organ. **[1 mark]**

   _____

   c Describe the function of this organ. **[1 mark]**

   _____

   _____

EXAM TIP

If you're not sure what the missing level is, go back to the Knowledge Organiser and look it up.

2 Gas exchange takes place inside the lungs.

   a **Figure 1** shows the gas exchange system.
      Label the main structures in Figure 1. Choose answers from
      the box. **[4 marks]**

   | ribs   diaphragm   alveoli (air sacs)   trachea |

Figure 1

   b Complete the description of the process of gas exchange by choosing
      the correct words in bold. **[3 marks]**

   When you inhale, you take in **oxygen / carbon dioxide**. This is used in
   photosynthesis / respiration to transfer energy to the cells. This
   process produces **oxygen / carbon dioxide**, which you then exhale.

EXAM TIP

Use a pencil to lightly cross out the answer. It is then easier to change your mind once you've read the whole paragraph.

3 The skeletal system has a number of functions.

   a Give **one** function of the skeletal system. Choose an answer from
      the box. **[1 mark]**

   | makes blood   digests food   produces eggs |

   _____

   b Give **one** other function of the skeletal system. **[1 mark]**

   _____

EXAM TIP

The use of the word 'other' in the question means you won't get any marks for repeating the answer to part a.

c Name the tissue that attaches bones to muscle. **[1 mark]**

_____

4 A number of changes take place in the body when you inhale.

a Tick **one** box in each row of **Table 1** to identify these changes.
[3 marks]

Table 1

	Increases	Decreases	Moves up	Moves down
ribcage				
diaphragm				
chest volume				

EXAM TIP

This question asks you to put one tick in each row. Rows are the boxes going across – any more than one tick will be wrong.

b A bell jar can be used to model these changes (**Figure 2**).

Figure 2

EXAM TIP

Reading both parts of the question, you can see that the lungs and the rubber sheet are in different parts. So the rubber sheet is not what represents the lungs.

i Which part of the model represents the lungs? **[1 mark]**

_____

ii What does the rubber sheet represent? **[1 mark]**

_____

5 Movement of the skeleton occurs at joints.

a Match each component of the joint to its function by drawing lines.
[2 marks]

Joint component	Function
cartilage	connects the bones together
ligament	lubricates the joint so bones slide over each other smoothly
fluid	prevents the ends of the bones from rubbing together

b   Muscles pull on bones to cause movement. Different muscles have different strengths.

Working in pairs, some students used the following technique to measure the strength of their biceps (**Figure 3**).

- Ask your partner to sit on top of the table.
- Put the scale underneath the table.
- Push up as hard as you can.
- Read the force your muscles exert using the scale.

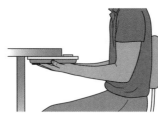

Figure 3

EXAM TIP

When stating units for forces it is really important to use the correct letter and to check whether it should be a capital or lowercase letter.

  i   State the unit used to measure muscle force.   **[1 mark]**

  _____

  ii   Suggest why the partner is asked to sit on the table.   **[1 mark]**

  _____

  _____

6   Both plants and animals contain reproductive systems.

a   Describe the function of the reproductive system.   **[1 mark]**

  _____

b   The reproductive system is an example of an organ system. State what is meant by an organ system.   **[1 mark]**

  _____

  _____

c   Explain the difference between multicellular and unicellular organisms.   **[2 marks]**

  _____

  _____

  _____

EXAM TIP

When the command word in a question is 'name', you generally only need to write one or two words. Any more is a waste of time.

7   Gas exchange takes place inside the lungs.

a   Name the tube through which air travels from the mouth towards the lungs.   **[1 mark]**

  _____

b State the function of the ribs. **[1 mark]**

_____

c The lungs contain millions of alveoli.

Describe **two** ways the alveoli are adapted to their function. **[2 marks]**

i _____

ii _____

8 **Figure 4** shows one way you can measure your lung volume. When you exhale (breathe out) into the tube, air from your lungs pushes the same volume of water out of the bottle.

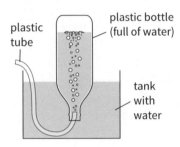

plastic tube

plastic bottle (full of water)

tank with water

Figure 4

a A student used this method to measure their total lung volume. They repeated the procedure three times. Add the missing value to complete the results in **Table 2**. **[1 mark]**

Table 2

Repeat number	Water in bottle before exhaling in cm³	Water in bottle after exhaling in cm³	Approximate lung volume in cm³
1	3000	400	2600
2	3000	350	
3	3000	360	2640

b Using the data in Table 2, calculate their average lung volume. **[2 marks]**

_____ cm³

c Another student carried out the same investigation. Their average lung volume was 2200 cm³. Suggest **one** reason why their lung volume may be lower. **[1 mark]**

_____

d Describe **two** ways that exhaled air differs from inhaled air.   **[2 marks]**

i _____

_____

ii _____

_____

9 **Figure 5** shows a pair of antagonistic muscles in the leg.

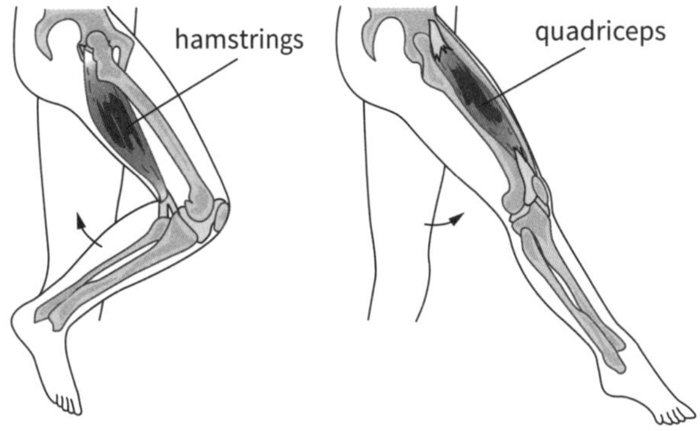

Figure 5

EXAM TIP

This is a four-mark question, so you're going to need to write more than one thing. Look at your answer at the end and see if you think it is worth four marks.

Using information from Figure 5 and your own knowledge, explain how these muscles control the bending of the knee.   **[4 marks]**

_____

_____

_____

_____

_____

10 Exhaled air contains less oxygen and more carbon dioxide than inhaled air.

a Explain this difference.   **[2 marks]**

_____

_____

_____

b State **one** other difference between exhaled air and inhaled air.

[1 mark]

_____

c Explain the changes that occur when a person exhales.   **[4 marks]**

_____

_____

_____

_____

_____

B1 **11** The following question is about cells.

a Which statement is the best definition of a cell? Tick **one** box. **[1 mark]**

group of tissues working together to form a function ☐

smallest type of living organism ☐

smallest unit of a living organism ☐

EXAM TIP

If a question tells you to only tick one box, then only tick one box. If you tick two boxes you won't get any marks.

b Match each cell component to its function by drawing lines. **[2 marks]**

Cell component	Function
cell wall	where respiration takes place
mitochondria	controls the cell, contains genetic material
nucleus	surrounds the cell, providing support

c Name the piece of equipment you would use to observe a cell. **[1 mark]**

_____

B1 **12** A student was shown some cells under the microscope (**Figure 6**).

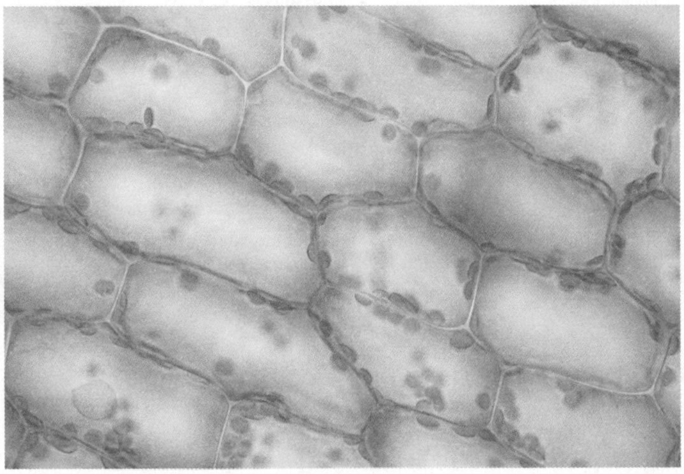

EXAM TIP

Identify which features are different between animal and plant cells and unicellular organisms.

Figure 6

a Where do these cells come from? Tick **one** box. **[1 mark]**

plant ☐ animal ☐

unicellular organism ☐

b Give **two** reasons for your answer **[2 marks]**

i _____

_____

ii _____

_____

c All cells need to respire. Name the cell component in which this chemical reaction takes place. **[1 mark]**

_____

B3 Reproduction in humans

Adolescence

The period of time during which a child changes into an adult is called **adolescence**. It includes both emotional and physical changes, caused by **sex hormones**. The physical changes are called **puberty**. These include the following changes:

Female	Both	Male
breasts develop	pubic hair grows	voice breaks (gets deeper)
ovaries start to release **egg cells**	underarm hair grows	**testes** and **penis** get bigger
periods start	body smell (body odour) becomes stronger	testes start to produce **sperm cells**
hips widen	growth spurt	shoulders widen
		hair grows on face and chest

Female reproductive system

The biological function of the female reproductive system is to produce egg cells and then grow a baby for long enough that it can be born and survive.

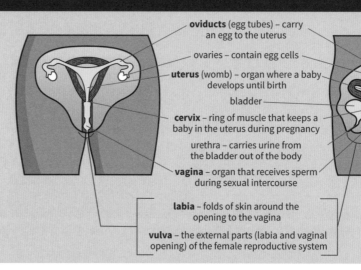

oviducts (egg tubes) – carry an egg to the uterus

ovaries – contain egg cells

uterus (womb) – organ where a baby develops until birth

bladder

cervix – ring of muscle that keeps a baby in the uterus during pregnancy

urethra – carries urine from the bladder out of the body

vagina – organ that receives sperm during sexual intercourse

labia – folds of skin around the opening to the vagina

vulva – the external parts (labia and vaginal opening) of the female reproductive system

Male reproductive system

The biological function of the male reproductive system is to produce sperm cells and release them inside the female reproductive system. The penis releases sperm into the vagina during sexual intercourse.

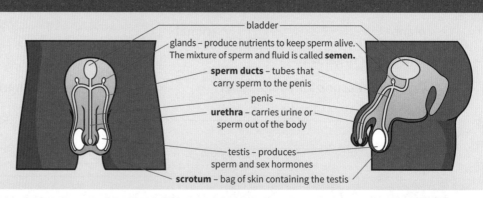

bladder

glands – produce nutrients to keep sperm alive. The mixture of sperm and fluid is called **semen.**

sperm ducts – tubes that carry sperm to the penis

penis

urethra – carries urine or sperm out of the body

testis – produces sperm and sex hormones

scrotum – bag of skin containing the testis

Key terms

Make sure you can write a definition for these key terms

adolescence cervix egg cell labia ovary oviduct penis puberty scrotum semen sex hormones sperm cells sperm ducts testes uterus urethra vagina vulva

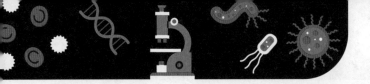

Fertilisation in humans

Gametes are reproductive cells. The male gamete is a sperm cell and the female gamete is an egg cell. To create a baby, the nucleus of the sperm and egg have to join together. This is called **fertilisation**.

When a male and a female have sexual intercourse, semen containing sperm is released into the vagina from the penis. This is known as **ejaculation**.

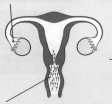

One egg is released from an ovary every month.

Sperm swim from the vagina, through the cervix, and into the uterus.

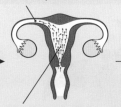

If a sperm meets an egg in the oviduct, fertilisation occurs.

Many sperm die before they reach the oviduct.

The fertilised egg travels down the oviduct and implants in the uterus lining. It then develops into an embryo.

The fertilised egg divides several times to form a ball of cells called an **embryo**. The embryo attaches to the lining of the uterus and begins to develop into a baby. This is called **implantation**.

Menstrual cycle

The **menstrual cycle** lasts about 28 days and is controlled by hormones.

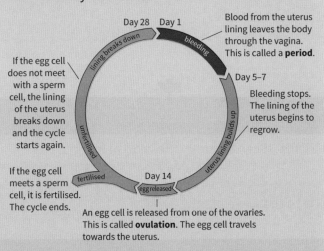

Blood from the uterus lining leaves the body through the vagina. This is called a **period**.

Day 5–7
Bleeding stops. The lining of the uterus begins to regrow.

If the egg cell does not meet with a sperm cell, the lining of the uterus breaks down and the cycle starts again.

If the egg cell meets a sperm cell, it is fertilised. The cycle ends.

An egg cell is released from one of the ovaries. This is called **ovulation**. The egg cell travels towards the uterus.

Preventing pregnancy

Pregnancy can be avoided by using **contraception**.

*   Condoms are a thin layer of latex that prevent semen being released into the vagina. They also prevent the spread of sexually transmitted infections (STIs).
*   The contraceptive pill contains hormones that stop ovulation.

Gestation (pregnancy)

Gestation is the time from fertilisation until birth. During early pregnancy, the embryo's cells divide and specialise. After eight weeks the embryo is called a **foetus**.

placenta – substances pass between the female's blood and the foetus' blood; acts as a barrier, stopping infections and harmful substances reaching the foetus

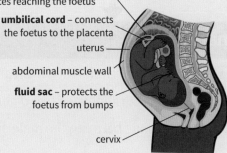

umbilical cord – connects the foetus to the placenta

uterus

abdominal muscle wall

fluid sac – protects the foetus from bumps

cervix

During pregnancy, the female should eat a healthy diet, not smoke, and avoid alcohol. Smoking can cause babies to be born early. Drinking alcohol can cause problems with brain development.

Birth

During birth, the cervix relaxes, and the muscles in the uterus wall contract. This pushes the baby out, through the vagina. The placenta is then pushed out.

 Key terms   **Make sure you can write a definition for these key terms**

contraception   ejaculation   embryo   fertilisation   fluid sac   foetus   gametes   gestation   implantation
menstrual cycle   ovulation   period   placenta   umbilical cord

Knowledge

B3 Reproduction in plants

Flower structure

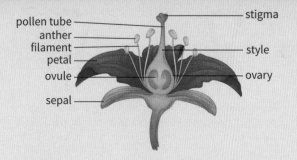

Stamen

The **male** part of the flower has:

- an **anther** that produces **pollen**
- a **filament** that holds up the anther.

Carpel

The **female** part of the flower has:

- a sticky **stigma** to catch pollen grains
- a **style**, which holds up the stigma
- an ovary containing **ovules**.

Types of flower

	Wind-pollinated flower	Insect-pollinated flower
Flowers	small flowers, brown or dull green	brightly coloured, sweet smelling
Nectar produced	no	yes
Pollen	large quantities, very light	small quantities, sticky or spiky
Anthers and stigma	loosely attached, dangle out of the flower	held firmly in the flower

Pollination

Pollination is the transfer of pollen from an anther to a stigma. It can occur by the wind or insects.

Cross-pollination occurs between two *different* plants.

Self-pollination occurs between the male and female parts of the *same* plant.

Fertilisation in plants

During fertilisation, the nucleus of the pollen and the ovule join.

After fertilisation, the **ovary** develops into the **fruit** and the ovules become **seeds**. All fruits contain seeds.

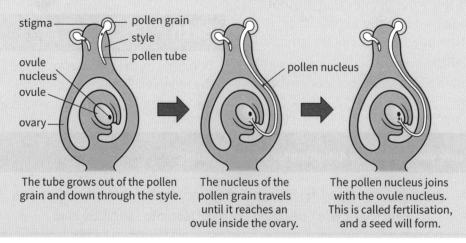

The tube grows out of the pollen grain and down through the style.

The nucleus of the pollen grain travels until it reaches an ovule inside the ovary.

The pollen nucleus joins with the ovule nucleus. This is called fertilisation, and a seed will form.

Germination

Germination is the period of time when a seed starts to grow.

A seed needs three things to germinate:

- water – to cause the seed to swell
- oxygen – to use in respiration, to transfer energy for growth
- warmth – to speed up reactions, speeding up germination

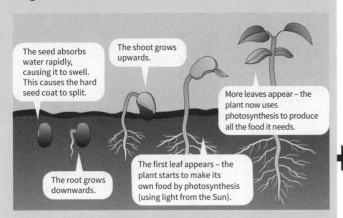

The seed absorbs water rapidly, causing it to swell. This causes the hard seed coat to split.

The shoot grows upwards.

More leaves appear – the plant now uses photosynthesis to produce all the food it needs.

The first leaf appears – the plant starts to make its own food by photosynthesis (using light from the Sun).

The root grows downwards.

Practical: Investigating seed dispersal

Seed dispersal can be investigated by studying the mechanism of wind dispersal. Measure the time taken for a model seed to fall to the ground. The longer the seed stays in the air, the further it is likely to be carried by the wind. Factors that could affect this time include:

- height of release
- length or surface area of the wings
- mass of seed
- wind speed.

To ensure data is valid, all other variables must be controlled effectively.

Seed structure

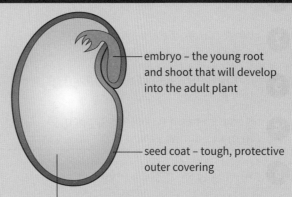

embryo – the young root and shoot that will develop into the adult plant

seed coat – tough, protective outer covering

food store – a store of food (starch) that the young plant uses until it can make its own food by photosynthesis.

Seed dispersal

Seeds are dispersed away from each other and the parent plant so they have space to grow and do not compete for resources. The table shows the main methods of **seed dispersal**.

Dispersal mechanism	Seed adaptations	Example
wind	light with extensions that act as parachutes or wings	sycamore seeds
animals (internal)	hard coats – eaten within fruits and spread in droppings	blackberries
animals (external)	hooks that stick to animals' fur	burdock seeds
water	light (float on water) or waterproof fruits	coconuts
explosion	fruits burst open when ripe, throwing seeds in all directions	pea pods

Key terms

Make sure you can write a definition for these key terms

anther   carpel   filament   fruit   germination   ovary   ovule   pollen
pollination   seed   seed dispersal   stamen   stigma   style

Retrieval

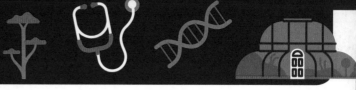

Learn the answers to the questions below and test yourself.

		B3 Questions	Answers
Adolescence	1	What is adolescence?	the time when a child changes into an adult – it involves physical and emotional changes
	2	What causes the changes that take place during adolescence?	sex hormones
	3	Name some changes that happen to females during puberty.	breasts develop, ovaries start to release eggs, periods start, hips widen
	4	Name some changes that happen to males during puberty.	voice gets deeper, testes start to produce sperm, shoulders widen, hair grows on face and chest
Male reproductive system	5	Where are sperm cells produced?	in the testes
	6	What are the sperm ducts?	tubes that carry sperm from the testes to the penis
	7	What is the urethra?	the tube that carries urine and semen out of the body
Female reproductive system	8	What is the uterus?	the organ where a foetus develops until birth
	9	What is the cervix?	the ring of muscle at the entrance to the uterus – it keeps the foetus in place whilst the individual is pregnant
	10	What is the vagina?	the organ that receives sperm during heterosexual intercourse
	11	What are the oviducts?	tubes that carry an egg to the uterus
	12	Where are egg cells produced?	in the ovaries
	13	What is a period?	the loss of the uterus lining through the vagina
	14	What is ovulation?	the release of an egg from an ovary
Pregnancy	15	What happens during heterosexual intercourse?	the penis releases sperm into the vagina
	16	Name the male and female gametes in an animal.	sperm (male), egg (female)
	17	What happens during fertilisation in animals?	the nucleus of a sperm cell joins with the nucleus of an egg cell
	18	What is implantation?	when an embryo attaches to the lining of the uterus
	19	What is gestation?	the time from fertilisation to birth
	20	What is the function of the placenta?	it is where substances pass between the female's blood and the foetus' blood
	21	What happens during birth?	the cervix relaxes and the muscles in the uterus wall contract, pushing the baby out of the body through the vagina
	22	What is contraception?	a method of preventing pregnancy

Put paper here Put paper here Put paper here Put paper here Put paper here Put paper here Put paper here Put paper here

Flowers	23 Name the male and female gametes in a plant.	pollen (male), ovule (female)
	24 Name the female parts of a flower.	carpel: stigma, style, ovary
	25 Name the male parts of a flower.	stamen: anther, filament
	26 What is pollination?	the transfer of pollen from the anther to the stigma
	27 Identify the main steps of fertilisation in plants.	pollen grain grows a tube down the style and into the ovary; pollen nucleus travels down the tube and fuses with the nucleus of an ovule
Seeds	28 Name the main parts of a seed.	seed coat, embryo, food store
	29 What do seeds need to germinate?	water, warmth, oxygen
	30 Name **four** ways seeds are dispersed.	wind, animals, water, explosion

Put paper here

Previous questions | Answers

1	What is a cell?	the smallest functional unit in an organism – the building block of life
2	Where does gas exchange take place in humans?	in the lungs
3	How does inhaled air compare with exhaled air?	it has more oxygen, less carbon dioxide, and the same amount of nitrogen
4	Name the **four** main functions of the skeleton.	support, movement, protection, make blood cells
5	How does the body move?	muscles pull on bones

Put paper here

Practice questions

1 Complete **Table 1** to identify some of the changes that happen to a person during puberty. Tick the correct boxes. **[4 marks]**

Table 1

Change	Occurs in males	Occurs in females	Occurs in both
ovaries release eggs			
pubic hair grows			
voices deepen			
periods start			

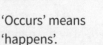

2 Flowers play an important role in plant reproduction.

a **Figure 1** shows the flower of a plant. Label the main structures in **Figure 1**. Choose answers from the box. **[4 marks]**

petal stigma ovary anther

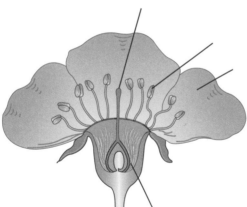

Figure 1

b Name the part of the flower that produces pollen. **[1 mark]**

_____

c Describe **one** way pollen is transferred between plants. **[1 mark]**

_____

3 For a baby to develop, an egg and a sperm cell need to join.

a Match each term in sexual reproduction to its definition by drawing lines. **[2 marks]**

Term	Definition
ovulation	the nuclei of the sperm and egg join together
fertilisation	an egg cell is released from the ovary
implantation	the fertilised egg attaches to the lining of the uterus

b Name the part of the body where a baby develops. **[1 mark]**

_____

4 a Complete the sentences about seeds. Choose answers from the box. Each answer may be used once, more than once, or not at all. **[4 marks]**

light   dispersed   fertilisation   competition   nutrients   warmth

Seeds are _____ away from the parent plant and other

plants to reduce _____. This increases their chances of

having enough space and _____ to grow. In order to

germinate, a seed needs water, oxygen, and _____.

b Give **two** ways seeds are dispersed. **[2 marks]**

i _____

ii _____

5 The female reproductive system works in a sequence called the menstrual cycle.

a State the approximate number of days this cycle takes. **[1 mark]**

_____

b Describe the main stages that take place during the menstrual cycle. **[4 marks]**

_____

_____

_____

_____

_____

6 **Figure 2** shows the main structures in the male reproductive system.

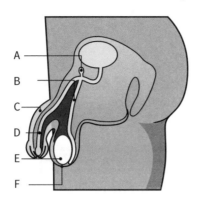

Figure 2

a Name structure F. **[1 mark]**

_____

EXAM TIP

Even though you only need to name structure F to answer this question, it's good revision to try and name all the other parts of the reproductive system.

b Identify the structure in Figure 2 that produces nutrients to keep the sperm alive. **[1 mark]**

_____

c Describe the structures that sperm pass through on their way out of the body. **[3 marks]**

_____

_____

_____

7 **Figure 3** shows the gestation period for some different organisms.

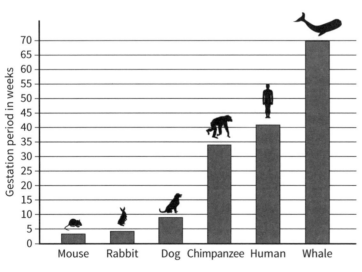

Figure 3

a Use Figure 3 to answer the questions.

i Identify the animal with the shortest gestation period. **[1 mark]**

_____

ii Calculate the difference in time between the gestation of a human and a chimpanzee. **[2 marks]**

iii Identify the trend shown in the graph. **[1 mark]**

_____

b Describe how a baby is protected from bumps as it develops. **[2 marks]**

_____

_____

8 A group of students want to investigate how the mass of a seed determines how far it is dispersed.

a State the independent variable in this investigation. **[1 mark]**

_____

b State **one** variable that should be controlled in this investigation. **[1 mark]**

_____

c Write a method for this investigation. **[4 marks]**

_____

_____

_____

_____

_____

9 During pregnancy, a baby develops in the uterus.

a Name **one** substance that must be passed from the pregnant person to the foetus. **[1 mark]**

_____

b Explain how substances are exchanged between the pregnant person and the foetus. **[4 marks]**

_____

_____

_____

_____

_____

c After 40 weeks, the baby is ready to be born. Explain the main stages of birth. **[4 marks]**

_____

_____

_____

_____

_____

EXAM TIP

For explain questions you need to say why something is happening.

10 Figure 4 shows the flowers of a sugar maple tree.

Figure 4

a Describe what is meant by pollination. **[2 marks]**

_____

_____

_____

b Explain **one** structure of the flower shown in Figure 4 that tells you it is wind pollinated. **[2 marks]**

_____

_____

_____

EXAM TIP

Don't worry if you've never heard of a sugar maple tree. You're expected to take what you have learnt in class and apply it to new situations.

c Explain **one** other feature of wind-pollinated flowers. **[2 marks]**

_____

_____

_____

B1 **11 Figure 5** shows a euglena. A euglena is an example of a unicellular organism.

a State the piece of equipment you would use to observe a euglena.

[1 mark]

_____

b Which of the following is a unicellular organism? Choose the answer from the box. **[1 mark]**

cactus   frog   amoeba   beetle

_____

Figure 5

EXAM TIP

Think of the size you expected a unicellular organism to be before you think of the equipment.

c Add an arrow to Figure 5 to identify the flagellum, which helps the euglena to move. **[1 mark]**

B2 **12** Three students investigated who had the stronger biceps muscles. They each measured their biceps strength using a newton scale. Their results are shown in **Table 2**.

Table 2

Student	Biceps strength in N			
	Test 1	Test 2	Test 3	Mean
A	470	420	430	440
B	440	470	440	
C	430	420	410	420

a Calculate the mean biceps strength for student B. **[2 marks]**

_____ N

EXAM TIP

This is just the same as working out the mean in maths.

b Identify who had the weakest biceps muscles. **[1 mark]**

_____

c Explain how the biceps muscle causes the arm to move. **[2 marks]**

_____

_____

_____

B3 Practice 31

B4 Health and lifestyle

Balanced diet

To remain healthy, you must eat a **balanced diet**. This means eating food containing the right nutrients in the correct amounts.

Food component	Role in the body	Examples
carbohydrates	provide energy	pasta, bread
lipids (fats and oils)	provide energy, provide insulation under the skin, protect organs from damage	cheese, olive oil
protein	growth and repair	fish, eggs
vitamins	keep you healthy	fruit, vegetables
minerals	keep you healthy	fruit, vegetables
water	needed in all cells and body fluids	water, tea
fibre	provides bulk to keep food moving through the gut, preventing constipation	beans, cereal

Practical: Food tests

To prepare a food solution for a **food test**:

1 Crush the food using a pestle and mortar.
2 Add a few drops of water and mix well.

Food test	Chemical	Colour change if nutrient present
starch	iodine	blue–black
lipid	ethanol	cloudy
sugar	Benedict's solution	orange–red
protein	biuret solution	purple

Digestive system

During **digestion**, large food molecules are broken down into small molecules of nutrients by the **digestive system**. They pass into the blood in the small intestine, where they are used by the body. **Villi** cover the small intestine wall, increasing the surface area so more nutrients can be absorbed.

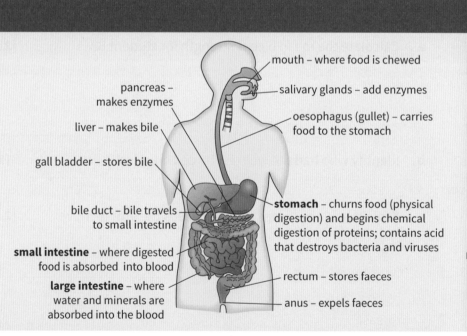

mouth – where food is chewed

salivary glands – add enzymes

oesophagus (gullet) – carries food to the stomach

pancreas – makes enzymes

liver – makes bile

gall bladder – stores bile

bile duct – bile travels to small intestine

small intestine – where digested food is absorbed into blood

large intestine – where water and minerals are absorbed into the blood

stomach – churns food (physical digestion) and begins chemical digestion of proteins; contains acid that destroys bacteria and viruses

rectum – stores faeces

anus – expels faeces

 Key terms — Make sure you can write a definition for these key terms

balanced diet   bile   carbohydrase   carbohydrate   catalyst   deficiency   digestion
digestive system   enzyme   fibre   food test   large intestine   villi

Unhealthy diet

Energy is needed for all body processes, even when sleeping. This energy comes from food. The energy in food is measured in joules (J) or kilojoules (kJ) – 1 kilojoule is the same as 1000 joules.

Too little energy	Energy needs	Too much energy

Too little energy

If the energy in the food eaten is less than the energy used, a person will lose body mass.
This leads to them being underweight and, in extreme cases, **starvation**. Underweight people:

- often suffer from health problems, for example, a poor immune system
- lack energy and are often tired
- may have a vitamin or mineral **deficiency**, such as rickets (lack of vitamin D) or scurvy (lack of vitamin C).

Energy needs

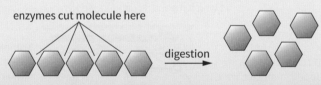

The amount of energy a person needs depends on their age (as this affects growth rate), body size, and how active they are.

Too much energy

If the energy in the food eaten is more than the energy used, a person will gain body mass, stored as fat.
If a person becomes extremely overweight, they are **obese**. Overweight people:

- are at greater risk of heart disease, stroke, and diabetes
- can have breathing problems or joint pain
- may have a vitamin or mineral deficiency.

Enzymes

Enzymes are special proteins that can break down large molecules of nutrients into small molecules. Enzymes are known as biological **catalysts** – they speed up digestion without being used up themselves.

enzymes cut molecule here

digestion

Type of enzyme	Digests
carbohydrase	carbohydrates (e.g., starch) → sugars
protease	protein → amino acids
lipase	lipids → fatty acids and glycerol

Lipid digestion takes place in the small intestine. It is helped by **bile**. Bile breaks the lipids into small droplets that are easier for the lipase enzymes to work on.

Bacteria

Helpful bacteria live in the large intestine. They live on fibre in the diet and make important vitamins (e.g., vitamin K) that are absorbed into the body. Vitamin K is a group of vitamins needed for blood clotting and helping wounds to heal.

Key terms

Make sure you can write a definition for these key terms

lipase   lipids   mineral
obese   protease   protein
small intestine   starvation
stomach   villi   vitamin

Drugs

Drugs are chemical substances that affect the way the body works. They alter chemical reactions inside the body.

Medicinal drugs:

- benefit health by curing or treating symptoms of a disease
- can have side effects, so doctors have to balance the benefits with the risks
- include antibiotics, which kill bacteria, and paracetamol, which relieves pain.

Recreational drugs:

- are taken for enjoyment, to relax, or to help stay awake
- normally have no health benefits and many are harmful
- can be illegal, like ecstasy, or legal, like caffeine – caffeine is a stimulant and speeds up body reactions.

Drug addiction

If a person's body gets used to the changes caused by a drug, they may become dependent on the drug. They have an **addiction**.

If a person with an addiction tries to stop taking the drug, they may suffer **withdrawal symptoms**. These include headaches, anxiety, and sweating.

Alcohol

Alcohol contains the drug **ethanol**. Ethanol is a **depressant**. It affects the nervous system, slowing down body reactions. Ethanol affects a person's ability to walk and talk, and in excess can cause death.

Drinking large amounts of alcohol over a long time can cause:

- stomach ulcers
- heart disease
- brain damage
- cirrhosis of the liver

Drinking alcohol whilst pregnant can damage the developing baby, increasing the risk of miscarriage, stillbirth, and premature birth. Alcohol can also reduce fertility, by affecting sperm production and ovulation.

Smoking

Tobacco smoke contains many harmful chemicals.

- Nicotine is a **stimulant**. It makes the heart beat faster and narrows the blood vessels. It is also addictive.
- Tar is a sticky black material that collects in the lungs. It irritates and narrows the airways. It contains chemicals that cause cancer.
- Carbon monoxide is a poisonous gas. It binds to red blood cells in place of oxygen.

Smoking increases the risk of:

- mouth, throat, and lung cancer
- heart attacks and strokes
- respiratory infections.

2 Tobacco smoke stops the cilla from moving, which means dirt and bacteria reach the lungs.

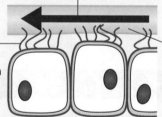

1 Dirt and bacteria are trapped in mucus, which is moved along the trachea by cillia. The mucus is destroyed in the stomach.

3 Smokers cough up the mucus, further damaging the lungs.

Smoking whilst pregnant increases the risk of miscarriage and affects foetal development. Smoking around a baby increases the risk of sudden-infant-death syndrome and respiratory illness.

Key terms

Make sure you can write a definition for these key terms

addiction   depressant   drug   ethanol   medicinal drug
recreational drug   stimulant   withdrawal symptom

Learn the answers to the questions below and test yourself.

B4 Questions | Answers

Balanced diet

#	Question	Answer
1	What are the main components of a balanced diet?	carbohydrates, lipids, protein, vitamins, minerals, water, fibre
2	How do you test for starch?	add iodine – food solution turns dark blue–black if starch is present
3	Identify **two** roles of lipids in the body.	provide energy, provide insulation under the skin, protect organs
4	How do you test for sugar?	add Benedict's solution and heat – food solution turns orange–red if sugar is present
5	What is the role of protein in the body?	growth and repair

Digestive system

#	Question	Answer
6	What happens during digestion?	large molecules are broken down into small nutrient molecules, which can then be absorbed
7	What is the function of the stomach?	to mix food with digestive juices and acid
8	What is the function of the small intestine?	to absorb small molecules of nutrients into the bloodstream
9	What is the function of the large intestine?	to absorb water back into the body, leaving a mass of undigested waste (faeces)

Enzymes and bacteria

#	Question	Answer
10	What are enzymes?	biological catalysts – they speed up digestion without being used up
11	What do carbohydrases do?	break down carbohydrates into sugar molecules
12	In which part of the digestive system do helpful bacteria live?	large intestine
13	What do lipases do?	break down lipids into fatty acids and glycerol

Drugs

#	Question	Answer
14	What is a drug?	a chemical substance that affects the way the body works
15	Name some examples of recreational drugs.	ethanol (alcohol), tobacco, caffeine

Put paper here

Previous questions | Answers

#	Question	Answer
1	What is a tissue?	a group of similar cells working together to perform a function
2	What is adolescence?	the time when a child changes into an adult – it involves physical and emotional changes
3	What is a period?	the loss of the uterus lining through the vagina
4	What is gestation?	the time from fertilisation to birth
5	What do seeds need to germinate?	water, warmth, oxygen

Put paper here

Practice questions

1   Drugs are chemicals that affect the way the body works. Answer the following questions. Choose answers from the box.

| addictive   medicinal   nicotine   ethanol   recreational   antibiotic |

EXAM TIP

Not all of these words are going to be used up.

a   Name the group of drugs that are taken to treat an illness.   **[1 mark]**

_____

b   Give an example of a recreational drug.   **[1 mark]**

_____

c   Name the drug found in alcohol.   **[1 mark]**

_____

2   **Figure 1** shows the digestive system.

a   Label the main structures in Figure 1. Choose answers from the box.

[4 marks]

| small intestine   large intestine   stomach   oesophagus |

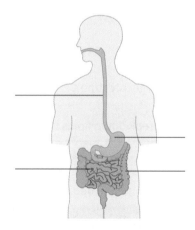

EXAM TIP

You could try to come up with a rhyme to help you remember the order of the parts of the digestive system.

Figure 1

b   Identify the part of the digestive system where food is absorbed.

[1 mark]

_____

c   Name **one** substance that is added to food in the stomach.   **[1 mark]**

_____

3 **Figure 2** shows how the length of time a person smokes relates to the number of deaths a year.

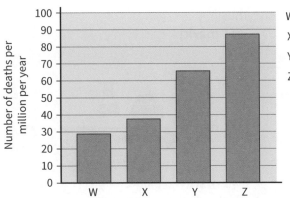

W – non-smokers

X – stopped smoking for more than ten years

Y – stopped smoking for less than ten years

Z – still smoking

EXAM TIP

When reading numbers from a graph, put your ruler at the top of the bar and draw a line across to the axis. This will help you work out the value for the answer.

Figure 2

a How many deaths were there for non-smokers? **[1 mark]**

_____ deaths per million per year

b Identify which statement about Figure 2 is true. Tick **one** box. **[1 mark]**

EXAM TIP

Use the data from the graph to select the correct box.

The less time a person smokes, the greater the risk of death. ☐

The longer a person smokes the greater the risk of death. ☐

There is no link between the length of time a person smokes and the risk of death. ☐

c Tobacco smoke contains a number of harmful chemicals. Match each chemical to its effect by drawing lines. **[2 marks]**

Chemical
tar
nicotine
carbon monoxide

Effect
makes the heart beat faster
reduces the amount of oxygen the blood can carry
can cause cancer

4 Enzymes are used in digestion.

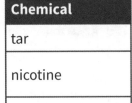

a Which of the following terms describes an enzyme? Choose the answer from the box. **[1 mark]**

an antibody a catalyst a hormone

_____

b Protease is an enzyme that breaks down proteins. Identify the molecules that are made when proteins are broken down. Choose the answer from the box. **[1 mark]**

| amino acids | sugars | fatty acids |

_____

c Name **one** organ in the digestive system where protease enzymes are found. **[1 mark]**

_____

5 Starch is an example of a carbohydrate.

a Name a food that is a good source of carbohydrates. **[1 mark]**

_____

b State the function of carbohydrates in the body. **[1 mark]**

_____

EXAM TIP

Read the whole question. This could also be asking for a starchy food.

c Describe how you would test a food source for the presence of starch. **[2 marks]**

_____

_____

_____

6 To remain healthy, you need to take in the correct amount of energy and the right balance of nutrients.

a If you eat too little over a period of time, you may become underweight.

Describe **two** health issues that are more likely if you are underweight. **[2 marks]**

i _____

_____

EXAM TIP

Just give two issues. Writing more won't get you more marks!

ii _____

_____

b If the energy content in the food you eat is more than the energy you use, you gain body mass. Over a period of time, this can lead to obesity.

Give **two** diseases that obesity increases the risk of developing. **[2 marks]**

i _____

ii _____

c Explain why a house builder needs to take in more energy than an officer worker. **[2 marks]**

_____

_____

_____

7 A student wants to test a cereal bar for the presence of fat. Write a method the student could follow to produce a sample of the cereal bar and test it. **[6 marks]**

_____

_____

_____

_____

_____

_____

_____

EXAM TIP

When writing method answers you can use bullet points. Imagine another person is reading your answer. Is it clear enough for someone else to follow?

8 A yoghurt company has released a new low-fat strawberry yoghurt. They claim that their new low-fat yoghurt contains 70% less fat than their original strawberry yoghurt (**Table 1**).

Table 1

Type of yoghurt	Fat content in g per 100 g	Sugar content in g per 100 g	Protein in g per 100 g
original	4.2	11.1	5.3
low fat	1.9	9.8	3.9

a State **one** health benefit of eating the original yogurt rather than the low-fat yoghurt. **[1 mark]**

_____

b Calculate the percentage change in fat content between the low-fat yoghurt and the original yoghurt. **[2 marks]**

EXAM TIP

To calculate a percentage change, use the formula:

percentage change = (new value – original value)/original value × 100%

_____%

c Do you agree with the company's claim? Give a reason for your answer. **[1 mark]**

_____

_____

9   **Figure 3** shows the cells that line the tubes in your air ways, such as the trachea.

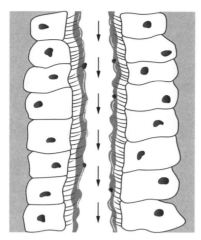

Figure 3

a   Describe how these cells are adapted to keep the lungs clean.   **[3 marks]**

_____

_____

_____

_____

EXAM TIP

There is lots of information in the image to help answer this question. Look at how these cells are adapted to their function.

b   Explain why many smokers develop a cough.   **[3 marks]**

_____

_____

_____

_____

10 **Figure 4** shows the lining of the small intestine.

Figure 4

a   Using Figure 4 and your own knowledge, explain how the small intestine is adapted to its function.   **[4 marks]**

_____

_____

_____

_____

_____

EXAM TIP

Try thinking in reverse. What is the function of the small intestine and how are these cells helping that function?

b It is essential that your diet contains some fat. Give **two** uses of fat in the body. [2 marks]

i _____

ii _____

c Fat digestion takes place inside the small intestine. Explain how bile supports the digestion of lipids. [3 marks]

_____

_____

_____

_____

EXAM TIP

There are two jobs that bile does and both are helpful here.

B3 **11** The statements describe the steps that take place in order for pregnancy to occur. Put the steps in order by writing the letters in the boxes. The first one has been done for you. [4 marks]

A Sperm may fertilise an egg if present in the oviduct.

B Embryo attaches itself to the uterus lining.

C Sperm swim through the cervix into the uterus.

D Sperm cells are released into the vagina.

E Fertilised egg divides several times to form a ball of cells.

_____

D → ☐ → ☐ → ☐ → ☐

EXAM TIP

D has already been used here, so you know it doesn't go anywhere else in the sequence.

B1 **12** Both plant and animal cells contain a nucleus.

a Name **two** other cell components found in both plant and animal cells. [2 marks]

i _____

ii _____

b Describe the function of a nucleus. [2 marks]

_____

_____

c Red blood cells are an example of a specialised cell. They do not contain a nucleus. Explain **one** other feature of a red blood cell. [2 marks]

_____

_____

B5 Biological processes

Photosynthesis

Plants make food through the process of **photosynthesis**. Photosynthesis is a chemical reaction in which plants take in carbon dioxide and water and convert them into glucose, a carbohydrate, using light energy transferred from the Sun. This provides the plant with food in the form of glucose. Plants also produce oxygen, which plants and animals then use in respiration, to transfer energy to the cells.

The word equation for the process of photosynthesis is:

$$\text{carbon dioxide + water} \xrightarrow{\text{light}} \text{glucose + oxygen}$$
$$\text{(reactants)} \qquad\qquad \text{(products)}$$

Photosynthesis takes place mainly in chloroplasts in the leaf cells, though a small amount happens in the stem.

Producers and consumers

Plants and algae are **producers** – they make their own food by photosynthesis. They convert materials from their environment into glucose, using sunlight.

Like plants, algae are green. However, they can be unicellular or multicellular organisms. They live underwater and do not have leaves, stems, or roots.

Animals are **consumers** – they have to eat other organisms such as plants or animals to survive. Consumers break down the organisms they eat during digestion, releasing nutrients, which are then used by the body.

Practical: Testing a leaf for starch

During photosynthesis, a plant produces glucose. It stores the glucose as starch in the leaf. To check that a plant has carried out photosynthesis, a leaf can be tested with iodine.

Step 1 Boil the leaf in water to remove the waxy layer.

Step 2 Put the leaf into a test tube of ethanol and place into boiling water. The ethanol dissolves the chlorophyll, removing it from the leaf.

Step 3 Wash the leaf in water to remove the ethanol and soften the leaf.

Step 4 Spread the leaf on a white tile and add a few drops of iodine. If the leaf turns black, starch is present.

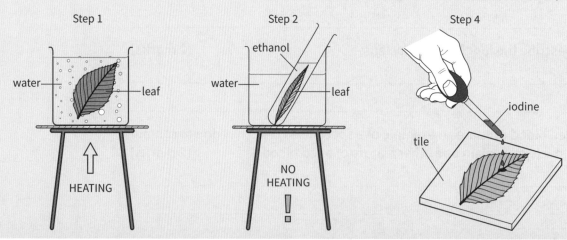

Key terms

Make sure you can write a definition for these key terms

consumer   fertiliser   guard cells   magnesium   nitrates
phosphates   photosynthesis   producer   stomata

Leaf adaptations

Leaves are specially adapted for photosynthesis:

- They are green due to the chlorophyll that absorbs sunlight. More chloroplasts are found at the top of the leaf, as this is where most sunlight hits the leaf.
- They are thin, which allows gases to diffuse in and out of the leaf.
- They have a large surface area to absorb as much light as possible.
- They have veins. These contain vessels to transport water and glucose.
- They have a waxy layer on the top of the leaf to prevent water evaporating.

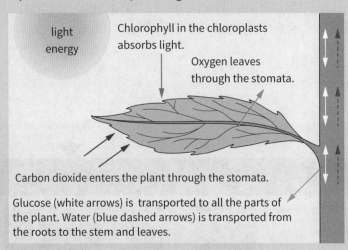

light energy

Chlorophyll in the chloroplasts absorbs light.

Oxygen leaves through the stomata.

Carbon dioxide enters the plant through the stomata.

Glucose (white arrows) is transported to all the parts of the plant. Water (blue dashed arrows) is transported from the roots to the stem and leaves.

Gas exchange

Stomata are found mainly on the underside of the leaf. They allow gases to enter and leave a leaf. Carbon dioxide diffuses into the leaf for photosynthesis and oxygen diffuses out. **Guard cells** open the stomata during the day and close them at night.

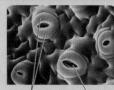

guard cells   stomata

Water transport

Water diffuses into the root hair cells. It is then transported around the plant in water vessels. As the water evaporates from the leaves more water is drawn up through the plant.

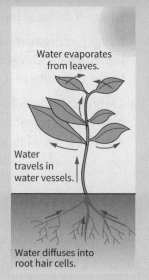

Water evaporates from leaves.

Water travels in water vessels.

Water diffuses into root hair cells.

Minerals

Plants need a range of minerals for healthy growth. Minerals dissolve in soil water, are absorbed through root hairs, and are then transported around the plant in the water vessels.

Mineral	Use in plant	Deficiency symptoms
nitrates (contain nitrogen)	making amino acids, which join together to make proteins needed for healthy growth	poor growth and yellowed older leaves
phosphates (contain phosphorus)	healthy roots	poor root growth and younger purple leaves
magnesium	making chlorophyll to absorb light	yellow leaves

Fertilisers and manure are used to replace minerals in the soil that are lost when the plants are harvested.

Respiration

Respiration

with oxygen	without oxygen
Aerobic respiration	**Anaerobic respiration (in animals)**

glucose + oxygen → carbon dioxide + water (+ energy)

glucose → lactic acid (+ energy)

reactants

- **Aerobic respiration** occurs in the **mitochondria** of cells when oxygen is present. This chemical reaction transfers the energy stored in food to the cell.

- Glucose is absorbed from the small intestine into the blood **plasma**. It is transported to the cells where it diffuses in.

- Oxygen is breathed in and diffuses into the bloodstream. Oxygen is then carried by haemoglobin to the cells where it diffuses in.

- Carbon dioxide diffuses out of the cells into the blood plasma. It is transported to the lungs where it diffuses into the alveoli (air sacs) and is exhaled.

products

- **Anaerobic respiration** occurs when there is not enough oxygen for aerobic respiration, such as during strenuous exercise.

- It transfers less energy than aerobic respiration.

- The lactic acid produced can cause muscle cramps. This causes increased inhalation to break down lactic acid – the oxygen needed is called the **oxygen debt**.

Fermentation

Fermentation is a type of anaerobic respiration carried out by microorganisms.

The word equation for fermentation is:

glucose   →   ethanol + carbon dioxide (+ energy)
(reactants)   (products)

Yeast, as shown in this image, is a microorganism used in food production. For example, it is used in the following types of food production:

- Bread production – flour, water, and yeast are mixed to make dough. The yeast ferments carbohydrates in the flour into ethanol and carbon dioxide. Carbon dioxide gas is trapped inside the dough and makes it rise. The ethanol evaporates as the dough is baked.

- Beer and wine production – beer is made by fermenting barley grains. Wine is made by fermenting grapes. In both cases, yeast ferments sugar into alcohol.

 Key terms

Make sure you can write a definition for these key terms

aerobic respiration   anaerobic respiration   fermentation
mitochondria   oxygen debt   plasma

 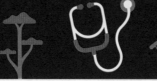 

⇄ Retrieval

Learn the answers to the questions below and test yourself.

B5 Questions | Answers

Photosynthesis

1 What are producers?

plants and algae that make their own food by photosynthesis

2 What is the word equation for photosynthesis?

carbon dioxide + water $\xrightarrow{\text{light}}$ glucose + oxygen

Starch test

3 How do you test a leaf for starch?

boil it, soak in warm ethanol, wash it, lay on a white tile, add a few drops of iodine

Leaf adaptations

4 Name **four** ways leaves are adapted to photosynthesis.

thin, green (contain chlorophyll), have a large surface area, contain veins

5 What are stomata?

tiny holes that allow gases to diffuse into and out of the leaf

6 State the function of guard cells.

to open and close the stomata

Plant minerals

7 Name **three** minerals plants need for healthy growth.

nitrates, phosphates, magnesium

8 Give some symptoms of a plant having a mineral deficiency.

poor root growth, stunted growth, yellow leaves

9 Name **two** ways farmers can add minerals back into the soil.

using fertilisers, using manure

Respiration

10 What is the word equation for aerobic respiration?

glucose + oxygen → carbon dioxide + water (+ energy)

11 What is the word equation for anaerobic respiration?

glucose → lactic acid (+ energy)

12 Why does the body normally respire aerobically?

it transfers more energy per glucose molecule and does not produce lactic acid, which can cause cramp

13 What is the name for anaerobic respiration in microorganisms?

fermentation

Fermentation

14 What is the word equation for fermentation?

glucose → ethanol + carbon dioxide (+ energy)

15 What are **three** useful products made by using fermentation?

bread, beer, wine

Put paper here

Previous questions | Answers

1 Name **three** examples of recreational drugs.

ethanol (alcohol), tobacco, caffeine

2 Name the male parts of a flower.

stamen – anther, filament

3 What is the uterus?

the organ where a foetus develops until birth

4 What are antagonistic muscles?

a pair of muscles that work together to control movement at a joint – as one muscle contracts, the other relaxes

5 Where does gas exchange take place in humans?

in the lungs

Put paper here

Practice

Practice questions

1 Leaves have a number of features to maximise photosynthesis.

Match each part of a leaf to its function by drawing lines. **[3 marks]**

Part of a leaf
veins
stomata
waxy layer
guard cells

Function
allow carbon dioxide into the leaf
open and close the stomata
transport water to the leaf cells
reduces the amount of water loss

EXAM TIP

Even if you're not 100% sure of the answer we can use some logic to help us. For example, stomata is on both sides of the box so those cannot connect to each other.

2 Plants need minerals for healthy growth.

a Complete the sentences. Choose answers from the box. Each answer may be used once, more than once, or not at all. **[4 marks]**

EXAM TIP

If you're not sure of the correct answer, try saying the line in your head with different words in and see which fits best.

> leaf   air   dissolve   soil   vessels   diffuse   root hair

Plants get the minerals they need from the _____

The minerals _____ in water and are absorbed into the

_____ cells.

Minerals are transported around the plant in the water _____.

b Name **one** mineral that plants need. **[1 mark]**

_____

c Give **one** way that farmers can add minerals back to the soil. **[1 mark]**

_____

3 Plants are producers.

a Name the reaction that plants use to make food. **[1 mark]**

_____

b State where in a plant cell this reaction occurs. **[1 mark]**

_____

c Complete the word equation to describe this process by choosing the correct words in bold. **[2 marks]**

oxygen / carbon dioxide + water → oxygen + **protein / glucose**

4 When a person is sprinting, they often respire anaerobically.

a Name the reactant used for anaerobic respiration. **[1 mark]**

_____

EXAM TIP

The reactants are on the left-hand side of an equation.

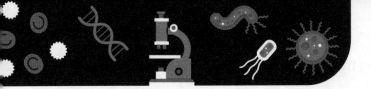

b Lactic acid is produced when an organism respires anaerobically. Describe **one** effect of lactic acid. **[1 mark]**

_____

c Microorganisms also respire anaerobically. Name **one** useful product made when a microorganism respires anaerobically. **[1 mark]**

_____

5 Respiration occurs in all cells.

a Complete the word equation for aerobic respiration. **[2 marks]**

_____ + _____ → _____ + _____

b State where respiration takes places in an animal cell. **[1 mark]**

_____

c Describe how carbon dioxide is removed from the cell. **[3 marks]**

_____

_____

_____

> **EXAM TIP**
>
> Remember: photosynthesis is reverse of respiration.

6 Plants need water for photosynthesis.

a State **one** other substance needed for photosynthesis to occur. **[1 mark]**

_____

b Describe how water is transported through a plant to be used in photosynthesis. **[3 marks]**

_____

_____

_____

_____

c Describe the role of stomata in photosynthesis. **[2 marks]**

_____

_____

_____

> **EXAM TIP**
>
> This is asking for the other reactant. Light is not the correct answer.

7 The rate at which an underwater plant is photosynthesising can be calculated by counting the number of bubbles of gas it gives off in a set time.

a Name the gas given off by the plant. **[1 mark]**

_____

b A student recorded the results in **Table 1** when they moved the plant different distances from the window.

EXAM TIP

There is a standard structure to these answers. Complete this sentence 'As the distance from the window increases, the mean number of bubbles per minute...'

Table 1

Distance from window sill in m	Mean number of bubbles per minute
0.0	45
0.5	40
1.0	32
1.5	20

State the conclusion that can be drawn from these results. **[2 marks]**

_____

_____

_____

8 Animals can respire aerobically and anaerobically. Compare the process of aerobic respiration and anaerobic respiration in humans. **[6 marks]**

EXAM TIP

For this compare question you need to state the things that aerobic and anaerobic respiration have in common **and** how they are different.

_____

_____

_____

_____

_____

_____

_____

9 A student carried out a test to show what reactants were needed for photosynthesis. The equipment was set up as shown in **Figure 1**.

- Leaf A was covered with a strip of black paper.
- Leaf B was placed in a bag containing soda lime, which absorbs carbon dioxide.
- Leaf C was placed in a bag containing hydrogencarbonate solution, which gives off carbon dioxide.
- The plant was kept in the dark for 48 hours then placed on a sunny windowsill.

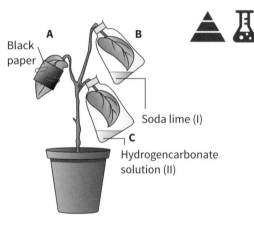

Figure 1

a After a few days, the student tested the leaves for the presence of starch. Describe how to test a leaf for starch. **[4 marks]**

_____

_____

_____

b The results are shown in **Figure 2**. Explain the students's findings. **[4 marks]**

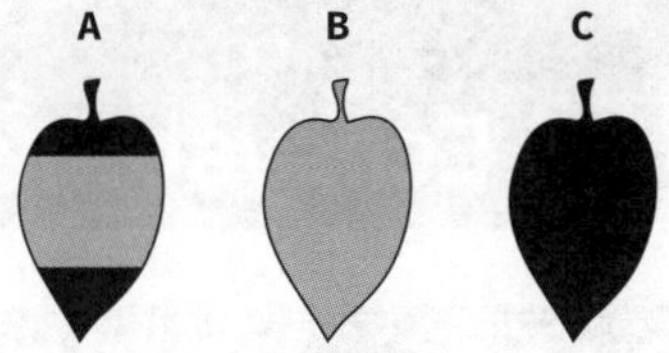

_____

_____

_____

_____

A   B   C

Figure 2

> **EXAM TIP**
>
> Write on the leaf images what each colour means. This will remind you when you're writing your answer.

c **i** The student carried out the same investigation with a variegated leaf (**Figure 3**).

Shade in the part of the unshaded leaf where starch is likely to be found. **[1 mark]**

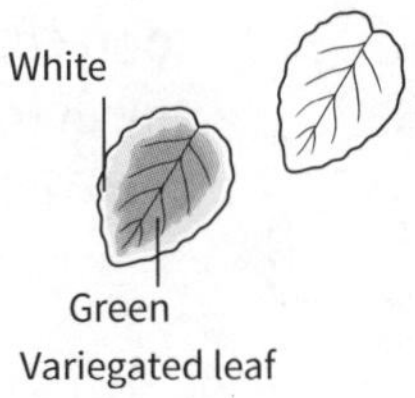

White

Green
Variegated leaf

Figure 3

ii Give a reason for your answer. **[2 marks]**

_____

_____

_____

B3 **10** Most plants reproduce by producing seeds.

a Name the process by which a seed starts to grow. **[1 mark]**

_____

b Put the statements in order to show how a seed is formed. **[4 marks]**

A Fertilisation occurs – the ovule and pollen nucleus join

B Pollen grain grows a tube, through the style, into the ovary

C Pollen is made by the anther

D Pollen grain is transferred to the stigma by an insect or the wind

E Ovule develops into a seed

F The pollen nucleus travels down the tube to meet with an ovule

C → ☐ → ☐ → ☐ → ☐ → E

> **EXAM TIP**
>
> You can cross off C and E straight away, then play around with the rest of the letters until it starts to make sense.

B2 **11** Multicellular organisms contain organ systems.

a State an organ system and describe its function. **[2 marks]**

_____

_____

b Describe the levels of organisation in an animal. **[4 marks]**

_____

_____

_____

B6 Ecosystems and adaptation

Interdependence

Interdependence is the way in which living organisms depend on each other to survive, grow, and reproduce.

For example, bees and flowers are interdependent. Flowering plants rely on bees for pollination, and bees depend on flowers for nectar.

Decreasing bee populations is a concern. If less pollination occurs, fewer crop plants may be fertilised, meaning human food supplies could decrease.

Food chains

A **food chain** is a diagram showing the transfer of energy between organisms, by showing what organisms eat. The first organism in a food chain is always a **producer**. The second organism is always a **herbivore** – they only eat plants. The third organisms are **carnivores** – they eat other animals. All animals are **consumers**.

The lion is called the top predator – this means it is not eaten by any other animals. The top predator is always the last link in the food chain.

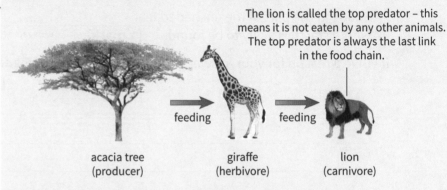

acacia tree (producer)   giraffe (herbivore)   lion (carnivore)

At each level in the chain, some energy is transferred to the organism's surroundings by heat and in waste products, meaning not all of the energy is passed on. Therefore, there are rarely more than four links as there is too little energy for further levels in the chain.

Food webs

A **food web** is a set of linked food chains. Food webs show the feeding relationships of organisms more realistically than food chains, as most animals eat more than one type of organism.

A **population** is the number of animals or plants of the same type that live in an area. In a food web, populations are interdependent – the population size of one type of organism has a direct effect on the population size of other types of organism.

If the population of the producer *decreases* then the populations of the consumers also *decrease*.

1 Grass (producer) dies
2 Rabbits, caterpillars, and snails die as there is no grass to eat.
3 Foxes, frogs, voles, and thrushes die.
4 Hawks die.

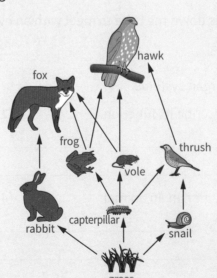

If the population of a consumer decreases, then other populations may *increase* or *decrease*.

1 Thrush population decreases.
2 Snail population may increase as nothing is eating the snails.
3 Hawk population may decrease as they have less food.

Decomposers are also found in food webs. These are organisms (bacteria and fungi) that break down dead plant and animal material. This releases nutrients back into the soil or water.

Bioaccumulation

Chemicals can also be passed along food chains. For example, **insecticides** (chemicals used to kill insects) can be washed into rivers from fields and end up in the sea.

4 One polar bear eats a lot of seals and so the insecticide accumulates dangerous levels in the polar bear's body. This makes the bear ill and can cause death.

3 Each seal eats several fish so the levels of chemical accumulate (build up) in their body. This is called **bioaccumulation**.

2 Fish absorb small amounts of the insecticide directly into their bodies from the water, where it is stored.

1 Insecticide enters the sea.

Ecosystems

An **ecosystem** is the name given to the plants and animals that are found in a particular location and the area in which they live.

The organisms in an ecosystem are known as a **community**. The area they live in is called a **habitat**. The conditions found in a habitat are known as the **environment**. These include the air, soil, and water.

The plants and animals in a community and a habitat co-exist. This means they live in the same place at the same time.

Practical: Sampling organisms

Scientists cannot study every organism in an ecosystem, so they take samples.

Quadrats are used to sample plants and slow-moving organisms like snails.

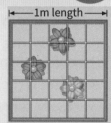

← 1m length →

Co-existing in an ecosystem

Each of the organisms living in an ecosystem has its own **niche**. A niche is a particular place or role that an organism has within the ecosystem. For example, they may live in a particular part of a tree or have a particular food source.

Tree canopy: many organisms live amongst the branches and leaves. For example, bees gather pollen and nectar when the tree is in blossom; squirrels gather acorns, and moths lay their eggs; small birds, such as sparrows, eat the caterpillars; hawks feed on the sparrows.

Trunk: the tree trunk provides food or shelter for a number of insects and caterpillars.

Roots and leaf litter: decomposers, woodlice, and earthworms live at the base of the tree. They break down old leaves, releasing nutrients that the tree can absorb and use for new growth.

Key terms

Make sure you can write a definition for these key terms

bioaccumulation carnivore community consumer decomposers
ecosystem environment food chain food web habitat herbivore
insecticides interdependence niche population producer quadrat

B6 Ecosystems and adaptation continued

Competition

In a habitat, there is a limited supply of resources. To survive, organisms compete with each other to get enough of these resources. This is known as **competition**.

Animals compete for food, water, space (for shelter and to hunt), and mates (to reproduce).

Plants compete for light, water, space, and minerals. Plants produce their own food by photosynthesis.

Predator-prey relationships

When a **predator** feeds on just one type of **prey**, the predator and prey populations are interdependent. A change in the population of one animal directly affects the population of the other. When plotted on a graph, this relationship shows a clear pattern:

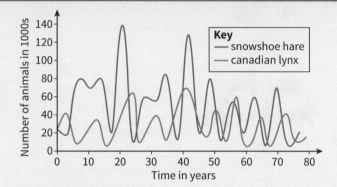

- When the prey population (hare) increases, the predators (lynx) have more to eat.
- The lynx survive longer and reproduce more. The number of predators increases.
- The growing predator population eats more prey. The prey numbers fall.
- Eventually, there is not enough food for all the predators, so their numbers fall.
- There are now fewer lynx feeding on the hares. The hare population increases and the cycle starts again.

Adaptations

Adaptations are characteristics that help an organism to survive and reproduce. For example, a cactus has spines, widespread roots, water-storing stems, and is covered in a waxy layer. These mechanisms save water in the desert. Large desert mammals can survive for long periods of time without drinking.

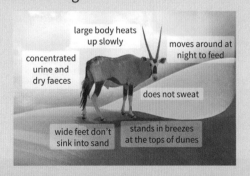

Seasonal adaptations

Adaptations for coping with seasonal changes, such as cold winters, include:

- **migration** – e.g., birds fly somewhere warmer or that has more food
- **hibernation** – e.g., bears sleep somewhere warm over the winter
- growing thick winter coats – e.g., sheep grow a thick coat of wool
- losing leaves – this saves energy, and the fallen leaves provide nutrients and a layer of warmth and protection around the base of the tree.

Key terms **Make sure you can write a definition for these key terms**

adaptation   competition   hibernation   migration   predator   prey

Retrieval

 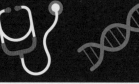 

Learn the answers to the questions below and test yourself.

B6 Questions | Answers

Food chains and webs

#	Question	Answer
1	What is a food chain?	a diagram that shows the transfer of energy between organisms
2	What is the first organism in a food chain?	a producer
3	What is a food web?	a diagram that shows a set of linked food chains
4	What is a decomposer?	an organism that breaks down dead plant and animal material
5	What is interdependence?	the way in which living organisms depend on each other to survive, grow, and reproduce
6	What is a population?	the number of plants or animals of the same species that live in an area
7	What is bioaccumulation?	the build-up of toxic chemicals along a food chain

Ecosystems

#	Question	Answer
8	What is a habitat?	the place where an organism lives
9	What is an ecosystem?	the living organisms in a particular area and the habitat in which they live
10	What is a niche?	the particular place or role that an organism has within an ecosystem

Competition

#	Question	Answer
11	What do animals compete for?	food, water, space, mates
12	What do plants compete for?	light, water, space, minerals

Adaptations

#	Question	Answer
13	What is an adaptation?	a characteristic that helps an organism to survive and reproduce
14	Name **four** adaptations of a cactus.	spines instead of leaves, stems that store water, widespread roots, covered in a thick waxy layer
15	Name **three** ways animals cope with the winter.	migration, hibernation, growing thick winter coats

Put paper here

Previous questions | Answers

#	Question	Answer
1	What is pollination?	the transfer of pollen from the anther to the stigma
2	How do you test for starch?	add iodine – food solution turns blue–black if starch is present
3	What is a drug?	a chemical substance that affects the way the body works
4	Name **four** ways leaves are adapted to photosynthesis.	thin, green (contain chlorophyll), have a large surface area, contain veins
5	What is the word equation for anaerobic respiration?	glucose → lactic acid (+ energy)

Put paper here

Practice questions

1 **Figure 1** shows a cactus. It has lots of adaptations to help it survive in its habitat.

Figure 1

a   Name the habitat where a cactus grows.   **[1 mark]**

_____

b   Match each adaptation of a cactus to its function (how it helps the cactus to survive) by drawing lines.   **[3 marks]**

Adaptation	Function
swollen stems	prevents water evaporating from the plant
thorns	collect water from a large area
waxy layer	stop animals eating it
widespread roots	store water

EXAM TIP

You don't have to start at the top of the list. Do the one you find easiest first.

2 **Figure 2** shows a food chain in a grassland.

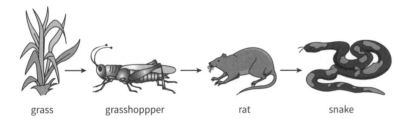

grass   grasshoppper   rat   snake

Figure 2

a   Identify the producer in the food chain.   **[1 mark]**

_____

b   Identify a predator in the food chain.   **[1 mark]**

_____

c   Describe what is meant by a consumer.   **[1 mark]**

_____

_____

3 Plants and animals compete for resources. Answer the following questions. Choose answers from the box.

mates	light	water	space	food

a Identify **one** resource that both animals and plants compete for.

[1 mark]

_____

EXAM TIP

There are lots of possible answers, but only give one. Give any more and you risk getting no marks.

b Identify **one** resource that only animals compete for. [1 mark]

_____

c **i** Identify **one** resource that only plants compete for. [1 mark]

_____

ii Give a reason for your answer. [2 marks]

_____

_____

_____

4 Organisms live within ecosystems.

a Identify the best definition of an ecosystem. Tick **one** box. [1 mark]

- the place where a plant or animal lives ☐

- the living organisms in a particular area and the habitat in which they live ☐

- the particular place or role that an organism has within an ecosystem ☐

b Name **two** things organisms living within an ecosystem depend on each other for. [2 marks]

i _____

ii _____

5 **Figure 3** shows a tree frog that lives in the rainforest and some of its adaptations.

nocturnal   very low body mass   green   sticky feet

Figure 3

EXAM TIP

Nocturnal means they are awake at night.

Suggest and explain **two** ways that the frog is adapted to living in the rainforest. [4 marks]

i _____

_____

ii _____

_____

6 A farmer investigated the number of thistles present in a field. She placed a 1 m² quadrat at four random locations in the field (**Figure 4**).

EXAM TIP

For this question you should only count plants that are fully inside the quadrat.

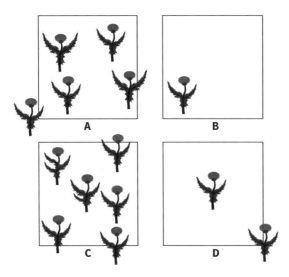

Figure 4

a Explain why the farmer should place the quadrat in random locations. [1 mark]

_____

_____

b Before calculating a mean, the famer decided that she would only count plants that were fully contained in the quadrat.

Complete **Table 1** and calculate the mean number of thistles per m². [2 marks]

Table 1

Quadrat	A	B	C	D	Mean
Number of thistles per m²	3	1		1	

c The field is 1500 m². Estimate the thistle population of the field. [2 marks]

_____

7 **Figure 5** shows the feeding relationships between organisms living in Africa.

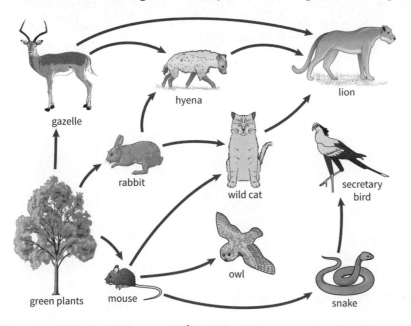

Figure 5

EXAM TIP

We can think of the arrows as 'eaten by'.

a Identify **one** organism that hyenas eat. **[1 mark]**

_____

b State and explain what would happen to the wild cat population if all the lions were removed from an area. **[2 marks]**

_____

_____

_____

c State and explain what would happen to the owl population if all the wild cats were eaten. **[2 marks]**

_____

_____

_____

EXAM TIP

There are two command words in the question. 'State' is telling you to give a simple statement. 'Explain' is asking you to say why that statement is happening.

8 Ladybirds are the predators of aphids. **Table 2** shows the variation in the numbers of aphids and ladybirds in an area over a 15-month period. **Figure 6** is a graph of this variation.

Month	Number of aphids in thousands	Number of ladybirds in thousands
0	10	5
3	80	25
6	100	45
9	30	60
12	20	30
15	70	10

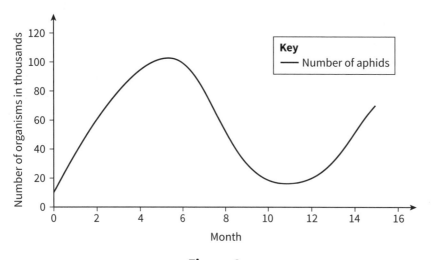

EXAM TIP

Use crosses to add the data and then draw a line of best fit.

Figure 6

a Add the data for ladybirds to the graph in Figure 6. **[3 marks]**

b Describe the patterns shown by the data. **[4 marks]**

EXAM TIP

Talk about any ups and downs in the graph, or any other change that you see, and link them to time.

_____

_____

_____

_____

_____

9 Organisms living in an ecosystem are said to be interdependent.

a Explain how flowering plants and bees are interdependent. **[2 marks]**

_____

_____

_____

b The food chain shows one source of food for a jaguar.

flower ⟶ butterfly ⟶ lizard ⟶ jaguar

Explain why food chains rarely have more than four links. **[4 marks]**

_____

_____

_____

_____

_____

c Explain why the Sun is the ultimate source of energy in food chains. **[3 marks]**

EXAM TIP

Think about what all food chains start with.

_____

_____

_____

_____

10 Mercury was used to make insecticides but is now banned, as it damages the nervous and reproductive systems of mammals, including humans.

In the sea, plankton (microscopic organisms) absorb the mercury. When the plankton are eaten by small fish, the mercury stays in the fish because it cannot be excreted. Larger fish, such as tuna, then eat the smaller fish. People eating contaminated tuna may get mercury poisoning.

a State what is meant by an insecticide. **[1 mark]**

_____

b Use the information to draw a food chain. Explain how mercury can poison humans but not the tuna. **[6 marks]**

EXAM TIP

Use highlighters to pull the important information out of the question, then use that to draw your food chain.

_____

_____

_____

_____

EXAM TIP

When it says 'draw' a food chain, you don't actually need to draw anything, just write the parts in order.

B5 **11** Photosynthesis takes place in plants.

a Name the cell component where photosynthesis occurs. **[1 mark]**

_____

b Complete the word equation for photosynthesis. **[1 mark]**

$$\text{carbon dioxide + water} \xrightarrow{\text{light}} \text{oxygen +} \rule{2cm}{0.4pt}$$

c Describe how carbon dioxide gets into the plant. **[2 marks]**

_____

_____

B4 **12** Enzymes are special proteins that play a crucial role in digestion.

a Describe the role of enzymes in digestion. **[1 mark]**

_____

b Explain why enzymes are called catalysts. **[2 marks]**

_____

_____

c Compare the digestion of carbohydrates with the digestion of proteins. **[4 marks]**

_____

_____

Knowledge

B7 Inheritance

Variation

Differences in characteristics within a **species** are known as **variation**. Organisms of the same species can reproduce to produce fertile offspring. These differences can be a result of the following types of variation.

Inherited variation	Both	Environmental variation
• Characteristics are passed from biological parents to offspring • Examples: genetic diseases, eye colour, blood group	• Many characteristics are affected by both types of variation • Examples: height, body mass, leaf surface area	• Surroundings affect your characteristics • Examples: dyed hair, tattoos, accent

Measuring variation

To study variation, scientists survey populations and take measurements of different characteristics. These data are then plotted on a graph so that patterns can be easily seen.

Discontinuous variation:

- This can only result in certain values, for example, blood group, eye colour.

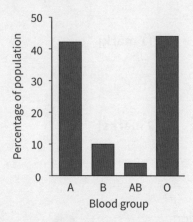

Continuous variation:

- This can take any value within a range, for example, height, hair length.

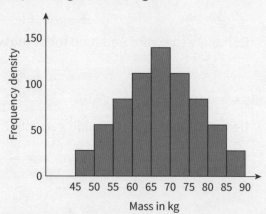

- Characteristics that show discontinuous variation should be plotted on a bar chart.
- Characteristics that occur only as a result of inherited variation normally show discontinuous variation.

- Characteristics that show continuous variation should be plotted on a histogram.
- Characteristics that occur as a result of both environmental and inherited variation usually show continuous variation.

 Key terms

Make sure you can write a definition for these key terms

chromosome   continuous variation   DNA   discontinuous variation
environmental variation   gene   inherited variation   species   variation

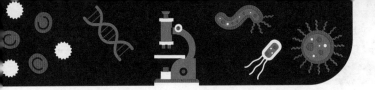

Genetic material

DNA contains all the information needed to make an organism. It is stored in the nucleus of cells.

DNA is arranged into long strands called **chromosomes**. An offspring inherits half of their chromosomes from their biological mother and half from their biological father. This is why offspring share some of their characteristics with each of their biological parents.

Each chromosome is divided into sections of DNA. Sections of DNA that contain information to produce a characteristic, such as eye colour, are called **genes**.

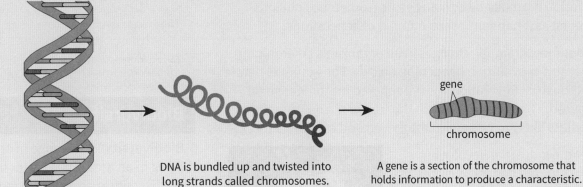

The shape of DNA is a double helix – a bit like a twisted ladder.

DNA is bundled up and twisted into long strands called chromosomes.

A gene is a section of the chromosome that holds information to produce a characteristic.

Inheriting genetic material

Different species have different numbers of chromosomes in the nuclei of their cells. Humans have 46 chromosomes, arranged in 23 pairs. One set of 23 chromosomes comes from a person's mother and one set of 23 chromosomes from their father.

Egg and sperm cells are the only cells to contain 23 chromosomes. They only have one copy of each chromosome. During fertilisation, the egg and sperm cells join together. When their nuclei join, their chromosomes pair up, producing an embryo with 46 chromosomes in each cell.

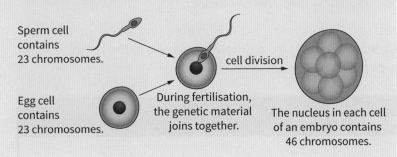

Sperm cell contains 23 chromosomes.

Egg cell contains 23 chromosomes.

During fertilisation, the genetic material joins together.

cell division

The nucleus in each cell of an embryo contains 46 chromosomes.

Discovering DNA

Four scientists worked together to produce a model of the structure of DNA:

- In the 1950s, Rosalind Franklin and Maurice Wilkins used X-rays to produce an image of the structure of DNA.

- James Watson and Francis Crick were also studying DNA. When they saw this image, it showed them that DNA had a helical shape.

- Through further investigations, Watson and Crick worked out that the structure of DNA is like a twisted ladder. This is known as a double helix.

B7 Inheritance continued

Evolution

All living organisms have evolved from a common ancestor through the process of **natural selection**.

Evolution started with unicellular organisms. These organisms, similar to bacteria, lived in water more than three billion years ago. Over time, they evolved to become multicellular organisms, which could live on land, in the air, and in water.

Evolution normally takes many years (sometimes millions of years) as it happens over a number of generations.

Sometimes, dramatic changes in an organism's environment can result in evolution happening quickly. For example, before the Industrial Revolution, most peppered moths were pale coloured. They blended in with the tree bark and, therefore, were less likely to be eaten, so survived and reproduced.

After the Industrial Revolution, dark coloured peppered moths were better adapted as they were camouflaged against the soot-covered trees. They, therefore, survived and reproduced, increasing the population of dark-coloured moths.

Natural selection

Organisms in a species show variation caused by differences in their genes.

Organisms with characteristics best suited to the environment survive and reproduce. This is called 'survival of the fittest'.

Genes that code for advantageous characteristics are passed onto the offspring.

The process is repeated many times.

Over a long time, this can lead to the formation of a new species.

Biodiversity

Biodiversity is the range of organisms living in an area. The greater the biodiversity in an area, the more stable the ecosystem is, as the animals living there have a range of food sources.

Species of plants and animals that have only a small population in the world are said to be **endangered**.

Extinction

If a species is not well-adapted to its environment, it will not survive and the organisms will die before reproducing. A species becomes **extinct** when there are no more individuals of that species left anywhere in the world.

Factors leading to extinction are:

- environmental changes
- habitat destruction
- new diseases

- new predators
- increased competition.

Fossils, like the one in the image, are the remains, or traces, of organisms that lived many years ago. They provide evidence for organisms that are now extinct.

Scientists are trying to prevent endangered species from becoming extinct by breeding in zoos, setting up nature reserves and using gene banks to store genetic samples from different species. In the future, these samples could be used for research or to produce new individuals.

Key terms

Make sure you can write a definition for these key terms

biodiversity   endangered   evolution   extinct   fossil   natural selection

 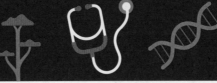

Retrieval

Learn the answers to the questions below and test yourself.

B7 Questions | Answers

Variation

1	What is variation?	differences in characteristics within a species
2	What is a species?	organisms that can mate to produce fertile offspring
3	What is inherited variation?	variation due to genetic information that is inherited from an organism's biological parents
4	What is environmental variation?	variation caused by an organism's surroundings and lifestyle
5	What is continuous variation?	a characteristic that can take any value within a range of values
6	What is discontinuous variation?	a characteristic that can only be certain values

Genetic material

7	What is DNA?	a chemical that contains all the information needed to make an organism
8	What is a chromosome?	a long strand of DNA that contains many genes
9	What is a gene?	a section of DNA that contains the information for a characteristic
10	How is genetic material inherited?	when the egg and sperm join during fertilisation
11	Name the **four** scientists who worked together to develop the model of DNA	Watson, Crick, Wilkins, Franklin

Evolution

12	What is evolution?	the development of a species over time
13	What is natural selection?	the process by which organisms with characteristics that are most suited to the environment survive and reproduce, passing on their genes

Extinction

14	What does extinct mean?	when no more individuals of a species are left anywhere in the world
15	What is biodiversity?	the range of organisms living in an area

Put paper here

Previous questions | Answers

1	What is the function of the cell nucleus?	controls the cell and contains genetic material
2	Name **three** minerals plants need for healthy growth.	nitrates, phosphates, magnesium
3	What is the word equation for fermentation?	glucose → ethanol + carbon dioxide (+ energy)
4	What is a habitat?	the place where an organism lives
5	What do plants compete for?	light, water, space, minerals

Put paper here

Practice questions

1 Variation can be caused by environmental variation, inherited variation, or both. Put each characteristic in the box under the correct heading in **Table 1**.   **[4 marks]**

| lobed ears | height | pierced ears | eye colour |

Table 1

Environmental variation	Inherited variation	Both

2 **Figure 1** shows a human cell.

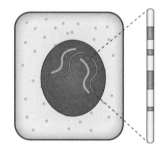

Figure 1

a Add labels to identify:

   i the nucleus   **[1 mark]**

   ii a chromosome   **[1 mark]**

   iii a gene   **[1 mark]**

b Name the chemical that contains the genetic information to make an organism.   **[1 mark]**

_____

> **EXAM TIP**
>
> Use a ruler to draw arrows and add labels around the diagram. Don't try to draw lines from the question to the diagram.

3 Many organisms are at the risk of extinction.

a Describe what is meant by the term *extinction*.   **[1 mark]**

_____

_____

b Identify **two** possible causes of extinction. Tick **two** boxes.   **[2 marks]**

creation of new habitats   ☐

outbreak of a new disease   ☐

change in the organism's environment   ☐

new food supplies   ☐

> **EXAM TIP**
>
> The question wants two answers. Even if you're not sure of a second one, just tick any other box. Don't tick three as that will lose you marks.

c Describe **one** way that scientists are trying to prevent organisms from becoming extinct. **[1 mark]**

_____

_____

4 The statements describe how a species evolves by the process of natural selection. Put the statements in order by writing the correct letter in each box. The first one has been done for you. **[4 marks]**

A This process is repeated many times until these characteristics become more common in the population.

B Over a long period of time, this may lead to the development of a new species.

C Organisms in a species show variation – this is caused by differences in their genes.

D The individuals with characteristics that are best adapted to their environment are most likely to survive.

E The successful individuals reproduce and pass on their useful characteristics.

EXAM TIP

Sometimes it is easier to start backwards when working out the order.

C → ☐ → ☐ → ☐ → ☐

5 The ladybirds in **Figure 2** show variation. One variation is their body mass.

a State **one** other way the ladybirds vary. **[1 mark]**

Figure 2

EXAM TIP

Do not write body mass for part a. This is not going to get you any marks.

_____

b Describe the causes of body mass variation. **[2 marks]**

_____

_____

_____

c State the type of chart that would be best to plot body mass variation. **[1 mark]**

_____

6 Characteristics are passed onto offspring through genetic material.

a State what is meant by a gene. **[1 mark]**

_____

b Describe how characteristics are inherited. **[3 marks]**

_____

_____

_____

_____

c Describe how scientists worked together to develop the DNA model. **[3 marks]**

_____

_____

_____

_____

7 The pie charts in **Figure 3** show the distribution of blood groups in India and the UK.

a Explain whether blood groups show inherited variation, environmental variation, or both. **[2 marks]**

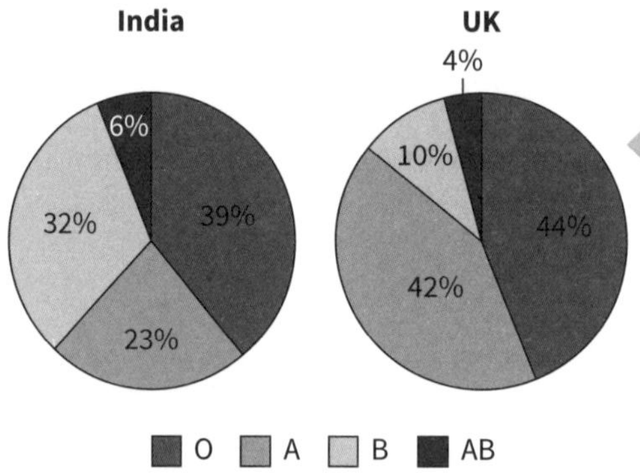

_____

_____

_____

_____

India

6%
32%   39%
23%

UK

4%
10%
44%
42%

O ■ A ■ B □ AB ■

Figure 3

EXAM TIP

When you're asked to compare data, make sure you give numbers in your answer.

b Compare the distribution of blood groups in India and the UK. **[3 marks]**

_____

_____

_____

_____

8 Use examples to describe the differences between continuous variation and discontinuous variation. **[6 marks]**

_____

_____

_____

_____

_____

EXAM TIP

You have to use examples here if you want to get the marks. Just saying what the difference is between continuous variation and discontinuous variation is not enough to get the marks.

9 Organisms within a species show variation.

a Use examples to describe the differences between inherited variation and environmental variation. **[4 marks]**

_____

_____

_____

_____

b Explain why some numerically measured characteristics show discontinuous variation. **[2 marks]**

_____

_____

_____

10 Describe how giraffes have evolved over a period of time to possess long necks. **[6 marks]**

_____

_____

_____

_____

_____

_____

B4 11 To remain healthy, you should eat a balanced diet.

a Match each component of the diet to its function by drawing lines. **[2 marks]**

Diet component	Function
protein	provides energy
carbohydrate	used to insulate the body and provide energy
lipid (fat)	used for growth and repair

b Identify the food that provides a good source of vitamins. Choose the answer from the box. **[1 mark]**

bread   cheese   orange

_____

 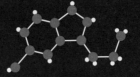 

Knowledge

C1 Particles

Materials and the particle model

Materials can be:

- a **substance** – this has one type of material only, like gold and water
- **mixtures** – these are made of more than one of type of substance, like wood and air.

All materials are made of very small (tiny) **particles**. All the particles in a substance are the same.

Every substance has its own **properties** (what it looks like and how it behaves). You can use the **particle model** to explain the properties of a substance. The properties depend on:

- the size, shape, and mass of the particles
- how the particles are arranged and separated
- how the particles move
- how strongly the particles are held together.

States of matter and their properties

Most substances can exist in three states – as a **solid**, a **liquid**, or a **gas**. These are the **states of matter**. You can explain the properties of a substance in its three states using the particle model.

solid	liquid	gas
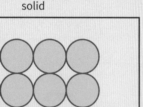	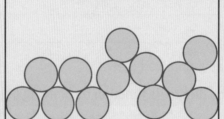	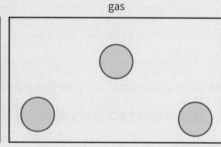
Particle arrangement of a solid.	Particle arrangement of a liquid.	Particle arrangement of a gas.

Property	Particle model explanation
solids have a fixed shape, do not flow, cannot be compressed	particles are touching, arranged in a pattern, vibrate but do not move from place to place
liquids flow, take the shape of the bottom of the container, cannot be compressed	particles are touching, can move around, move randomly, sliding over each other
gases fill containers, can be compressed	particles are far apart, moving quickly and randomly

Key terms   **Make sure you can write a definition for these key terms**

boiling   boiling point   change of state   condensing   conserved   density   evaporation   freezing   freezing point   gas   liquid   mass   melting   melting point   mixture   particle   particle model   property   reversible   solid   states of matter   sublimation   substance   volume

Density

Density is a measure of the mass (amount of stuff) in a given volume.

Mass is in grams (g) or kilograms (kg). **Volume** is in cm^3 or m^3.

The density of a substance depends on the mass and arrangement of its particles, as well as its state.

- The density of a substance in the gas state is much less than its density in the liquid and solid states.
- The density of a substance is about the same in the solid and liquid states.

Water is unusual – it is less dense in the solid state than in the liquid state.

Changes of state

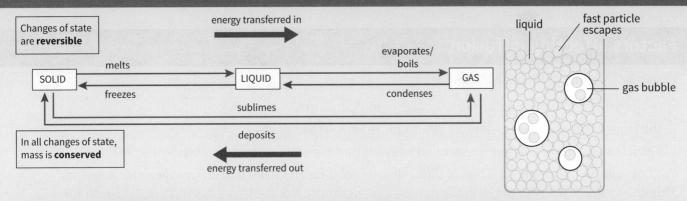

Examples of **changes of state** include melting, boiling, evaporation, and sublimation.

- In **melting**, particles vibrate more, and move out of their positions until they slide over each other.
- In **sublimation**, particles in a solid state break free and escape.

- In **boiling**, bubbles of gas form in the liquid and escape from it. This only happens at a certain temperature – the **boiling point**.
- In **evaporation**, fast-moving particles escape from the surface of a liquid.
- Evaporation happens at *any* temperature above the freezing point

Freezing and condensing

- In freezing, particles move more slowly until they get into a fixed pattern and vibrate.

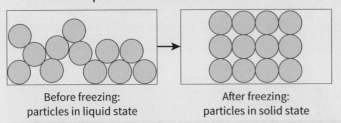

Before freezing: particles in liquid state

After freezing: particles in solid state

- In **condensing**, particles move more slowly and get closer together until they are sliding over each other.
- A substance changes from the solid state to the liquid state at the **melting point** of the substance.

Boiling point

A pure substance has a unique boiling or melting point.

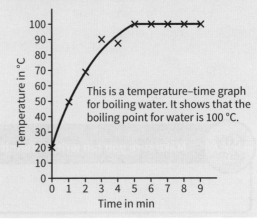

This is a temperature–time graph for boiling water. It shows that the boiling point for water is 100 °C.

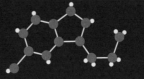

C1 Particles continued

Diffusion

In **diffusion**, particles move from an area of higher **concentration** to an area of lower concentration. Diffusion happens in the liquid and gas states because particles are free to move.

A substance diffuses more slowly in the liquid state than in the gas state.

In this demonstration, bromine diffuses into the upper gas jars. The particle diagram shows this.

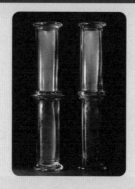

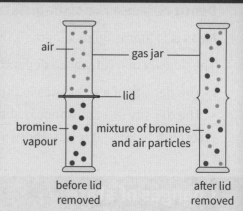

Factors affecting diffusion

How quickly diffusion happens depends on:

- temperature – particles move faster at higher temperatures
- the state of the substance – liquids diffuse more slowly than gases
- particle size – more massive (bigger and heavier) particles diffuse more slowly.

For example, in this demonstration of diffusion, the solid forms closer to the hydrogen chloride end. This shows that the hydrogen chloride particles diffuse more slowly. This is because hydrogen chloride particles are more massive than ammonia particles.

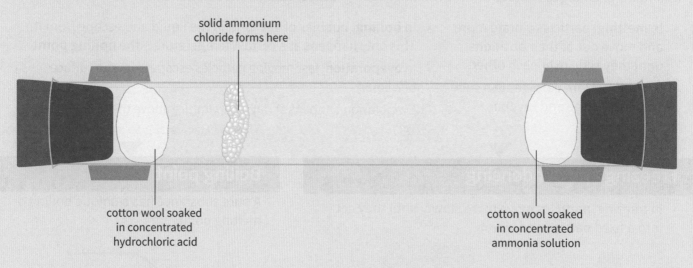

solid ammonium
chloride forms here

cotton wool soaked
in concentrated
hydrochloric acid

cotton wool soaked
in concentrated
ammonia solution

Key terms

Make sure you can write a definition for these key terms

concentration   diffusion

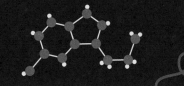
Learn the answers to the questions below and test yourself.

	C1 Questions		Answers
Materials	1. What are all substances made of?		particles/atoms
	2. What is a property?	Put paper here	what something looks like and how it behaves, for example, shiny, magnetic
States of matter	3. What is a state of matter?		whether a substance is solid, liquid, or gas
	4. How are particles arranged in a solid?		touching, regular pattern
	5. How are particles arranged in a liquid?	Put paper here	touching, not a regular pattern
	6. How are particles arranged in a gas?		moving very fast, not in a regular pattern
Density	7. What is density?		the amount of mass in a given volume
	8. Which state is usually the least dense?	Put paper here	gas state
	9. In terms of density, which substance is unusual?		water
Changes of state	10. What is the name of the process when a substance changes from the solid state to the liquid state?	Put paper here	melting
	11. What is the name of the process when a substance changes from the liquid state to the solid state?	Put paper here	freezing
	12. What is the process of boiling?		going from a liquid state to a gas state
	13. What is the process of condensing?		changing rapidly from the gas state to the liquid state
	14. What does melting point mean?	Put paper here	the temperature at which a substance melts
	15. What name is given to the temperature at which a substance boils?	Put paper here	boiling point
	16. How is the melting point of a substance shown on a temperature–time graph?	Put paper here	by a horizontal line
	17. How is boiling different from evaporating?		boiling only happens at the boiling point, evaporation happens at any temperature (above freezing)
Diffusion	18. What is diffusion?	Put paper here	movement of substances from an area of higher concentration to an area of lower concentration
	19. In which **two** states does diffusion happen?		gas state and liquid state
	20. Give **three** factors that affect how quickly diffusion happens.		temperature, state, particle size

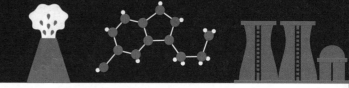

Practice

Practice questions

1 All substances are made of particles. The properties of a substance depend on the particles in it. Complete the sentences about properties and particles by drawing lines. **[3 marks]**

The mass of 1 cm³ of a substance depends on	the arrangement of the particles.
How easy a substance is to scratch depends on	the mass of the particles and how they are arranged.
Whether a substance flows depends on	how strongly the particles are held together.
How much space 1 g of a substance takes up depends on	whether the particles can move.

> **EXAM TIP**
>
> Each box on the left only connects to one box on the right hand side. Draw lines carefully using a pencil and a ruler.

2 **Figure 1** shows the particle model of the changes of state of a substance.

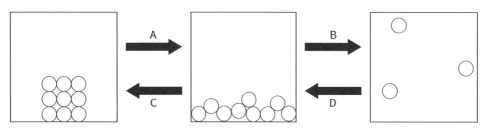

Figure 1

a Give the letter of the state change that shows melting. **[1 mark]**

_____

b Give the letter of the state change that shows condensation. **[1 mark]**

_____

> **EXAM TIP**
>
> Don't write too much here – all you need to do is write the letter.

c Give the letter of a change of state that would involve a large *increase* in density. **[1 mark]**

_____

d Complete the sentence. **[1 mark]**

In a solid state, particles _____ but do not move from place to place.

3 Which **two** statements are correct for a substance in a solid state?
Tick **two** boxes. **[2 marks]**

The substance takes the shape of its whole container. ☐

The particles move from place to place. ☐

The particles touch each other. ☐

The substance can be compressed only a tiny bit. ☐

The particles are not in a regular arrangement. ☐

4 **Figure 2** shows three temperature–time graphs. In each case, a substance
changes from the liquid state to the gas state.

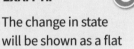

Figure 2

a Which graph(s) show a pure substance? Give the letter(s). **[1 mark]**

_____

b Look at graph C. Give the boiling point of the substance. Choose the
answer from the box. **[1 mark]**

| 0 °C | 20 °C | 100 °C |

_____

> **EXAM TIP**
>
> The change in state
> will be shown as a flat
> section of the graph.

c Complete the sentences about change of state. Choose answers
from the box. Each word may be used once, more than once,
or not at all. **[2 marks]**

| vibrate | reflect | density | temperature |

As the temperature increases, the particles move faster or

_____ more.

When the state of a substance changes, the _____ does
not change.

5 The particle model can explain diffusion. **Figure 3** shows some particles of a substance in a box of air. The air particles are not shown.

box A   box B   box C

Figure 3

EXAM TIP

This is chemistry, not art – don't spend too long getting perfect circles.

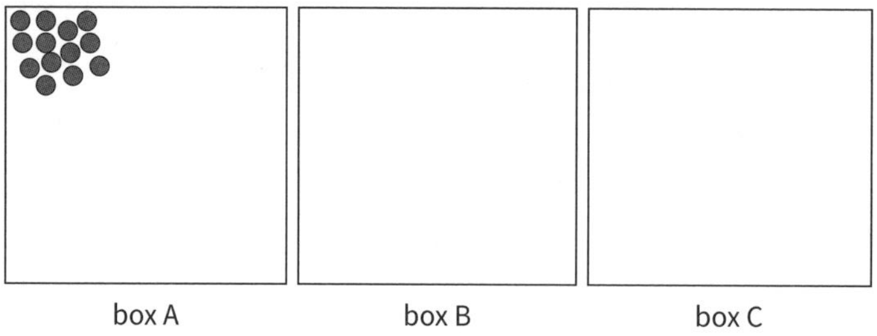

a Complete boxes B and C to show what happens to the particles as the substance diffuses and fills the box. **[2 marks]**

b Changing the conditions can make a substance diffuse faster or slower.

Identify the **one** change that would *increase* the rate of diffusion. Tick **one** box. **[2 marks]**

increasing the temperature ☐

increasing the size of the box ☐

adding more particles ☐

6 A student draws the particles in a substance in the liquid state, as shown in **Figure 4**.

Figure 4

EXAM TIP

If you're not sure, you can compare this image to the ones in the previous questions.

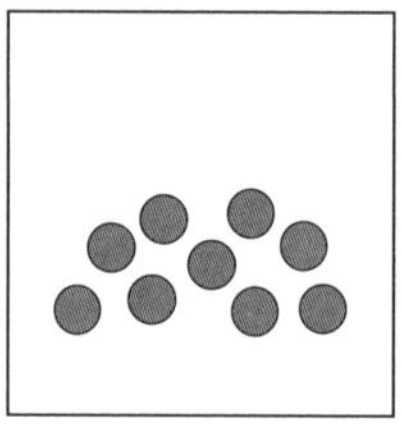

a Describe **one** mistake that the student has made. **[1 mark]**

_____

_____

b The liquid is left in a shallow dish. Describe what happens to the particles as the liquid evaporates. **[2 marks]**

_____

_____

c Describe **one** similarity and **one** difference between evaporation and boiling. **[2 marks]**

Similarity _____

Difference _____

7 You can use the particle model to explain the properties of substances in different states. Read the following sentences.

A student pours water into a glass. They pick up a solid lump of ice. They put the ice in the water and the ice floats.

For each of the sentences, identify the property and explain it using the particle model.

a *A student pours water into a glass.* **[2 marks]**

Property _____

Explanation _____

b *They pick up a solid lump of ice.* **[2 marks]**

Property _____

Explanation _____

c *They put the ice in the water and the ice floats.* **[2 marks]**

Property _____

Explanation _____

EXAM TIP

It's important to use key words in your answer to show you understand that you know what you are talking about. In this question, you must use the word 'particle'.

8 A student wants to investigate how the number of teaspoons of salt added to water affects its boiling point. **Figure 5** shows their results and the axes for their graph.

Number of spoonfuls of salt	Boiling temperature in °C
0	100
1	102
2	104
3	101
4	108
5	110

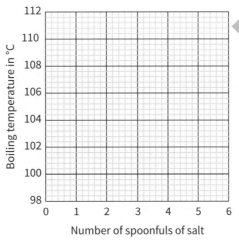

EXAM TIP

Always draw your points using a cross. It is much clearer for an examiner to understand.

Figure 5

a The student has seen that pure water boils at 100 °C and salty water boils at 104 °C. Write a hypothesis based on this information. **[1 mark]**

_____

_____

b Plot the data on the graph in Figure 5. Draw a line of best fit. Circle the anomalous result. **[3 marks]**

c Suggest whether or not the data supports your hypothesis from part a.

[1 mark]

_____

_____

EXAM TIP

The anomaly is the point that doesn't fit in with the rest.

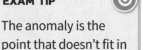

d Suggest **one** improvement the student could make to the investigation. **[1 mark]**

EXAM TIP

Think of any possible errors that could have been made or how you could make the experiment more accurate.

_____

_____

9 **Figure 6** shows the melting points of six metals.

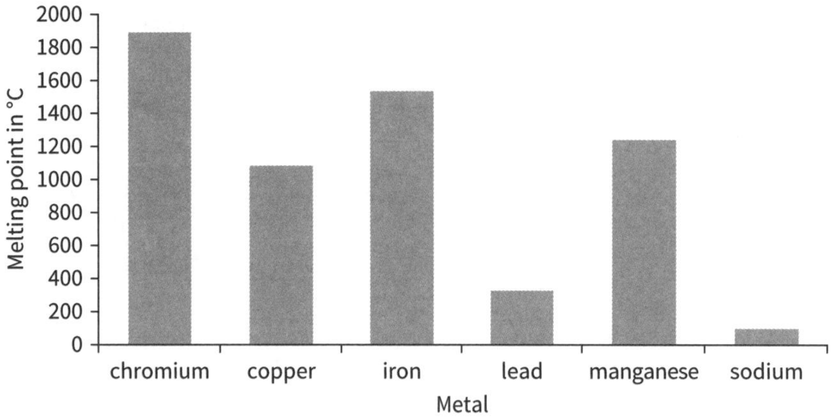

Figure 6

a Describe in terms of particles what happens when a substance melts.

[2 marks]

_____

_____

_____

b Name the substance in Figure 6 with the highest melting point.

[1 mark]

EXAM TIP

This is asking for the name of the metal, not the value of the boiling point.

_____

c Suggest why the melting points of the metals are different. **[1 mark]**

_____

d A student does an experiment with an unknown metal and finds that its melting point is 1200 °C. Suggest which metal in **Figure 6** it is likely to be. **[1 mark]**

_____

10 A student watches a video about mercury. Mercury is in a liquid state at room temperature. It freezes at −40 °C and evaporates at room temperature.

a Suggest how the densities of mercury in the solid, liquid, and gas state are similar or different. **[2 marks]**

_____

_____

b Explain the different densities of mercury you have described in part a.

[2 marks]

_____

_____

c Water is also a liquid at room temperature. Suggest why the density of water is different from the density of mercury when they are both in a liquid state.

[1 mark]

_____

_____

11 Look at the melting points and boiling points in **Table 1**.

Table 1

Substance	Melting point in °C	Boiling point in °C
water	0.0	100.0
chlorine	−101.0	−34.0
bromine	−7.3	58.0
mercury	−39.0	357.0
ethanol	−114.0	78.0

EXAM TIP

When dealing with a mix of negative and positive numbers, it can help to sketch out a number line and write points on, so you don't get confused.

a Name the substance with the highest melting point. [1 mark]

_____

b Explain why some boiling points are higher than others. [2 marks]

_____

_____

c Identify the state of bromine at 20 °C. Explain your answer. [2 marks]

_____

_____

d Identify which element is liquid for the largest range of temperatures. Justify your answer with calculations. [3 marks]

EXAM TIP

You have to use a calculation in your answer or you won't get full marks.

_____

_____

_____

_____

C2 Elements, atoms, and compounds

Elements

An **element** is a substance that cannot be broken down into other substances. For example, gold, silver, oxygen, chlorine, and helium.

There are about 100 elements. Each element is identified using **chemical symbols** – for example, hydrogen is H, oxygen is O. They are all listed in the **Periodic Table**. Elements with similar properties are grouped together.

Atoms

An **atom** is the smallest part of an element that can exist.

- An element contains just one type of atom.
- All the atoms in an element are identical.
- There are about 100 elements and, therefore, about 100 types of atom.
- Atoms of different elements have different masses and are different sizes.
- A single atom on its own does not have properties.

The Periodic Table

Alkali metals
Noble gases
Halogens

relative atomic mass	chemical symbol	name	atomic (proton) number

| 1.0 | H | hydrogen | 1 |

	Group																	4 He helium 2
	1	2										3	4	5	6	7	0/8	
Period 2	7 Li lithium 3	9 Be beryllium 4										11 B boron 5	12 C carbon 6	14 N nitrogen 7	16 O oxygen 8	19 F fluorine 9	20 Ne neon 10	
3	23 Na sodium 11	24 Mg magnesium 12										27 Al aluminium 13	28 Si silicon 14	31 P phosphorus 15	32 S sulfur 16	35.5 Cl chlorine 17	40 Ar argon 18	
4	39 K potassium 19	40 Ca calcium 20	45 Sc scandium 21	48 Ti titanium 22	51 V vanadium 23	52 Cr chromium 24	55 Mn manganese 25	56 Fe iron 26	59 Co cobalt 27	59 Ni nickel 28	63.5 Cu copper 29	65 Zn zinc 30	70 Ga gallium 31	73 Ge germanium 32	75 As arsenic 33	79 Se selenium 34	80 Br bromine 35	84 Kr krypton 36
5	85.5 Rb rubidium 37	88 Sr strontium 38	89 Y yttrium 39	91 Zr zirconium 40	93 Nb niobium 41	96 Mo molybdenum 42	(98) Tc technetium 43	101 Ru ruthenium 44	103 Rh rhodium 45	106 Pd palladium 46	108 Ag silver 47	112 Cd cadmium 48	115 In indium 49	119 Sn tin 50	122 Sb antimony 51	128 Te tellurium 52	127 I iodine 53	131 Xe xenon 54
6	133 Cs caesium 55	137 Ba barium 56	139 La* lanthanum 57	178.5 Hf hafnium 72	181 Ta tantalum 73	184 W tungsten 74	186 Re rhenium 75	190 Os osmium 76	192 Ir iridium 77	195 Pt platinum 78	197 Au gold 79	201 Hg mercury 80	204 Tl thallium 81	207 Pb lead 82	209 Bi bismuth 83	210 Po polonium 84	(210) At astatine 85	222 Rn radon 86
7	(223) Fr francium 87	(226) Ra radium 88	(227) Ac# actinium 89	(261) Rf rutherfordium 104	(262) Db dubnium 105	(266) Sg seaborgium 106	(264) Bh bohrium 107	(277) Hs hassium 108	(268) Mt meitnerium 109	(271) Ds darmstadtium 110	(272) Rg roentgenium 111	Cn copernicium	Nh nihonium	Fl flerovium	Mc moscovium	Lv livermorium	Ts tennessine	Og oganesson

*58–71 Lanthanides	140 Ce cerium 58	141 Pr praseodymium 59	144 Nd neodymium 60	(145) Pm promethium 61	150 Sm samarium 62	152 Eu europium 63	157 Gd gadolinium 64	159 Tb terbium 65	163 Dy dysprosium 66	165 Ho holmium 67	167 Er erbium 68	169 Tm thulium 69	173 Yb ytterbium 70	175 Lu lutetium 71
#90–103 Actinides	232 Th thorium 90	231 Pa protactinium 91	238 U uranium 92	237 Np neptunium 93	239 Pu plutonium 94	243 Am americium 95	247 Cm curium 96	247 Bk berkelium 97	252 Cf californium 98	(252) Es einsteinium 99	(257) Fm fermium 100	(258) Md mendelevium 101	(259) No nobelium 102	(260) Lr lawrencium 103

Elements and atoms

	Elements	Atoms
properties	have physical properties such as colour, smell, hardness, shine	do not have colour or smell, are not shiny, do not have any other physical properties
state	are in the solid, liquid, or gas state depending on the temperature	do not exist in a state
change of state	can change state	change their arrangement and motion depending on the state of the element

 Key terms **Make sure you can write a definition for these key terms**

atom   chemical symbol   compound   element   molecule   Periodic Table

Compounds

Compounds are substances made up of atoms of more than one element. The atoms are joined together strongly. For example, water is a compound as it contains atoms of the elements hydrogen and oxygen, joined together strongly.

Molecules are groups of two or more atoms joined together strongly.

- If all the atoms in a molecule are the *same*, the substance is an element.
- If there is *more than one* type of atom in a molecule, the substance is a compound.

Molecules of elements and compounds

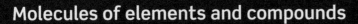

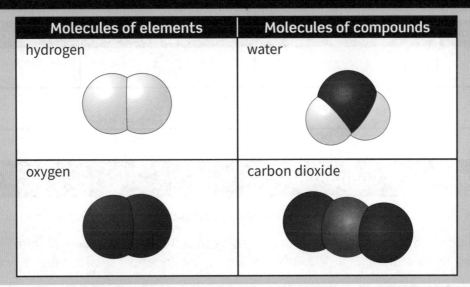

Molecules of elements	Molecules of compounds
hydrogen	water
oxygen	carbon dioxide

The properties of elements and compounds

A compound does *not* have the same properties as the elements whose atoms are in it. For example:

- Hydrogen is a colourless gas at room temperature. A hydrogen molecule is made up of 2 hydrogen atoms, joined together strongly.
- Oxygen is a colourless gas at room temperature. An oxygen molecule is made up of 2 oxygen atoms, joined together strongly.
- A molecule of water has 3 atoms – 2 hydrogen atoms and 1 oxygen atom. Water is a colourless liquid at room temperature.
- The boiling points of hydrogen and oxygen are lower than the boiling point of water.

Not all compounds exist as molecules. For example:

- Sodium is a shiny silver metal that fizzes in water.
- Chlorine is a smelly, green, poisonous gas at room temperature.
- The compound sodium chloride (salt) is a white solid (which we eat) made of sodium atoms and chlorine atoms joined together, but not as molecules.

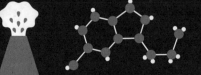

C2 Elements, atoms, and compounds continued

Chemical formulae of elements

You represent elements using **chemical formulae**, using the chemical symbols from the Periodic Table.

For some elements, the chemical formula is the same as the chemical symbol. For example, Mg for magnesium.

For elements that exist as molecules, the formula includes a number. The number shows the number of atoms in the molecule. For example, the 2 in H_2 means that there are 2 hydrogen atoms. You must write the number below (not above) the chemical symbol and to the right.

Atoms and molecules

Name	Made up of	Diagram	Chemical formula
helium	1 helium atom		He
hydrogen	2 hydrogen atoms		H_2

Chemical formulae of compounds

The chemical formula of a substance shows the **relative number** of atoms of each element in it.

For example, sulfuric acid has 2 hydrogen atoms and 4 oxygen atoms for every 1 sulfur atom. So, the formula is H_2SO_4. Oxygen combines with elements to form compounds that are oxides such as magnesium oxide, or MgO.

Some elements can combine with oxygen to form more than one type of oxide. For example, carbon dioxide, CO_2, carbon monoxide, CO. A few elements react with oxygen to make trioxides.

Molecules and formulae

Name	Made up of	Diagram	Chemical formula
carbon monoxide	1 carbon atom 1 oxygen atom		CO
carbon dioxide	1 carbon atom 2 oxygen atoms		CO_2
sulfur dioxide	1 sulfur atom 2 oxygen atoms		SO_2
sulfur trioxide	1 sulfur atom 3 oxygen atoms		SO_3

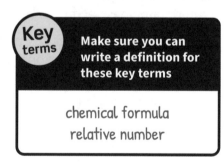

Key terms Make sure you can write a definition for these key terms

chemical formula
relative number

Learn the answers to the questions below and test yourself.

C2 Questions | Answers

Atoms and elements

	Question	Answer
1	What is an element?	a substance made up of only one type of atom – it cannot be split into other substances
2	Where are all the elements listed?	in the Periodic Table
3	Approximately how many naturally occurring elements are there?	approximately 100 (there are exactly 118)
4	What is a chemical symbol?	the one-letter or two-letter code that represents an element
5	What is an atom?	the smallest part of an element that can exist
6	How do atoms of different elements differ from each other?	they differ by mass and size
7	What is a compound?	a substance made up of atoms
8	What is a molecule?	a group of two or more atoms, joined together strongly

Compounds

	Question	Answer
9	Is every substance that is made of molecules a compound?	no
10	How many atoms are joined together in an oxygen molecule?	2
11	What does a chemical formula show?	it shows the number of atoms in a molecule of an element, or the relative number of atoms of each element in a compound
12	What does the 2 in H_2O mean?	there are 2 atoms of hydrogen in the molecule

Formulae

	Question	Answer
13	Give the name of the compound with the formula NO_2.	nitrogen dioxide
14	Write the formula of the compound whose molecules are made up of 1 sulfur atom and 3 oxygen atoms.	SO_3

Put paper here

Previous questions | Answers

	Question	Answer
1	What are all substances made of?	particles/atoms
2	How are particles arranged in a gas?	moving very fast, not touching, not in a regular pattern
3	What is density?	the amount of mass in a given volume
4	How is the melting point of a substance shown on a temperature–time graph?	by a horizontal line
5	In which **two** states does diffusion happen?	gas state, liquid state

Put paper here

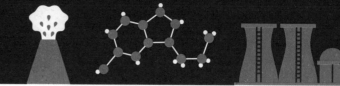

Practice questions

1 a Which is the correct definition of an element?
Tick **one** box.   **[1 mark]**

a pure substance ☐

a substance that contains only one type of atom ☐

a substance that contains more than one type of atom ☐

a substance that has a high melting point ☐

b Match each element to its chemical symbol by drawing lines. **[3 marks]**

Element	Chemical symbol
carbon	Ca
magnesium	Mg
sodium	C
calcium	Na

> **EXAM TIP**
>
> Use the Periodic Table to look these up. It's not always obvious and you shouldn't guess.

2 Complete the sentences about atoms by choosing the correct words in bold.   **[3 marks]**

An atom is the **biggest / smallest** part of an element that can exist. The atoms of one element are **different from / the same as** the atoms of a different element.

In a silver ring, there are billions of atoms. A single silver atom **does / does not** have the same properties as the silver ring.

3 Atoms can be represented by circles. You can show different types of atom using different colours or shading. Look at **Figure 1**.

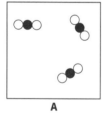
A

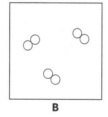
B

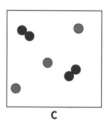
C

> **EXAM TIP**
>
> You could use highlighters to make this clearer for you.

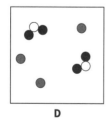
D

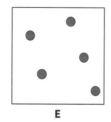
E

Figure 1

a Give the letter of the box that contains an element that exists as single atoms. **[1 mark]**

_____

b Give the letter(s) of the box(es) that contain only molecules. **[1 mark]**

_____

EXAM TIP

For these you might need to give more then one letter.

c Give the letter(s) of the box(es) that contains molecules of a compound. **[1 mark]**

_____

4 a Complete the sentences by choosing the correct words in bold. **[3 marks]**

A molecule contains **one / more than one** atom. A molecule of an element contains **more than one / only one** type of atom. A molecule of a compound contains **more than one / only one** type of atom.

Figure 2 shows three compounds, A, B, and C. The key shows what the shading in the diagram means.

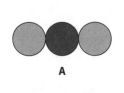

A

B

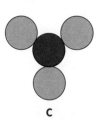

C

Key

 oxygen atom    carbon atom   sulfur atom

Figure 2

b Complete the sentences. Choose answers from the box. Each answer may be used once, more than once, or not at all. **[3 marks]**

EXAM TIP

Mono means 1, bi means 2, and tri means 3.

| oxygen | carbon dioxide | carbon monoxide |
| sulfur dioxide | sulfur trioxide | |

Compound A is _____.

Compound B is _____.

Compound C is _____.

5 A student looks at the Periodic Table.

a Describe what the Periodic Table shows. **[2 marks]**

_____

_____

b Give the chemical symbols of these elements. **[3 marks]**

iron _____

copper _____

chlorine _____

EXAM TIP

You will have to look these up. You're not expected to remember these.

c Give the approximate number of elements in the Periodic Table. **[1 mark]**

_____

6 A water molecule is made up of 2 hydrogen atoms joined to 1 oxygen atom.

a Complete **Table 1**. **[4 marks]**

Table 1

Substance	State at room temperature	Colour
hydrogen		
oxygen		

b Compare the properties of hydrogen and oxygen at room temperature with the properties of water. **[2 marks]**

_____

_____

_____

7 You can use chemical formulae to show the numbers and types of atoms in compounds. Here are the chemical formulae of some compounds.

H_2O CO_2 NO_2 SO_3 N_2O_5

a Compare the number of elements in each compound. **[1 mark]**

_____

EXAM TIP

'Compare' means you have to point out the similarities and differences.

b Compare the number of atoms in each compound. **[2 marks]**

_____

_____

8 Chlorine is in the gas state at room temperature and its molecules are made up of two atoms. Helium is also in the gas state at room temperature and exists as separate atoms. Draw the particle pictures of chlorine and helium in the boxes. You can use any colour. **[4 marks]**

EXAM TIP

Think about the spacing of the gases as well as the number of atoms that are together.

chlorine	**helium**

C1 9 A liquid can change to a gas by evaporation or boiling. For each statement in **Table 2**, state whether it is describing evaporation, boiling, or both. **[4 marks]**

Table 2

Statement	Evaporation, boiling, or both?
particles leave the surface of the liquid only	
bubbles of the substance in its gas state form throughout the liquid	
happens at the boiling point	
happens at any temperature	

C1 10 **Figure 3** shows elements in different states.

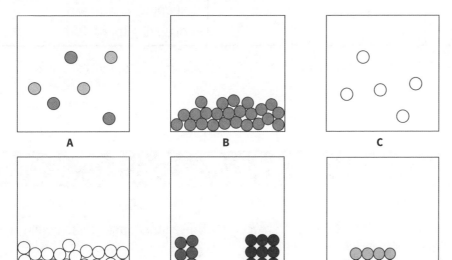

Figure 3

a Sort the boxes in Figure 3 into **three** categories. Use the particle model to explain your choice. **[2 marks]**

Category 1 _____

Category 2 _____

Category 3 _____

_____

_____

EXAM TIP

You get to pick the categories here; just make sure you can justify your choices.

b Sort the boxes in **Figure 3** into **two** categories. Use the particle model to explain your choice. **[2 marks]**

Category 1 _____

Category 2 _____

_____

_____

C3 Chemical reactions

Chemical reactions and physical changes

All **chemical reactions** make new substances *and* transfer energy to or from the surroundings. Chemical reactions are different from **physical changes**. It is usually difficult to reverse chemical reactions but easy to reverse physical changes.

Evidence of chemical reaction	Chemical reactions are used for	Energy transferred usefully in these chemical reactions
• a smell • flames or sparks • fizzing • a temperature change • a permanent colour change.	• medicines • fabrics • building materials • body tissues.	• cooking • burning petrol to make cars work • keeping us warm • digesting food.

Not all chemical reactions are useful. For example, the rusting of metal and rotting of food are also chemical reactions.

Catalysts are substances that speed up chemical reactions without being used up.

Oxidation and combustion

An **oxidation reaction** is a chemical reaction in which a substance reacts with oxygen to form an oxide.

A **combustion reaction** is an oxidation reaction. Combustion occurs when a substance reacts quickly with oxygen and transfers energy to the surroundings.

Fuels take part in combustion:

• Coal, oil, and gas are **non-renewable** fuels.
• Hydrogen and biomass are examples of **renewable** fuels.

Decomposition reactions

In a **decomposition reaction**, a compound breaks down into simpler compounds and/or elements.

When a substance breaks down when heated, the reaction is a **thermal decomposition** reaction. Heating a metal carbonate is an example of thermal decomposition. The carbon dioxide made in this reaction turns limewater milky.

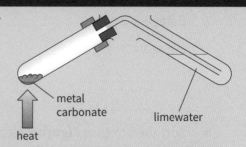

metal carbonate

limewater

heat

Key terms

Make sure you can write a definition for these key terms

catalyst   chemical reaction   combustion reaction   decomposition reaction
endothermic change   exothermic change   fuel   non-renewable   oxidation reaction
physical change   product   reactant   renewable   thermal decomposition   word equation

Chemical equations

The starting substances in reactions are **reactants**. The substances produced are **products**.

Word equations show the reactants and products in a chemical reaction. The arrow means *reacts to make*. It is different from the = sign in maths.

Chemical reactions

The table shows examples of chemical reactions.

Chemical reaction	Word equation and/or particle diagram
combustion of hydrogen	four hydrogen atoms from a fuel + oxygen molecule in the air → two water molecules go out in the exhaust. Key: oxygen atom, hydrogen atom. hydrogen + oxygen → water
combustion of methane	methane + oxygen → carbon dioxide + water. Key: carbon atom.
decomposition of hydrogen peroxide	hydrogen peroxide molecules → water molecules + oxygen molecules
thermal decomposition of a carbonate	*copper carbonate → copper oxide + carbon dioxide*

Exothermic and endothermic changes

	Exothermic change	Endothermic change
Energy transferred	• Energy is transferred *to* the surroundings from the substances that are reacting, changing state, or dissolving.	• Energy is transferred *from* the surroundings to the substances that are reacting, changing state, or dissolving.
Temperature change	• Immediately after the reaction, the products are at a higher temperature than the surroundings.	• Immediately after the reaction, the products are at a lower temperature than the surroundings.
Examples	• Combustion, heat packs.	• Thermal decomposition, cold packs.

Conservation of mass

Worked example: Calculating masses

Calculate the mass of oxygen that reacts with 0.72 g of magnesium to make 1.20 g of magnesium oxide.

mass of oxygen + mass of magnesium = mass of magnesium oxide

mass of oxygen + 0.72 g = 1.20 g

mass of oxygen = 1.20 g – 0.72 g

= 0.48 g

Worked example: Ratios

A **ratio** is a way of comparing values. In the previous Worked example, the ratio of the mass of magnesium to the mass of oxygen (Mg:O) is 0.72:0.48 or 72:48.

$$Mg:O = 72:48$$

You can simplify this ratio by dividing both numbers by a number common to both values – in this case, 24.

$$Mg:O = 3:2$$

Balanced formula equations

Formula equations give more information about what is happening in a reaction.

Each chemical symbol (one or two letters) represents an atom of an element. The numbers indicate whether there is more than one atom of that element.

A **balanced formula equation** gives the ratios of the amounts of reactants and products in a reaction.

Worked example: Balancing equations

1 Write the equation. Count the atoms on either side of the arrow.

$$Mg + O_2 \rightarrow MgO$$

2 Add a 2 in front of the MgO to balance the oxygen atoms.

$$Mg + O_2 \rightarrow 2MgO$$

3 Add a 2 in front of the Mg to balance the magnesium atoms.

$$2Mg + O_2 \rightarrow 2MgO$$

Worked example: Balancing equations

1 Write the equation. Count the atoms on either side of the arrow.

$$CH_4 + O_2 \rightarrow CO_2 + H_2O$$

2 Add a 2 in front of the H_2O to balance the hydrogen atoms.

$$CH_4 + O_2 \rightarrow CO_2 + 2H_2O$$

3 Add a 2 in front of the O_2 to balance the oxygen atoms. There is the same number of carbon atoms on both sides.

$$CH_4 + 2O_2 \rightarrow CO_2 + 2H_2O$$

 Key terms — Make sure you can write a definition for these key terms

balanced formula equation   conservation of mass   formula equation   ratio

 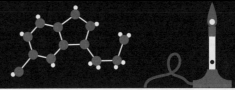

Retrieval

Learn the answers to the questions below and test yourself.

C3 Questions | Answers

Chemical reactions

#	Question	Answer
1	What is a chemical reaction?	a change in which atoms are rearranged and join together differently to make new substances
2	Give **two** signs that a chemical reaction has taken place.	two from: sparks/flames, odour/smell, substance gets hotter or colder, sounds, fizzing
3	What is a catalyst?	something that speeds up a chemical reaction without being used up
4	What is combustion?	a chemical reaction in which a substance reacts quickly with oxygen and transfers energy
5	What is oxidation?	a chemical reaction in which a substance reacts with oxygen
6	What is decomposition?	a chemical reaction in which a compound breaks down into one or more elements and/or new compounds

Chemical equations

#	Question	Answer
7	What is a reactant?	a starting substance in a reaction
8	What is a product?	a substance that is made in a reaction
9	What happens to atoms in a chemical reaction?	they are rearranged and joined together differently
10	Compare the numbers of atoms in reactants and products.	the numbers of atoms of each element are the same

Reaction principles

#	Question	Answer
11	What is an exothermic reaction?	a reaction that transfers energy to the thermal store of the surroundings
12	What is an endothermic reaction?	a reaction that transfers energy from the thermal store of the surroundings
13	What is the law of conservation of mass?	mass of reactants = mass of products
14	What is a balanced formula equation?	an equation that gives the relative amounts of reactants and products

Put paper here

Previous questions | Answers

#	Question	Answer
1	How are particles arranged in a gas?	random arrangement, moving very fast, not touching
2	What is density?	the amount of mass in a given volume
3	What is a chemical symbol?	the one-letter or two-letter code that represents an element
4	What is a molecule?	a group of two or more atoms, joined together strongly
5	What does the 2 in H_2O mean?	there are 2 atoms of hydrogen in the molecule

Put paper here

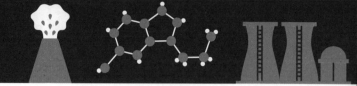

Practice

Practice questions

1 a Complete the sentences. Choose answers from the box.
Each answer may be used once, more than once, or not at all. **[5 marks]**

substance	reactants	products	rearrange
	catalyst	reaction	

In a chemical reaction, the starting substances are called

_____. They react to make _____. During

the reaction, the atoms _____ and join together

differently to make a new _____. A _____

speeds up a chemical reaction without being used up.

> **EXAM TIP**
>
> Not all of these words are going to be used, so don't worry about having some left over at the end.

b Which examples of chemical reactions are useful? Tick **two** boxes.

[2 marks]

rusting of metals ☐

burning fuels ☐

food going bad ☐

cement hardening ☐

2 There are different types of chemical reaction.

a Complete the sentences about reactions by drawing lines. **[3 marks]**

In a combustion reaction	a compound breaks down into different compounds or elements.
In a thermal decomposition reaction	a substance reacts with oxygen to form an oxide.
In an oxidation reaction	a substance reacts quickly with oxygen and transfers energy.
In a decomposition reaction	a compound that is heated breaks down to make different compounds or elements.

> **EXAM TIP**
>
> Take this slowly – some of these definitions are confusing.

b In any reaction, mass is conserved. Complete the sentences by choosing the correct words in bold. **[2 marks]**

The law of conservation of mass states that the mass of the products is **different from / the same as** the mass of the reactants. This is the same as saying that atoms **can / cannot** be created or destroyed in a reaction.

c Identify the hazard symbol for *highly flammable* in **Figure 1**. **[1 mark]**

EXAM TIP

Even if you're not sure, you can have a good guess at this question.

A · · · B · · · C

Figure 1

_____

3 Some reactions are exothermic and other reactions are endothermic. Complete the sentences. Choose answers from the box.

| from | evaporation | a combustion reaction | to |

[4 marks]

Exothermic reactions transfer energy _____ the

surroundings. An example is _____ .

Endothermic reactions transfer energy _____ the

surroundings. An example is _____ .

4 A student decides to investigate the combustion of fuels. They know that people burn charcoal on barbecues. Charcoal is a form of carbon.

a One of the products of the combustion of carbon is carbon dioxide. Give the word equation for this reaction. **[2 marks]**

_____

The student investigates the combustion of fuels used in a spirit burner. They use different fuels to heat a beaker of water. They collect data and put it in a table (**Table 1**).

EXAM TIP

You need to work out the other reactant for this equation; what do we need for combustion?

Table 1

| Fuel | Temperature change in °C | | | |
	First time	Second time	Third time	Mean
methanol	42	38	40	
ethanol	45	45	48	46
propanol	54	53	55	54
butanol	81	59	59	59

b Name the variables in this investigation. **[3 marks]**

Independent variable _____

Dependent variable _____

One control variable _____

EXAM TIP

The control variables are the ones that don't change. This could be a wide range of things.

c **i** Circle the anomaly in the table. **[1 mark]**

ii Calculate the missing mean. **[1 mark]**

d Justify the type of graph the student should plot with the data. **[1 mark]**

_____

_____

5 You can use ratios to describe the relative numbers of different types of atoms in compounds.

a The ratio of hydrogen atoms to oxygen atoms in water is 2 : 1. Explain what this means. **[1 mark]**

_____

b Give the ratio of the number of sulfur atoms to oxygen atoms in sulfur trioxide. **[1 mark]**

_____

EXAM TIP

'Tri' means 3.

c **i** The formula of butane is C_4H_{10}. Give the ratio of the number of hydrogen atoms to carbon atoms in this formula. **[1 mark]**

_____

ii Simplify the ratio. **[1 mark]**

_____

d The balanced symbol equation for the combustion of magnesium is:

$$2Mg + O_2 \rightarrow 2MgO$$

Use the equation to explain why you need 10 molecules of oxygen to react with 20 atoms of magnesium. Show your working. **[2 marks]**

_____

_____

6 You can determine the equation for a chemical reaction using particle diagrams. Look at the reaction in **Figure 2**.

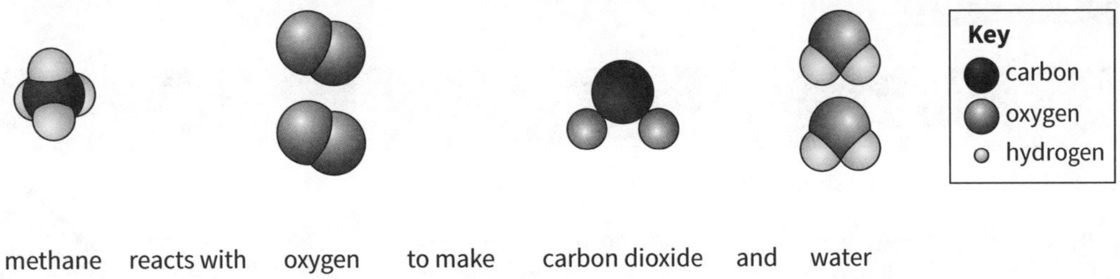

Key
● carbon
◓ oxygen
○ hydrogen

methane   reacts with   oxygen   to make   carbon dioxide   and   water

Figure 2

a Use the particle diagram in Figure 2 to give the balanced symbol equation for this reaction. **[2 marks]**

_____

_____

EXAM TIP
Just count the number of atoms.

b Another fuel is propane (C_3H_8). Determine the balanced symbol equation for the reaction of propane with oxygen. **[4 marks]**

_____

_____

_____

_____

C2 7 **Figure 3** shows particle diagrams of different substances.

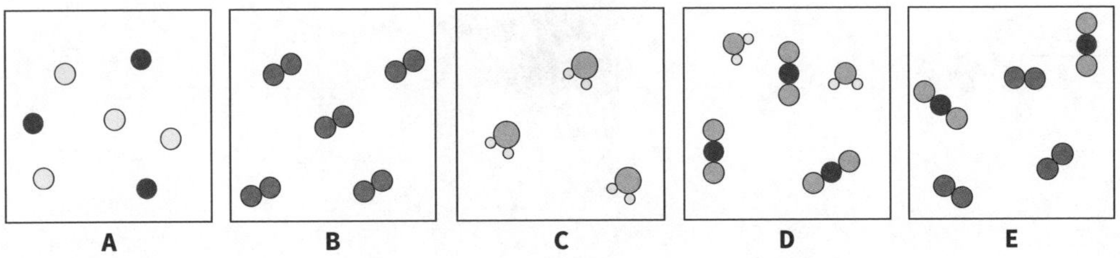

| A | B | C | D | E |

Figure 3

a Give the letter of the box containing one type of compound. **[1 mark]**

_____

EXAM TIP
Not all of the boxes are going to be answers.

b Give the letter of the box containing one type of element. **[1 mark]**

_____

c Give the letter of the box containing an element and a compound. **[1 mark]**

_____

d In what physical state are all the substances? **[1 mark]**

_____

Knowledge

C4 Acids and alkalis

Acids and alkalis

Acids and **alkalis** are chemically opposite and have different uses.

- Acids taste sour – examples include lemon juice and vinegar.
- Alkalis feel soapy – examples include soap and toothpaste.

(Note: You should never taste a substance or touch a solution in the laboratory.)

Corrosive

Acids and alkalis may be **corrosive**. When using acids or alkalis in the laboratory, do a **risk assessment**. This includes identifying **hazards** and working out how to reduce **risks** from these hazards.

The pH scale

strong acid	1	sulfuric acid nitric acid hydrochloric acid
	2	lemon juice cola drinks
	3	vinegar
weak acid	4	
	5	saliva tea
	6	
neutral	7	water blood (7.4)
	8	
weak alkali	9	toothpaste milk of magnesia
	10	
	11	
	12	
strong alkali	13	drain cleaner
	14	sodium hydroxide potassium hydroxide

Indicators and pH

An **indicator** tells you whether something is an acid or alkali. For example:

	Red litmus paper	Blue litmus paper
Acidic solution	Stays red	Turns red
Neutral solution	Stays red	Stays blue
Alkaline solution	Turns blue	Stays blue

You can make indicators out of natural substances, such as cabbage or flowers.

Indicators

Universal indicator (UI) shows you how acidic or alkaline a solution is on the **pH scale**.

- Acids have a pH less than 7 – the lower the pH, the more acidic the solution.
- **Neutral** solutions have a pH of 7.
- Alkalis have a pH more than 7 – the higher the pH, the more alkaline the solution.

Neutralisation

Anything that can neutralise an acid is called a **base**.

A base that dissolves in water is called an alkali. When you add a base or an alkali to an acid, a **neutralisation reaction** takes place.

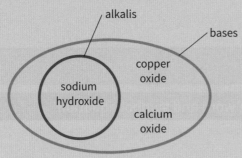

The pH of an alkali solution changes as you add acid to it:

- The solution becomes less alkaline and the pH gets lower.
- When the acid has been neutralised, the solution becomes neutral (pH 7).
- If you continue to add acid, the pH continues to get lower.
- The solution becomes acidic.

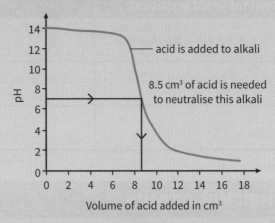

Uses of neutralisation

- Crops – some plants grow better in acidic soil, while some grow better in alkaline soil.
- Digestion – if you have too much stomach acid, you can take an indigestion tablet that neutralises the acid.
- Acid lakes – sulfur dioxide from burning coal dissolves in lakes and makes the water acidic. Adding a base to the lake can help to neutralise the water.

 Key terms Make sure you can write a definition for these key terms

acid   alkali   base   corrosive   hazard   indicator   neutral   neutralisation reaction
pH scale   risk   risk assessment   universal indicator

 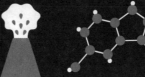 

Knowledge

C4 Acids and alkalis continued

Salts

All acids contain hydrogen atoms. For example, hydrochloric acid (HCl) and sulfuric acid (H_2SO_4).

An alkali, a metal, or a metal oxide may neutralise an acid. In the reaction, the hydrogen atoms of an acid are replaced by atoms of a metal element.

One of the products is always a **salt**. A salt is a compound in which the hydrogen atom of an acid is replaced by an atom of a metal.

Reactions with acids

General word equation	Example word and symbol equation
acid + metal → salt + hydrogen	$2HCl \quad + \quad Mg \quad \rightarrow \quad MgCl_2 \quad + \quad H_2$ hydrochloric acid + magnesium → magnesium chloride + hydrogen
acid + metal oxide → salt + water	$2HCl \quad + \quad MgO \quad \rightarrow \quad MgCl_2 \quad + \quad H_2O$ hydrochloric acid + magnesium oxide → magnesium chloride + water
acid + alkali → salt + water	$2HCl \quad + \quad Mg(OH)_2 \quad \rightarrow \quad MgCl_2 \quad + \quad 2H_2O$ hydrochloric acid + magnesium hydroxide → magnesium chloride + water

Practical: Making salts

Some salts exist in nature, like sodium chloride (which makes the sea salty).

You can make a salt using the technique below if the base does not dissolve in water. Here are the steps for making copper sulfate crystals:

Step 1 neutralisation – add lots of copper oxide to sulfuric acid

Step 2 filtration – filter out the excess (left over) copper oxide

Steps 3 and **4** evaporation – heat gently in an evaporating basin and allow to evaporate

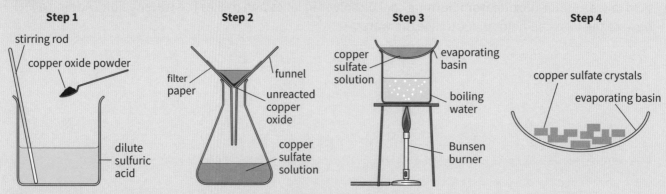

Key terms   Make sure you can write a definition for this key term

salt

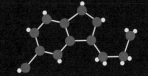
Learn the answers to the questions below and test yourself.

C4 Questions | Answers

Acids and alkalis

#	Question	Answer
1	Give an everyday example of an acid.	vinegar, lemon juice
2	How do acids taste?	sour
3	What is an alkali?	a soluble base, chemical opposite of an acid
4	How do most alkalis feel?	soapy
5	What is the meaning of corrosive?	can burn your skin and eyes

Indicators and pH

#	Question	Answer
6	What is an indicator?	a substance that changes colour to show whether a solution is acidic or alkaline
7	What colour does red litmus turn with an alkaline solution?	blue
8	Which indicator shows a colour change for acids and alkalis?	universal indicator
9	Give the name of the scale that shows how acidic or alkaline a solution is.	pH scale
10	What is the pH of a neutral solution?	pH 7

Neutralisation

#	Question	Answer
11	What is a base?	a substance that neutralises an acid
12	What is a neutralisation reaction?	the reaction between an acid and a base to produce a neutral (pH7) solution
13	What element do all acids contain?	hydrogen
14	What **two** products do you get if you react an acid with a base?	a salt, water
15	What **two** products do you get if you react an acid with a metal?	a salt, hydrogen

Put paper here

Previous questions | Answers

#	Question	Answer
1	What is a state of matter?	whether a substance is solid, liquid, or gas
2	How do atoms of different elements differ from each other?	they differ by mass and size
3	How many atoms are joined together in an oxygen molecule?	2
4	Give **two** signs that a chemical reaction has taken place.	two from: sparks/flames, odour/smell, substance gets hotter or colder, loud bang/fizzing
5	What is an exothermic reaction?	a reaction that transfers energy to the thermal store of the surroundings

Put paper here

Practice questions

1 a **Figure 1** shows some hazard symbols. You may find the symbol for *corrosive* on a bottle containing acid or alkali. Identify the hazard symbol for *corrosive* in Figure 1. **[1 mark]**

A

B

C

D

Figure 1

_____

b Which **two** things could you do to reduce the risks from the hazard of using acids or alkalis? Tick **two** boxes. **[2 marks]**

wear goggles ☐

wait before opening the bottle ☐

pour the liquids quickly ☐

wear gloves ☐

2 Neutralisation is an important reaction. Complete the sentences by choosing the correct words in bold. **[4 marks]**

A base is anything that **dilutes / neutralises** an acid. An alkali is a base that **does / does not** dissolve in water. In a neutralisation reaction, you add a base to an acid until it reaches a pH of **7 / 14**. When you neutralise an acid with a base or alkali, a **soap / salt** is formed.

3 The statements describe how to make a salt from sulfuric acid and copper oxide powder. Give the correct order of the statements. **[3 marks]**

A Place over a beaker of boiling water until about half the water has evaporated.

B Neutralise the acid by adding a base.

C Filter the neutral solution to remove any unreacted copper oxide.

D Put the solution of copper sulfate in an evaporating basin.

E Place the evaporating basin and its remaining contents in a warm, dry place for a few days.

☐ → ☐ → ☐ → ☐ → ☐

4   You use indicators to work out if solutions are acids or alkalis. Acids can be concentrated or dilute.

   a   Complete the sentences. Choose answers from the box.
       Each answer may be used once, more than once,
       or not at all.   **[4 marks]**

blue   shallow   concentrated   dilute   red   yellow

   If you add an acid to blue litmus paper, the paper will turn _____.

   If you add an alkali to red litmus paper, the paper will turn _____.

   If there are lots of acid particles in a solution, then the acid is

   _____. If there are not many acid particles, then the

   solution is _____.

   > **EXAM TIP**
   > There is a change in colour, so the answer to the first one is not going to be blue!

   b   Complete the sentences about universal indicator (UI)
       by drawing lines.   **[3 marks]**

   > **EXAM TIP**
   > You need to link three boxes together, just two won't be enough.

A very acidic solution	will turn UI purple	which is pH 1.
A solution that is a little acidic	will turn UI green	which is pH 14.
A neutral solution	will turn UI red	which is pH 7.
A very alkaline solution	will turn UI yellow	which is pH 5.

5   A student investigates the reaction between vinegar (an acid) and bicarbonate of soda (a base). There is fizzing when these two substances react. They put 10 cm³ of vinegar in a beaker. They add 10 cm³ of bicarbonate solution and time how long it takes for the fizzing to stop.

   a   The student investigates this question:

       How does the volume of bicarbonate solution affect the time of reaction?

       Name the independent variable.   **[1 mark]**

       _____

   b   The student collects the data in **Table 1**. Plot the data in
       Table 1 on the graph in **Figure 2**.   **[1 mark]**

   Table 1

Volume of bicarbonate solution in cm³	Time for bubbling to stop in s
10	25
20	27
30	39
40	27

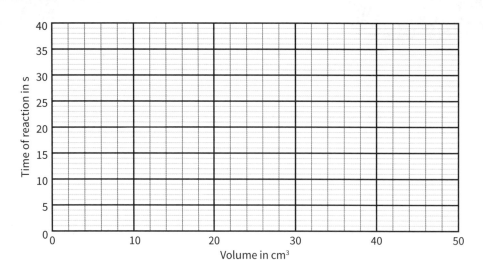

Figure 2

EXAM TIP

Always use crosses to plot points.

c Circle the anomaly on the graph in Figure 2. **[1 mark]**

d Suggest a conclusion for this investigation. **[1 mark]**

_____

_____

6 A student takes safety precautions and tests two cleaning solutions that they find at home with universal indicator (UI). Complete the sentences.

[2 marks]

Solution A turns UI purple so it is an _____

Solution B turns UI yellow so it is an _____

7 A student has 100 cm³ of hydrochloric acid and an equal volume of sodium hydroxide, as shown in **Figure 3**. The solutions are the same concentration. They pour the sodium hydroxide into the acid.

EXAM TIP

They are an acid or an alkali.

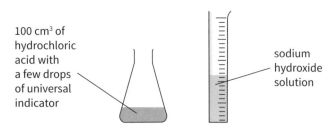

100 cm³ of hydrochloric acid with a few drops of universal indicator

sodium hydroxide solution

Figure 3

a Complete the table below. Write the correct colours in the middle column, and the pH number in the third column. **[1 mark]**

EXAM TIP

Start with the result for the zero value of alkali, then work out the result for the mixture.

Table 2

Volume of alkali in cm³	Indicator colour	pH
0		
100		

b The chemical formula of sodium hydroxide is NaOH. Using the formulae in the box, give the balanced symbol equation for this neutralisation reaction. **[2 marks]**

HCl   NaOH   NaCl H_2O

_____

c Give the name of the salt that is formed in this reaction (not the formula). **[1 mark]**

_____

8 A teacher dissolves 30 g of solid sodium hydroxide in water. They add water to make 500 cm³ of solution. This is solution A.

The teacher makes another solution by dissolving 40 g of sodium hydroxide in water. They add water to make 1000 cm³ of solution. This is solution B.

Which is the more concentrated solution, A or B? Justify your answer by doing calculations or using ratios. **[3 marks]**

EXAM TIP

Clearly show all of your working here.

_____

_____

_____

_____

_____

C1 **9** A teacher shows the class some ice and some dry ice. Dry ice sublimes. Complete the sentences by choosing the correct words in bold. **[4 marks]**

When ice and dry ice are in a solid state, their particles are **not touching / touching**. They are arranged in a **random / regular** pattern.

When the ice melts, the particles **are still / are not** touching. When dry ice sublimes, the particles **are still / are not** touching.

C3 **10** Hydrogen reacts with oxygen to produce water.

a Name the reactant(s) and product(s) in this reaction. **[2 marks]**

Reactant(s) _____

Product(s) _____

EXAM TIP

Reactants are the parts that react together.

b Give the word equation for this reaction. **[1 mark]**

_____

c A student gives this symbol equation for the reaction.

$$H_2 + O_2 \rightarrow H_2O$$

Explain how you know that this equation is **not** balanced. **[1 mark]**

_____

_____

Knowledge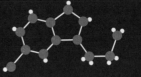

C5 The Periodic Table

The Periodic Table

The **Periodic Table** shows the names and symbols of all the elements that have been discovered. Dmitri Mendeleev organised the elements by their **chemical properties** and **physical properties**.

- Vertical columns are called **groups**.
- Horizontal rows are called **periods**.
- **Metals** are found to the left of the stepped line.
- **Non-metals** are found to the right of the stepped line.

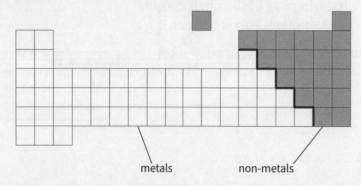

metals   non-metals

Elements in a group (vertical column) normally have similar properties, and there are patterns in properties within groups. This means that you can predict properties of elements based on their position in the Periodic Table.

Physical properties

The physical properties of a substance are the properties you can observe or measure without changing the substance. For example, its melting or boiling point, whether it conducts electricity, or its density.

Chemical properties

Chemical properties describe how a substance behaves in terms of its chemical reactions. For example, how vigorous its chemical reactions are with other substances and the products it forms in reactions.

Examples of elements

Three examples of elements are copper, sulfur, and germanium. They have different properties.

Copper, Cu

- metal
- easy to hammer into thin sheets
- excellent conductor of electricity
- shiny
- used in electrical wiring and in thin sheets to cover buildings

Germanium, Ge

- metalloid
- hard
- brittle
- shiny
- used to make fibre-optic cables and electronic components

Sulfur, S

- non-metal
- does not conduct electricity
- brittle (breaks easily)
- not shiny (dull)
- used to make fertilisers and to vulcanise (harden) rubber

Physical properties of metals and non-metals

Typical properties of a metal	Typical properties of a non-metal
good conductor of electricity	poor conductor of electricity
good conductor of thermal energy	poor conductor of thermal energy
shiny	dull
high density	low density
malleable (can be hammered into different shapes)	brittle (breaks easily when solid)
ductile (can be pulled into wires)	brittle
sonorous (makes a ringing sound when hit)	not sonorous
high melting point and boiling point	low melting point and boiling point

The elements near the stepped line in the Periodic Table, like germanium and silicon, are **metalloids**. Their properties are between those of metals and non-metals.

Chemical properties of metals and non-metals

When an element reacts with oxygen, it forms an **oxide**.

For example:

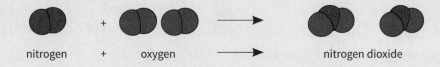

nitrogen + oxygen → nitrogen dioxide

Most metal oxides:

• are bases
• form alkaline solutions if they dissolve in water
• are in the solid state at room temperature.

Most non-metal oxides:

• are acidic
• form acidic solutions if they dissolve in water
• are in the gas state at room temperature.

Key terms — Make sure you can write a definition for these key terms

chemical property   group   metal   metalloid   non-metal
oxide   Periodic Table   period   physical property

C5 The Periodic Table continued

The Group 1 elements

Group 1 elements are called **alkali metals**. For metals, they have unusually low melting and boiling points, and they are relatively soft with low density. They are very **reactive** and react vigorously (strongly) with water.

From top to bottom:

- reactivity *increases*
- melting point *decreases*.

They always produce a metal hydroxide (which is alkaline) and hydrogen gas when they react with water.

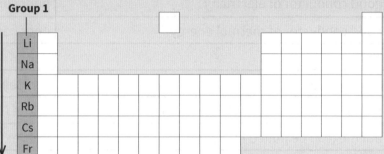

The Group 7 elements

Group 7 elements are called the **halogens**. They are reactive non-metals.

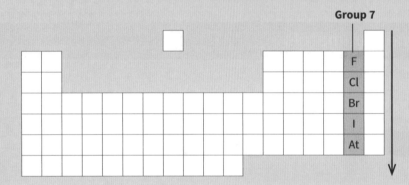

From top to bottom:

- reactivity *decreases*
- melting point *increases*
- colour gets darker
- the state changes from gas to solid.

Fluorine is a very pale yellow gas, chlorine is a pale green gas, bromine is a dark red liquid, and iodine is a grey solid.

The Group 0 elements

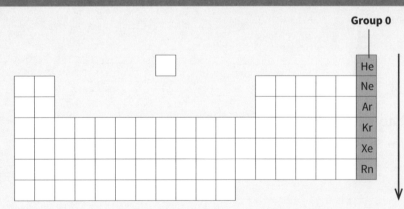

Group 0 elements are called **noble gases**. They are **unreactive** non-metals, which are in the gas state at room temperature.

From top to bottom, reactivity *increases slightly*. Helium, at the top of the group, is not known to take part in any chemical reactions.

Key terms

Make sure you can write a definition for these key terms

alkali metals   halogens   noble gases   reactive   unreactive

Retrieval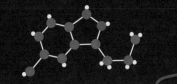

Learn the answers to the questions below and test yourself.

C5 Questions | Answers

The Periodic Table

#	Question	Answer
1	Define physical property.	a property you can observe or measure without changing the substance
2	Define chemical property.	how a substance behaves in its chemical reactions
3	How is a group shown on the Periodic Table?	by a vertical column
4	How is a period shown on the Periodic Table?	by a horizontal row
5	Where are metals found on the Periodic Table?	to the left of the stepped line

Properties of metals and non-metals

#	Question	Answer
6	List some physical properties of metals.	good conductor of electricity and thermal energy, shiny, malleable, ductile
7	List some physical properties of non-metals.	poor conductor of electricity and thermal energy, dull, brittle
8	What is formed when an element reacts with oxygen?	an oxide
9	Name **one** chemical property of a typical non-metal oxide.	it is acidic
10	Name **one** chemical property of a typical metal oxide.	it is a base

Groups 1, 7, and 0

11	List some properties of elements found in Group 1.	reactive, low melting points and boiling points, soft, low density
12	Which gas is produced when elements in Group 1 react with water?	hydrogen
13	List some properties of elements found in Group 7 (the halogens).	reactive, low melting points and boiling points
14	List some properties of elements found in Group 0 (noble gases).	unreactive, very low melting and boiling points, colourless gases at room temperature
15	Name some examples of noble gases.	helium, neon, argon

Put paper here

Previous questions | Answers

#	Question	Answer
1	What is an atom?	the smallest part of an element that can exist
2	What is a compound?	atoms of two or more elements that are joined together strongly
3	What is a catalyst?	something that speeds up a chemical reaction without being used up
4	What colour does red litmus turn with an alkaline solution?	blue
5	What **two** products do you get if you react an acid with a metal oxide?	a salt, water

Put paper here

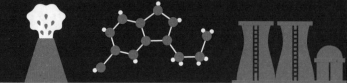

Practice

Practice questions

1 **a** Sort the physical properties in the box into properties of metals and properties of non-metals. **[4 marks]**

> dull   ductile   good electrical conductor   brittle

Properties of metals	Properties of non-metals

b Identify the metal. Choose the answer from the box. **[1 mark]**

> sulfur   hydrogen   aluminium   water

_____

2 The Periodic Table arranges elements according to their properties.

a Match each component of the Periodic Table with its description by drawing lines. **[3 marks]**

Periodic Table component
group
period
left of the stepped line
right of the stepped line

Description
location of the metals
a column in the table
location of the non-metals
a row in the table

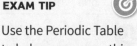

EXAM TIP

Use the Periodic Table to help you answer this question. Metals are found to the left of the stepped line.

b Identify the scientist who discovered the modern Periodic Table. Choose the answer from the box. **[1 mark]**

> Curie   Dalton   Mendeleev

_____

3 The sentences describe properties of the Group 1 elements. Complete the sentences. Choose answers from the box. Each answer may be used once, more than once, or not at all. **[3 marks]**

> hard   high   up   down   low   soft

Group 1 elements have _____ melting points compared to other metals.

Group 1 elements are _____ metals.

The reactivity of the Group 1 metals increases as you move

_____ the group.

4 Chlorine, bromine, and iodine are all elements of the same group in the Periodic Table.

   a Name the group that contains these elements. **[1 mark]**

   _____

   b Match each element to its colour and state at room temperature by drawing lines. **[3 marks]**

Element
chlorine
bromine
iodine

Colour
dark grey
red–brown
pale green

State
solid
liquid
gas

> **EXAM TIP**
> You can find a clue to their state in their position on the Periodic Table.

5 **Table 1** shows some properties of elements in Group 7 of the Periodic Table.

Table 1

Element	Melting point in °C	Boiling point in °C
fluorine	−220	−118
chlorine	−101	−35
bromine	7	59
iodine	114	184

   a Describe the pattern shown by the melting points as you move down the group. **[1 mark]**

   _____

   b Astatine is found below iodine in Group 7. Estimate the boiling point of astatine. **[1 mark]**

   _____ °C

> **EXAM TIP**
> Estimate means give a sensible answer. It doesn't have to be 100% correct.

   c Describe **one** physical property of the elements found in Group 7. **[1 mark]**

   _____

6 Elements in Group 7 are reactive.

   a Explain what is meant by the term *reactive*. **[1 mark]**

   _____

   _____

> **EXAM TIP**
> The compound that is formed in the reaction is the product and goes on the right-hand side.

   b Chlorine reacts vigorously with iron to form the compound iron chloride. Write a word equation for this reaction. **[3 marks)**

   _____

   _____

c Suggest how the reaction between iodine and iron is different from the reaction between chlorine and iron. **[1 mark]**

_____

_____

d Name the compound formed when iodine reacts with iron. **[1 mark]**

_____

7 **Figure 1** shows part of the Periodic Table.

1	**1**	**2**		H														**3**	**4**	**5**	**6**	**7**	**0** He
2	Li	Be																B	C	N	O	F	Ne
3	Na	Mg																Al	Si	P	S	Cl	Ar
4	K	Ca	Sc	Ti	V	Cr	Mn	Fe	Co	Ni	Cu	Zn	Ga	Ge	As	Se	Br	Kr
5	Rb	Sr	Y	Zr	Nb	Mo	Tc	Ru	Rh	Pd	Ag	Cd	In	Sn	Sb	Te	I	Xe
6	Cs	Ba	La	Hf	Ta	W	Re	Os	Ir	Pt	Au	Hg	Tl	Pb	Bi	Po	At	Rn

Figure 1

a Give the group number of calcium, Ca. **[1 mark]**

_____

b Name **one** other element in the same period as chlorine, Cl. **[1 mark]**

_____

c Name **one** element that is likely to react in a similar way to potassium, K. **[1 mark]**

_____

EXAM TIP

You will need to look this up on the Periodic Table.

d Give the chemical symbol of an element that will react more vigorously than bromine, Br. **[1 mark]**

_____

8 **Figure 2** shows the Periodic Table with the element names removed.

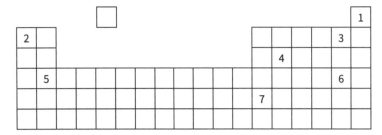

Figure 2

EXAM TIP

The groups increase in number as you go from left to right on the Periodic Table.

a Use the numbers in the Periodic Table to answer the questions.

i Identify an element that is in Group 2. **[1 mark]**

_____

ii Identify **one** element that reacts vigorously with water. **[1 mark]**

_____

iii Which **two** numbered elements have similar chemical reactions?

[1 mark]

_____

EXAM TIP

Elements in the same group react in a similar way.

b A teacher reacts element 2 with water. Name the gas produced in this reaction. **[1 mark]**

_____

9 Elements in Group 0 are the noble gases.

a Name **one** noble gas. **[1 mark]**

_____

b State **one** chemical property of all noble gases. **[1 mark]**

_____

c **Figure 3** shows a bar chart with the densities of some of the elements in Group 0, and part of the Periodic Table, showing the positions of the elements of Group 0.

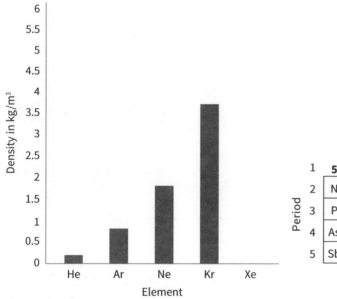

Figure 3

i Give the density of the element Ne. **[1 mark]**

_____

ii Describe the trend in the density of the noble gases. **[2 marks]**

_____

_____

EXAM TIP

'Describe the trend' means that you need to say if it is going up or down.

iii Predict the density of the element Xe. **[2 marks]**

_____

10 Compare the physical and chemical properties of the elements in Group 1 and Group 7 of the Periodic Table. **[6 marks]**

_____

_____

_____

_____

_____

_____

_____

EXAM TIP

For a compare question, you need to give things that are the same and things that are different.

11 **Table 2** shows the boiling points of elements in Group 0.

Table 2

Element	He	Ne	Ar	Kr	Xe
Period	1	2	3	4	5
Boiling point in °C	−269	−246	−186		−108

a i Predict the boiling point of krypton, Kr. **[1 mark]**

_____

ii Write down the state of argon, Ar, at room temperature. **[1 mark]**

_____

iii Describe the trend shown by the boiling points of the noble gases. **[1 mark]**

_____

_____

b Read the following extract from a practical science magazine.

> _Welding metal parts together requires the pieces to be heated strongly. This briefly melts the metals. As the pieces cool, they fuse together, forming a strong joint._
>
> _However, some metals react with gases in the atmosphere to form compounds such as metal oxides. These compounds can weaken the strength of a welded joint. Reactions between metals and gases in the atmosphere take place slowly at room temperature, but can occur rapidly at high temperatures._
>
> _To ensure welded joints are as strong as possible, welders use an argon shield whilst welding metal pieces together._

EXAM TIP

Use highlighters to pull out important bits of information from the text.

Suggest why an argon shield is used in welding to ensure welded joints are as strong as possible. **[4 marks]**

_____

_____

_____

_____

C4 **12 Figure 4** shows the pH scale.

a Label Figure 4 to show what each section of the pH scale is classified as. Choose answers from the box. **[3 marks]**

neutral alkali acid

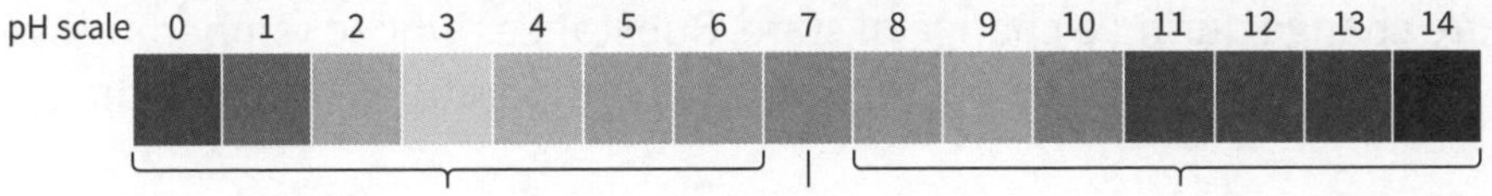

pH scale 0 1 2 3 4 5 6 7 8 9 10 11 12 13 14

Figure 4

EXAM TIP

The parts of the pH scale come up a lot so it is important to learn them.

b State the colour universal indicator would turn in a neutral solution. **[1 mark]**

_____

c Name another solution that can be used to determine if a substance is acidic. **[1 mark]**

_____

C3 **13** A student watches some combustion experiments and learns about oxidation.

a Compare combustion and oxidation. **[2 marks]**

_____

_____

_____

The student uses 10.4 g of iron wool. They burn the iron wool and measure the mass again. The mass is 11.2 g.

b Calculate the change in mass. **[2 marks]**

_____ g

EXAM TIP

This is asking how much the mass has gone up by.

c Give the word equation for the reaction. **[1 mark]**

_____

d Explain why the mass has increased. **[2 marks]**

_____

_____

e The student then burns some charcoal. Explain why the mass decreases. **[2 marks]**

_____

_____

Knowledge
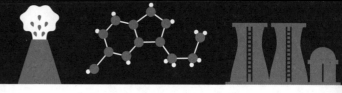

C6 Separation techniques

Pure and impure substances

A **pure substance** has no other substances mixed with it. All of its particles are the same. Pure substances can be elements or compounds. An **impure substance** has other substances mixed with it.

You can tell the difference between a pure substance and an impure substance by heating the substance and measuring the temperature change during a change of state. Substances whose temperature remains constant during a change of state are pure. Those showing a range of temperatures during a change of state are mixtures.

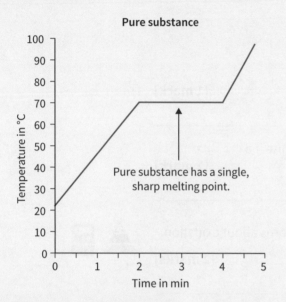

Pure substance has a single, sharp melting point.

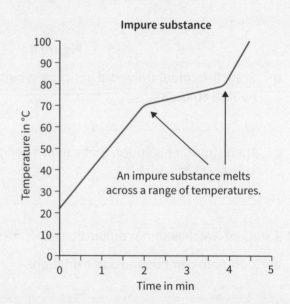

An impure substance melts across a range of temperatures.

Mixtures

A **mixture** is made up of substances that are not chemically joined together. The substances in a mixture keep their own properties. They can often be separated from each other.

Most materials are mixtures. Examples include air, seawater, and most rocks.

Differences between mixtures and compounds

	Mixture of elements	Compound
Are the substances chemically joined?	no	yes
Properties	substances within the mixture keep own properties	usually different to those of its elements
Are its elements easy to separate?	yes (usually)	no
Relative amounts of each substance	can change	cannot change

Key terms

Make sure you can write a definition for these key terms

dissolve   impure substance   insoluble   mixture   pure substance   saturated solution
solubility   soluble   solute   solution   solvent

Solutions

Solute: The substance that is added to the solvent and dissolves in it.

Solvent: The liquid that makes up most of the solution.

Solution: A type of mixture made of two parts – the solute and the solvent.

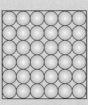

Particles of solid sugar.

Particles of liquid water.

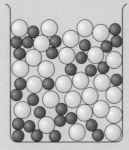

Particles not to scale

The particles of sugar mix with the particles of water to make a solution.

The complete mixing of a solute with a solvent is called **dissolving**. When sugar dissolves, its particles separate from each other. They then mix randomly with the water particles.

Solubility

Soluble substances can dissolve. Substances that are soluble in water include sugar, salt, and coffee.

Insoluble substances cannot dissolve. Substances that are insoluble in water include chalk, wood, and sand.

The **solubility** of a solute is the mass of solute that can dissolve in 100 g of water. For many substances, increasing the temperature increases the solubility. Different solutes have different solubilities.

When so much solute has been added to the solvent that no more can dissolve, the mixture is a **saturated solution**. Any additional solute that is added will not dissolve. You can see that this solution is saturated, as some solute remains at the base of the beaker.

Key terms

Make sure you can write a definition for these key terms

chromatogram chromatography condenser distillation
evaporation filtrate filtration residue

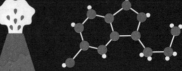

Practical: Filtration

Filtration is used to separate a mixture of an undissolved solid and a liquid.

For example, to separate sand from water, and small pieces of solids from gases, such as coronavirus particles from the air.

1 Filter paper has tiny holes in it.
2 Particles in a liquid or solution are so tiny that they can fit through the holes.
3 The pieces of the solid are too big to fit through the holes. They remain in the paper.

The **residue** is the solid left behind in the filter paper. The **filtrate** is the liquid that passes through the filter paper.

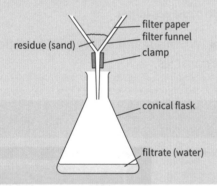

Practical: Distillation

Distillation is used to separate a solvent from a solution.

For example, to separate pure water from salt water, or essential oils from a plant solution.

1 Heat the solution until it boils. Some of the solvent leaves the solution as a gas.
2 The gas cools in the **condenser**, where it changes to the liquid state.

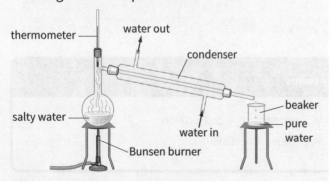

Practical: Chromatography

Chromatography is used to separate mixtures that are soluble in the same solvent.

For example, to separate dyes in a felt-tip pen or colours in sweet coatings.

1 Place a mixture, like ink, on a piece of paper. Place the bottom of the paper in a solvent.
2 As the solvent moves up the paper, it separates all the different constituents (parts) of the ink, producing a **chromatogram**.

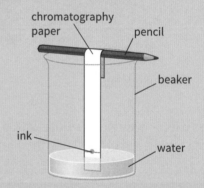

Practical: Evaporation

Evaporation is used to separate a solute and a solvent, keeping the solute.

For example, to separate salt from salt water or copper sulfate crystals from copper sulfate solution.

1 Heat the solution until tiny crystals of solid start to form around the edge of the solution.
2 Remove the heat and leave the mixture in a warm, dry place to allow the remaining solvent to evaporate.
3 The solute is left behind as a solid.

 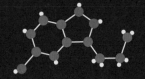
Learn the answers to the questions below and test yourself.

C6 Questions / Answers

Purity

1	What is a pure substance?	substance with no other substances mixed with it
2	How can you identify a pure substance?	it has a fixed melting point
3	What is a mixture?	two or more substances that are not chemically joined together

Solutions

4	What is a solution?	a mixture of a liquid with a solid or a gas, in which all parts of the mixture are the same
5	What is a solvent?	the liquid in which a solid or gas dissolves
6	What is a solute?	the solid or gas that dissolves in a liquid
7	What happens when a solute dissolves?	it mixes with a liquid (the solvent) to make a solution

Solubility

8	What is solubility?	the mass of a substance that dissolves in 100 g of water
9	What is a saturated solution?	a solution in which no more solute will dissolve
10	What does insoluble mean?	that a substance cannot dissolve in that solvent

Separation techniques

11	How can you separate an insoluble solid from a liquid?	by filtering
12	How can you separate a dissolved solid from a solution?	by evaporating the liquid, leaving the solid behind
13	How can you separate a solvent from a solution?	by distillation
14	What are the **two** processes involved in distillation?	boiling, condensing
15	What is chromatography?	a technique used to separate mixtures of liquids that are soluble in the same solvent

Put paper here

Previous questions / Answers

1	What is a compound?	atoms of two or more elements that are joined together strongly
2	What is decomposition?	a chemical reaction in which a compound breaks down into one or more elements and/or new compounds
3	Which solution is more acidic – one of pH 2 or one of pH 4?	pH 2
4	Define physical property.	a property you can observe or measure
5	Which gas is produced when elements in Group 1 react with water?	hydrogen

Put paper here

Practice

Practice questions

1 **Figure 1** shows the equipment used in distillation to separate pure water from seawater.

   a Label the equipment in **Figure 1**. Use answers from the box. **[4 marks]**

round bottomed flask   beaker   condenser   thermometer

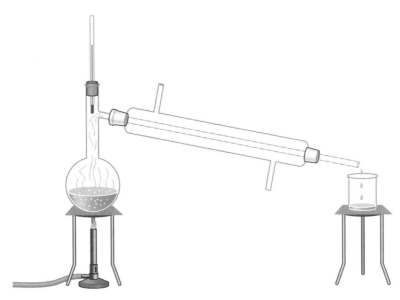

Figure 1

   b State where the pure water would be collected. **[1 mark]**

   _____

EXAM TIP

For part b use one of the labels from part a.

2 The sentences describe the process of filtration. Complete the sentences to describe how to separate a mixture of sand and salt. Choose answers from the box. **[6 marks]**

filter   insoluble   funnel   water   soluble   salt water   sand

   Add _____ to the sand and salt, and stir the mixture.

   The _____ salt dissolves.

   Pour the mixture through the filter paper in the _____.

   The _____ passes through.

   The _____, which is _____, is left behind in the filter paper.

EXAM TIP

Read the whole paragraph before you start adding in answers, as it will give you some clues.

3 Match each term to its correct definition by drawing lines.　**[3 marks]**　

Term	Definition
solvent	the process of mixing a solute and a solvent to make a solution
solute	a solid or gas dissolved in a liquid
solution	the substance that dissolves in a liquid
dissolving	the liquid in which a substance is dissolved

4 **Figure 2** shows the temperature of a substance as it is heated. To start with, the substance is in the solid state.

a Add a label to the graph to show when the substance is melting.

[1 mark]

> **EXAM TIP**
>
> Melting is a change in state, so look for when the graph changes.

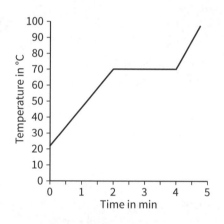

Figure 2

b The substance is a pure substance. Which is the best definition of a pure substance? Tick **one** box.　**[1 mark]**

a mixture of a liquid with a solid or a gas, in which all parts of the mixture are the same ☐

a substance that has no other substances mixed with it ☐

two or more substances that are not joined together chemically ☐

5 **Figure 3** shows a chromatogram with ink from three pens.

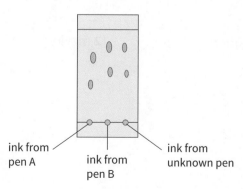

ink from pen A　ink from pen B　ink from unknown pen

Figure 3

a Describe how to use chromatography to separate the substances in a mixture. [3 marks]

_____

_____

_____

_____

b Suggest whether the unknown ink is from pen A or pen B. Give a reason for your answer. [1 mark]

_____

_____

EXAM TIP

Draw lines across from the known sample and match them up.

c Give **one** other use of chromatography. [1 mark]

_____

6 **Figure 4** shows a mixture of sugar and water particles.

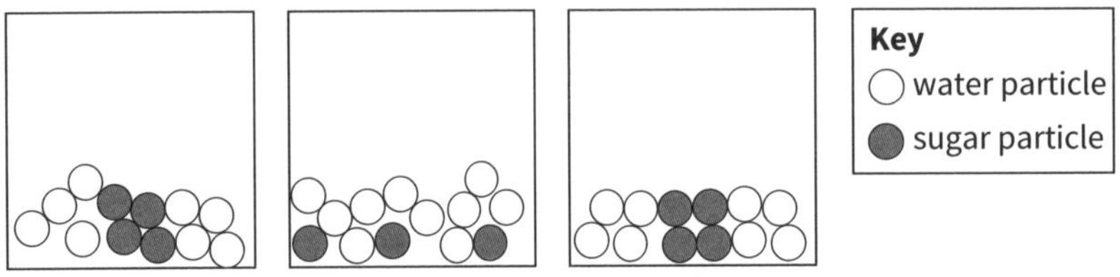

Key
○ water particle
● sugar particle

A   B   C
not to scale

Figure 4

a **i** Give the letter of the diagram that best represents sugar dissolved in water. [1 mark]

_____

ii Give a reason for your choice. [1 mark]

_____

_____

EXAM TIP

Think about what it looks like when sugar dissolves in water.

b Calculate the mass of sugar solution produced when 15 g of sugar is dissolved in 150 g of water. [1 mark]

_____ g

c Explain what is meant by a saturated solution. [2 marks]

_____

_____

_____

7 A group of students takes a sample of stearic acid and heat it to 80 °C. Stearic acid is in the solid state at room temperature and liquid at 80 °C. They remove the heat source and take the temperature of the sample every minute for 15 minutes. **Figure 5** shows their apparatus and results.

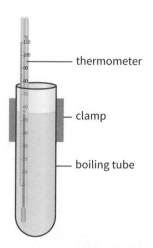

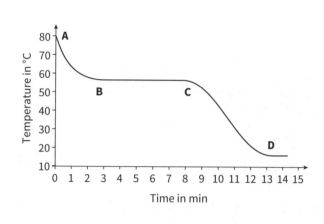

Figure 5

a State what is happening to the stearic acid between points A and B on the graph in Figure 5. **[1 mark]**

_____

_____

EXAM TIP

Don't worry if you've never heard of stearic acid before. You can apply what you have learnt in class to this new context.

b Identify the freezing point of stearic acid. Explain the reason for your choice. **[2 marks]**

_____

_____

_____

c Describe the trend shown between points C and D on the graph in Figure 5. **[2 marks]**

_____

_____

_____

EXAM TIP

Your answer should go: 'As the time in minutes increases, the temperature...'

8 Seawater is an example of a mixture, whereas carbon dioxide is an example of a compound. Compare the similarities and differences between mixtures and compounds. **[6 marks]**

_____

_____

_____

_____

_____

_____

_____

9   Ethanol has a boiling point of 78 °C. Using your knowledge
    of the particle model of matter, explain how distillation can be used to
    produce a pure sample of ethanol from a mixture of ethanol
    and water.   [6 marks]

EXAM TIP

Think about the boiling
point of water.

_____

_____

_____

_____

_____

_____

_____

10 The graph in **Figure 6** shows how the solubility of two salts, A and B,
    changes with temperature.

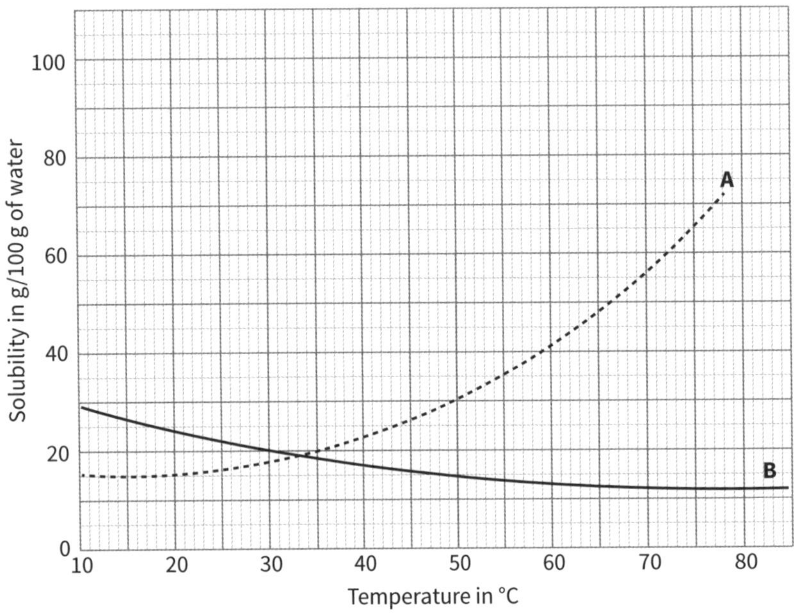

Figure 6

a   Describe how the solubility of salt A changes with
    temperature.   [2 marks]

_____

_____

_____

b   Identify the temperature at which the solubilities of salt A
    and salt B are identical.   [1 mark]

_____ °C

EXAM TIP

Look at where the lines
meet.

c Identify **two** differences in the effect of temperature on the solubilities of salt A and salt B. **[2 marks]**

_____

_____

_____

C5 **11** Elements have a number of different properties. Answer the questions. Choose answers from the box.

> high melting point   sonorous   brittle   forms an acidic oxide
> low boiling point   forms a basic oxide   ductile

a Identify **two** physical properties of metals. **[2 marks]**

i _____

ii _____

b Identify **one** chemical property of a non-metal. **[1 mark]**

_____

c State where non-metal elements are found in the Periodic Table. **[1 mark]**

_____

> **EXAM TIP**
>
> You should be able to define all the words in the box, even if you're not using them for this question.

C2 **12** In **Figure 7**, atoms are represented by different circles.

A	B	C

Figure 7

For each diagram, A, B, and C, identify whether it represents an element, a compound, or a mixture by circling the correct answer. Then, explain the reason for your choice. **[6 marks]**

A **element**   **mixture**   **compound**

Reason _____

B **element**   **mixture**   **compound**

Reason _____

C **element**   **mixture**   **compound**

Reason _____

> **EXAM TIP**
>
> This is a 6 mark question, suggesting you get one mark for circling the correct answer, so have a go even if you're not sure.

Knowledge

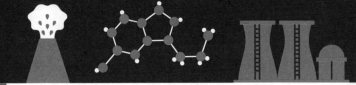

C7 Metals and other materials

Metals and acids

When a **metal** reacts with an acid, a type of substance known as a salt is produced. Hydrogen gas is also released because all acids contain the element hydrogen.

For example:

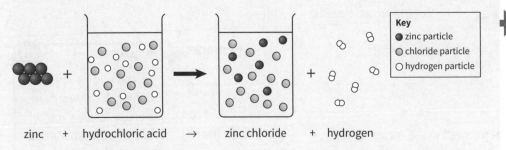

zinc + hydrochloric acid → zinc chloride + hydrogen

When acids and salts are dissolved in water, their particles are free to move around separately. (In this diagram, the water particles are not shown).

The type of salt produced depends on the acid used. For example, when reacting magnesium with different acids:

Acid used	Salt type	Name of salt
hydrochloric acid	chloride	magnesium chloride
sulfuric acid	sulfate	magnesium sulfate
nitric acid	nitrate	magnesium nitrate

Practical: Testing for hydrogen

The gas produced when reacting a metal and a salt can be collected in an upturned test tube.

Insert a lit splint into the upturned test tube. If the gas is hydrogen, there will be a squeaky pop sound.

Metals and oxygen

Many metals react with oxygen from the air to make a metal oxide.

For example:

aluminium + oxygen → aluminium oxide

However, some metals need to be heated before they can react, such as copper.

Metals and water/steam

Very reactive metals, like sodium, will react with cold water to produce a metal hydroxide and hydrogen gas.

sodium + water → sodium hydroxide + hydrogen

Other metals, like magnesium, only react with steam (not cold water) and produce a metal oxide and hydrogen.

magnesium + steam → magnesium oxide + hydrogen

Magnesium can be reacted with steam using the experimental set-up shown.

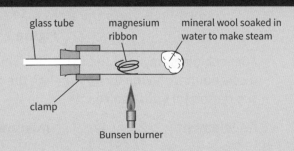

glass tube   magnesium ribbon   mineral wool soaked in water to make steam

clamp

Bunsen burner

 Key terms   Make sure you can write a definition for these key terms

displacement reaction   metal   ore   reactive   reactivity series   unreactive

Reactivity

A substance is **reactive** if it reacts vigorously with substances, such as dilute acids and water. A substance is **unreactive** if it takes part in only a few chemical reactions.

The more reactive a metal is, the more vigorously bubbles of hydrogen gas are made when the metal is placed in an acid.

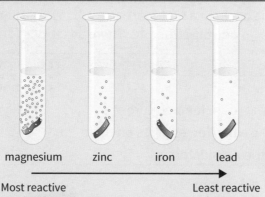

magnesium   zinc   iron   lead

Most reactive   Least reactive

The reactivity series

The **reactivity series** lists metals in order of how vigorous their reactions are.

most reactive

potassium
sodium
calcium
magnesium
aluminium
zinc
iron
lead
hydrogen
copper
mercury
silver
gold

least reactive

Displacement reactions

In a **displacement reaction**, a more reactive element displaces, or pushes out, a less reactive element from its compound. In metals, this means that the *more reactive* metal will become part of a compound and the *less reactive* metal will become an element.

For example:

- Aluminium is more reactive than iron. It is higher in the reactivity series. On adding aluminium metal to iron sulfate solution:

  aluminium + iron sulfate → aluminium sulfate + iron

- Zinc is more reactive than copper. On heating zinc metal with copper oxide:

  zinc + copper oxide → zinc oxide + copper

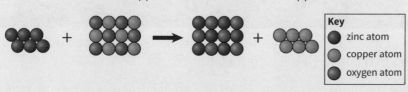

Key
- zinc atom
- copper atom
- oxygen atom

Extracting metals

Only very unreactive metals, like gold and platinum, are found as pure metals in nature. Most metals exist in Earth's crust as compounds, called minerals. Minerals that contain enough metal to be worth extracting are called **ores**.

Metal displacement reactions can be used to extract the metal element from its compound.

Using carbon to extract metals

Although carbon is a non-metal, it can be placed in the reactivity series. This shows part of the reactivity series, including carbon:

Carbon can displace metals lower in the reactivity series from their compounds. It is readily available in coke, a product formed from coal. For example:

iron oxide + carbon → iron + carbon monoxide

The carbon has displaced the iron from its compound.

magnesium
carbon
zinc
iron
copper

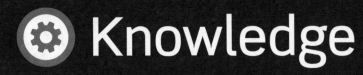 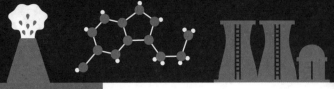

⚙ Knowledge

Ceramics

A **ceramic** is a hard, brittle material made by firing a material, such as clay, at a high temperature. In ceramic materials, millions of atoms join together in one big structure. There are strong forces between the atoms.

Physical properties		Chemical properties
• hard	• brittle	• do not react with water, acids, or alkalis.
• stiff	• solid at room temperature	
• very high melting points	• strong when forces press on them	
• easy to break when pulled	• electrical insulators.	

These properties make them very useful. For example:

- bricks – strong, durable
- jet engine turbine blades – high melting points
- crockery – does not react with water, acids, or alkalis.

Polymers

A **polymer** is a substance with very long molecules. A polymer molecule has identical groups of atoms, repeated many times.

Natural polymers include:

- wool – wool fibres trap air between them and are, therefore, good thermal insulators, making wool useful for clothing
- rubber – flexible, waterproof, and durable, making it suitable for bicycle and car tyres.

Synthetic polymers are made in laboratories and factories. These include the polymer poly(ethene).

Composites

Composite substances are mixtures of two or more different materials. The properties of the composite material are a combination of the properties of the materials it is formed from.

Two examples of composite materials are:

- reinforced concrete – the concrete is made stronger by adding steel bars as the concrete is being poured
- carbon fibre reinforced plastic (CFRP) – carbon fibres are added to a polymer, which acts to hold the fibres together. CFRP is extremely strong and lightweight.

Key terms

Make sure you can write a definition for these key terms

ceramic   composite   durable   natural polymer   polymer   synthetic polymer

Retrieval

Learn the answers to the questions below and test yourself.

C7 Questions | Answers

Reactions of metals

1	Which gas is formed when a metal reacts with acid?	Put paper here	hydrogen
2	Name the type of salt formed when a metal reacts with hydrochloric acid.		chloride
3	Name the type of salt formed when a metal reacts with sulfuric acid.		sulfate
4	Name the type of salt formed when a metal reacts with nitric acid.	Put paper here	nitrate
5	What is formed when a metal reacts with oxygen?		metal oxide

Reactivity

6	Which metal is less reactive – lead or gold?	Put paper here	gold
7	What is the reactivity series?		a list of metals in order of how vigorously they react
8	What is a displacement reaction?	Put paper here	where a more reactive metal displaces a less reactive metal from its compound
9	What is an ore?		a rock that you can extract a pure metal from

Ceramics, polymers, and composites

10	Name **four** physical properties of ceramics.		hard, brittle, high melting point, electrical insulator
11	What is a polymer?	Put paper here	a substance made up of very long molecules
12	Name **two** examples of natural polymers.		wool, rubber
13	Name **three** examples of synthetic polymers.		poly(ethene)/polythene, nylon, PVC
14	What is a composite?	Put paper here	a mixture of materials – its properties are a combination of the properties of the materials it is made from
15	What is carbon fibre?		a material made of thin tubes of carbon

Previous questions | Answers

1	What is the law of conservation of mass?	Put paper here	*mass of reactants = mass of products*
2	What is a base?		a substance that neutralises an acid
3	Name **one** chemical property of a typical non-metal oxide.		it is acidic
4	What is a pure substance?	Put paper here	a substance that has no other substances mixed with it
5	How can you separate a solvent from a solution?		by distillation

Practice

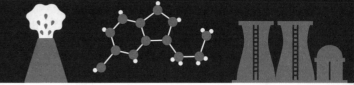

1 **Figure 1** shows an example of the structure of a polymer.

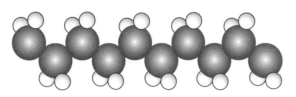

Figure 1

a Which **two** statements about polymers are true?
Tick **two** boxes. **[2 marks]**

a polymer has very long molecules ☐

a polymer has short molecules ☐

a polymer has identical groups of atoms, repeated many times ☐

a polymer contains a random order of atoms ☐

> **EXAM TIP**
> Never leave questions like this unanswered – even if you don't know the answer, tick two boxes.

b Choose the item in the box that is made from a polymer. **[1 mark]**

| rubber bungee cord | carbon fibre car body panel | ceramic tile |

_____

2 **Figure 2** shows part of the reactivity series of metals.
Use Figure 2 to answer the questions.

potassium
sodium
magnesium
zinc
iron
copper
gold

a Name the most reactive metal. **[1 mark]**

_____

b Name **one** metal that is more reactive than zinc. **[1 mark]**

_____

c Name **one** metal that is less reactive than iron. **[1 mark]**

_____

Figure 2

3 Ceramics have many uses in everyday life.

a Match each use of ceramics to the property that makes it particularly suitable for that use by drawing lines. **[4 marks]**

Use	Most important property
bricks	high melting point
overhead power line insulators	strong in compression
plates and cups	hard
jet engine turbine blades	do not conduct electricity
scratch-resistant tiles	unreactive with water, acids, or alkalis

> **EXAM TIP**
> Use a pencil to draw these lines – that way it is easier to change your answer if you need to.

b Name **one** property of ceramics not listed in part a. **[1 mark]**

_____

4 A student added a small piece of metal to a test tube containing
hydrochloric acid, as shown in **Figure 3**.

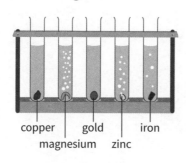

copper | gold | iron
magnesium | zinc

Figure 3

a Identify **one** metal that did not react with the
hydrochloric acid. **[1 mark]**

_____

b Identify which of the metals is the most reactive. Give a
reason for your answer. **[2 marks]**

_____

_____

_____

c Identify which gas is given off when a metal reacts with hydrochloric
acid. Choose the answer from the box. **[1 mark]**

sulfur dioxide   oxygen   hydrogen

_____

> **EXAM TIP**
> A reaction can be seen
> by bubbles being
> given off.

5 A science class recorded the time taken for different metals to react with
oxygen when exposed to air at room temperature. The time was measured
by noting how long it took for the metal to change from shiny to dull grey
after the metal was freshly cut. The box shows notes taken by a student.

Metals	Time
lithium	2 minutes
potassium	5 seconds
magnesium	4 weeks
sodium	30 seconds

> **EXAM TIP**
> The change from shiny
> to dull metal happens
> as the metal reacts,
> so look at the time
> this takes.

a List the metals in order of reactivity, from most reactive to
least reactive. **[3 marks]**

_____   _____   _____   _____

(most reactive)   (least reactive)

b Complete the word equation for when lithium reacts with oxygen. **[1 mark]**

lithium + oxygen → ______________________________

6 To test how reactive a metal is, small pieces of metal can be added to an acid. The hazard symbol in **Figure 4** was shown on the bottle of one of the acids used.

> **EXAM TIP**
> These symbols are important to keep you safe in the lab. It's really important that you know what they all mean.

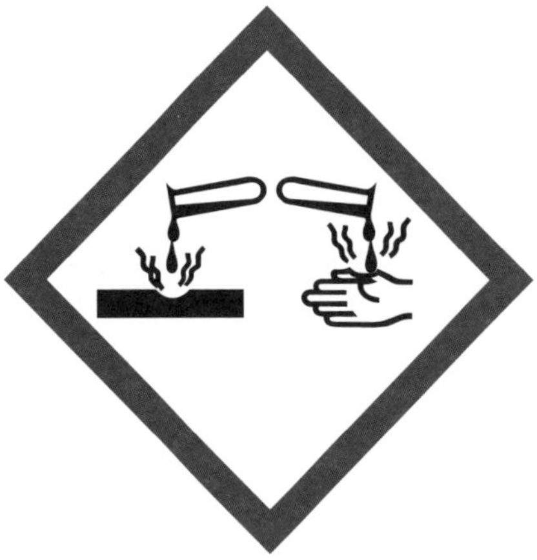

Figure 4

a **i** State what the symbol means. **[1 mark]**

____

ii State **one** safety precaution the scientist should follow when using the acid. **[1 mark]**

____

b State **two** observations that show if a metal has reacted with the acid. **[2 marks]**

____

____

c When a metal reacts with an acid, a salt is made. Match the acid used to the salt formed by drawing lines. **[2 marks]**

> **EXAM TIP**
> Look at the start of each word for a clue. The acid and the salt have a similar start to their names.

Acid used
hydrochloric acid
sulfuric acid
nitric acid

Salt formed
sulfate
chloride
nitrate

7 **a** State what is meant by a displacement reaction. **[2 marks]**

____

____

b Give **one** use of displacement reactions. **[1 mark]**

____

c A group of students reacted four metals with compounds containing each of the four metals. Their results are shown in **Table 1**. A tick means a reaction took place.

Table 1

Metal compound	Metal			
	copper	magnesium	iron	zinc
magnesium sulfate	✗		✗	✗
copper chloride		✓	✓	✓
zinc carbonate	✗	✓	✗	
iron nitrate	✗	✓		✓

i Using the information in Table 1, place the metals in order of reactivity. **[3 marks]**

_____ (most reactive)

_____

_____

_____ (least reactive)

ii Explain how you worked out the order of reactivity. **[2 marks]**

_____

_____

8 a State what is meant by a metal ore. **[1 mark]**

_____

_____

b A company extracts 5000 kg of iron ore, which contains 15% iron. Calculate the mass of iron that the rocks contain. **[2 marks]**

_____ kg

c The sentences describe the process used to extract pure iron from iron ore. Correctly order the sentences by writing the letters in the boxes. The last one has been done for you. **[4 marks]**

A Finally, the pure iron is collected from the reaction vessel.

B A displacement reaction takes place because carbon is more reactive than iron.

C The products of the displacement reaction are iron and carbon dioxide.

D Separate the iron oxide from any other compounds in the rock.

E Heat the iron oxide strongly in the presence of carbon.

F Mine the rocks containing iron ore from the ground.

□ → □ → □ → □ → □ → A

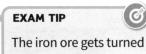

EXAM TIP

The iron ore gets turned into iron oxide.

9 **Table 2** shows some properties of two polymers, polythene and synthetic rubber.

Table 2

Property	Synthetic rubber	Polythene
water resistance	high	high
density in g/cm³	1.15	0.85
can be rolled to thin sheets	no	yes
relative hardness	50	25
relative elasticity	100	10
colour	black	any colour

a Match each polymer to its use by drawing lines. **[1 mark]**

Polymer
polythene
synthetic rubber

Use
car tyres
carrier bags

b Using information from Table 2 and your own knowledge, explain the reasons for your choices in part a. **[6 marks]**

_____

_____

_____

_____

_____

_____

_____

EXAM TIP

You have to use data from the table to answer this question.

C4 **10** Some solutions are acidic and some are alkaline.

a Which **two** statements are correct? Tick **two** boxes. **[2 marks]**

a neutral solution has a pH of 7 ☐

an alkaline solution has a pH less than 7 ☐

the more acidic a solution, the higher its pH ☐

you cannot use litmus paper to find out the pH of a solution ☐

EXAM TIP

Even if you're not sure, just tick any two boxes – you might be correct!

b When you add an acid to an alkali, there is a reaction. Which is the correct type of reaction? Choose the answer from the box. **[1 mark]**

combustion   evaporation   neutralisation   oxidation

_____

C2 **11** Nitrogen can react with oxygen to form nitrogen monoxide. **Figure 5** shows the particle diagram of the reaction.

before   **after**

Figure 5

a Define the term chemical reaction. **[1 mark]**

_____

_____

EXAM TIP

Use the information in the main part of the question to work out the reactants and the products.

b Give the word equation for this reaction. **[2 marks]**

_____

c Does the particle diagram show that mass is conserved? Explain your answer. **[2 marks]**

_____

_____

C8 The Earth

Structure of Earth

Earth is made up of four layers – two outer layers and two inner layers.

The crust and the mantle are the outer layers. They are made of rock.

The inner layers, called the core, are made from iron and nickel.

crust – a solid layer around 40 km thick. It contains many different compounds.

mantle – this layer is mostly solid rock, but it can flow.

outer core – a layer of hot, liquid metal around 2000 km deep.

inner core – the central part of Earth, around 2500 km in diameter. The inner core has very high temperatures and pressures.

Structure of the atmosphere

The **atmosphere** is a layer of gas that surrounds Earth. The part of the atmosphere nearest Earth is the **troposphere**. It is mostly made up of nitrogen and oxygen.

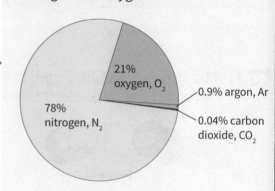

21% oxygen, O_2

0.9% argon, Ar

78% nitrogen, N_2

0.04% carbon dioxide, CO_2

The rock cycle

There are three types of rock that make up Earth's crust – **sedimentary**, **igneous**, and **metamorphic** rocks. These are formed by different processes in the **rock cycle** and have different properties. The rock cycle shows how rocks change and how their materials are recycled over millions of years.

The Earth's crust moves – very slowly – all the time. When continents collide, huge forces from inside Earth push rocks upwards. This is called **uplift** and can cause mountains to form.

volcano | lava | mountain — weathering

cooling and freezing

transport

uplift

lake

igneous rock

heating and/or pressure

cooling and freezing

metamorphic rock

melting

heating and/or pressure

deposition

magma

sedimentary rock

compaction and/or cementation

melting

Uplift provides evidence for the rock cycle. It brings rocks and fossils to the surface that were once buried.

Sedimentary rocks

Sedimentary rocks are made of separate grains with small gaps between them. Air or water can get into the gaps, so the rocks are **porous**. Examples include chalk and limestone. Sedimentary rocks are formed through a four-stage process:

Stage 1: **Weathering** – older rocks are broken up into smaller rocks and sediments by:

- chemical weathering
- freeze–thaw weathering or other types of physical weathering
- biological weathering (action of animals or plants).

Stage 2: **Transport** – sediment is moved away from the original rock by wind, water, or ice. Stages 1 and 2 together (the breaking of rock into sediments and its movement) are known as **erosion**.

Stage 3: **Deposition** – sediment settles in one place. Layers of different types of sediment may settle on one another.

Stage 4: New rock forms by two possible processes:

- **compaction** – the weight of sediment above squeezes the sediment below into rocks
- **cementation** – another substance sticks the sediments together.

Igneous rocks

Igneous rocks are made up of crystals. Examples include granite and basalt. Igneous rocks are formed when molten rock cools down.

- **Magma** (liquid rock underground) cools slowly, forming rocks with large crystals.
- **Lava** (liquid rock above the ground) cools quickly, forming rocks with small crystals.

Metamorphic rocks

Metamorphic rocks contain crystals. Examples include marble and slate. Metamorphic rocks are formed when heat and/or pressure change existing rocks. For example:

- marble forms when limestone is heated
- slate forms when high pressure compresses mudstone, squeezing out water and making new layers of very fine crystals.

Uses of sedimentary rocks

Uses: building materials and making concrete.

Properties:

- some types are porous
- strong in compression
- soft – grains are easy to break apart as forces between them are weak

Uses of igneous rocks

Uses: kitchen worktops and paths.

Properties:

- not porous
- strong and durable
- hard – crystals are locked tightly together

Uses of metamorphic rocks

Uses: sculptures (marble) and roof tiles (slate).

Properties:

- not porous
- hard

C8 Earth continued

Carbon cycle

The **carbon cycle** shows how carbon atoms move between carbon dioxide in the atmosphere and carbon compounds on Earth. Places where carbon remains for a long time are called **carbon stores**. These include the atmosphere, sedimentary rocks, fossil fuels, living organisms, and soil.

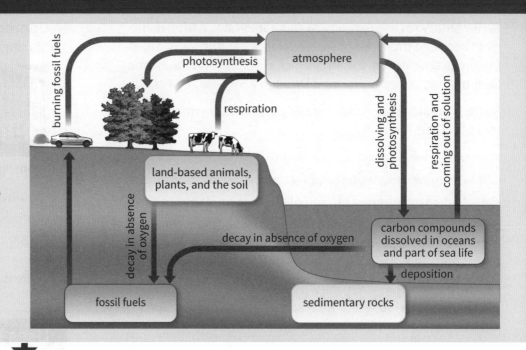

Changes to atmospheric carbon

Carbon dioxide is *added* to the atmosphere by:

- **respiration**, when energy is transferred from food to cells in plants and animals

    glucose + oxygen → carbon dioxide + water

- **combustion**, when fossil fuels and wood are burnt, for example

    methane + oxygen → carbon dioxide + water

Carbon dioxide is *removed* from the atmosphere by:

- **photosynthesis**, when plants make glucose

    carbon dioxide + water → glucose + oxygen

- dissolving in the oceans

Key terms

Make sure you can write a definition for these key terms

atmosphere   cementation   compaction   crust   deposition   erosion   igneous
inner core   lava   magma   mantle   metamorphic   outer core   porous   rock cycle
sedimentary   transport   troposphere   uplift   weathering

Greenhouse effect

Some gases in the atmosphere prevent some of the radiation from the Sun that hits Earth's surface from being lost back into space. This keeps the temperature warm close to Earth's surface.

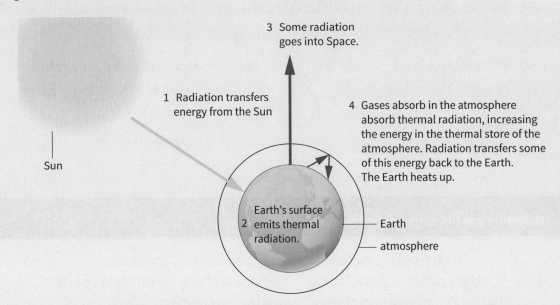

3 Some radiation goes into Space.

1 Radiation transfers energy from the Sun

4 Gases absorb in the atmosphere absorb thermal radiation, increasing the energy in the thermal store of the atmosphere. Radiation transfers some of this energy back to the Earth. The Earth heats up.

Sun

Earth's surface
2 emits thermal radiation.

Earth

atmosphere

The absorption of radiation by gases in the atmosphere is known as the **greenhouse effect**. Carbon dioxide and methane are examples of **greenhouse gases** because they absorb a lot of radiation.

Global heating

Over time, the atmospheric temperature has increased. This is known as global warming or **global heating**. Scientific evidence has shown that human activities that release extra carbon dioxide into the atmosphere are responsible. These include:

- burning fossil fuels for transport, electricity, and heating
- sea level rise
- increase in extreme weather events
- changes in distribution of pests and diseases
- **deforestation** – removing trees for agriculture and building; this reduces photosynthesis and further adds carbon dioxide to the atmosphere if the trees are burnt
- farming animals, which increases carbon dioxide and methane emissions.

Impacts of global heating include:

- glaciers and polar ice melting, leading to a rise in sea levels and flooding
- global weather patterns changing, for example, wet areas getting wetter (causing flooding), and dry areas becoming drier (causing droughts).

Long-term changes to weather patterns are called **climate change**. This has led to some animals and plants becoming extinct, and it being harder for people to grow food.

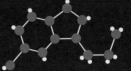 
Recycling

All the materials that people use come from Earth's crust, atmosphere, or oceans. The faster the materials are extracted, the sooner they will run out. **Recycling** means collecting and processing used objects so their materials can be used again. Materials that can be recycled include paper, metals, and plastics.

Advantages:

- natural resources will last longer
- less energy is needed than when using new materials
- reduces waste and landfill

Disadvantages:

- takes effort for people to sort their waste
- recycling lorries use fuel and make pollution

Key terms

Make sure you can write a definition for these key terms

carbon cycle   carbon stores   climate change   combustion
deforestation   global heating   greenhouse effect   greenhouse gas
photosynthesis   recycling   respiration

Retrieval

Learn the answers to the questions below and test yourself.

C8 Questions | Answers

Earth

#	Question	Answer
1	Name the **four** layers of the structure of Earth.	crust, mantle, outer core, inner core
2	Name the **two** most common gases in the atmosphere.	nitrogen, oxygen

Rocks and the rock cycle

#	Question	Answer
3	What are sedimentary rocks?	rocks that are made of separate grains, formed from sediments by compaction or cementation
4	Name **three** examples of sedimentary rocks.	chalk, limestone, sandstone
5	What are igneous rocks?	rocks formed of crystals, made when magma or lava cools and freezes
6	Name **three** examples of igneous rocks.	basalt, granite, obsidian
7	What are metamorphic rocks?	rock formed by the action of heat and/or pressure on sedimentary or igneous rocks
8	Name **three** examples of metamorphic rocks.	marble, slate, gneiss
9	What does the rock cycle show?	how rocks change and how their materials are recycled into new rocks over millions of years

Environmental chemistry

#	Question	Answer
10	Name the main processes in the carbon cycle.	photosynthesis, respiration, combustion, dissolving in the oceans
11	Name **two** examples of greenhouse gases.	carbon dioxide, methane
12	What is the greenhouse effect?	the absorbing of energy by gases in the atmosphere
13	What is global heating?	the gradual increase in Earth's air temperature
14	What is recycling?	collecting and processing used materials to make new objects
15	Name **four** materials that can be recycled.	paper, plastic, aluminium, glass

Put paper here

Previous questions | Answers

#	Question	Answer
1	List some properties of elements found in Group 7 (halogens).	reactive, low melting points, low boiling points
2	What happens when a solute dissolves?	it mixes with a liquid (the solvent) to make a solution
3	What is chromatography?	a technique used to separate mixtures of liquids that are soluble in the same solvent
4	What is a displacement reaction?	where a more reactive metal displaces a less reactive metal from its compound
5	What is a composite?	a mixture of materials – its properties are a combination of the properties of the materials it is made from

Put paper here

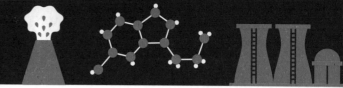

Practice

Practice questions

1 **Figure 1** shows the structure of Earth.

    a Label the layers. Choose answers from the box.   **[4 marks]**

inner core	magma	outer core	mantle	crust	lava

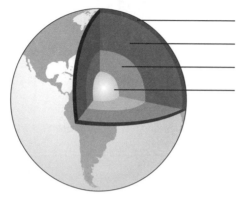

Figure 1

    b Earth's atmosphere is a mixture of gases. Which is the best
description of the atmosphere? Tick **one** box.   **[1 mark]**

      the atmosphere contains mainly oxygen and carbon dioxide   ☐

      the atmosphere is a mixture of solids, liquids, and gases   ☐

      the atmosphere contains mainly nitrogen   ☐

2 **Figure 2** shows how the mean global air temperature has changed
over time.

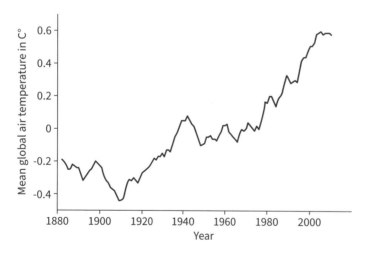

Figure 2

    a Complete the sentences to describe the overall trend shown
by the graph in Figure 2.   **[2 marks]**

      Since 1910, the mean temperature of Earth has _____.

      In the year 2000, the mean temperature of Earth was
_____ °C.

b Name **one** impact on the environment of this change. **[1 mark]**

_____

3 Chalk is an example of a sedimentary rock.

a Predict **one** property of chalk. **[1 mark]**

_____

b Name another example of a sedimentary rock. **[1 mark]**

_____

c Sedimentary rocks are formed through four main stages. Put the stages in the box in the correct order. **[3 marks]**

| compaction | transport | deposition | weathering |

_____ → _____ → _____ → _____

4 **Figure 3** shows the main stages in the carbon cycle.

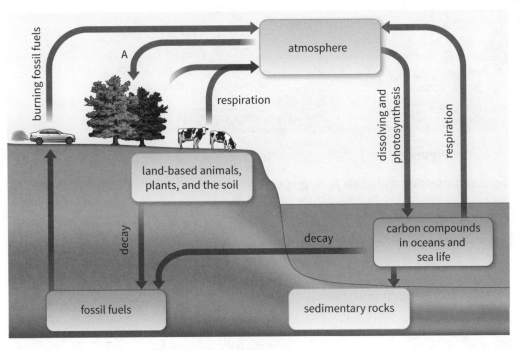

Figure 3

a Identify the process represented by A. **[1 mark]**

_____

b Fossil fuels are a store of carbon. Identify **two** other carbon stores in Figure 3. **[2 marks]**

i _____

ii _____

c   Carbon dioxide is released into the atmosphere when fossil fuels are burnt.

   i   Name **one** example of a fossil fuel.   [1 mark]

_____

   ii Give the scientific name for the process of burning.   [1 mark]

_____

5   **Figure 4** shows the rock cycle.

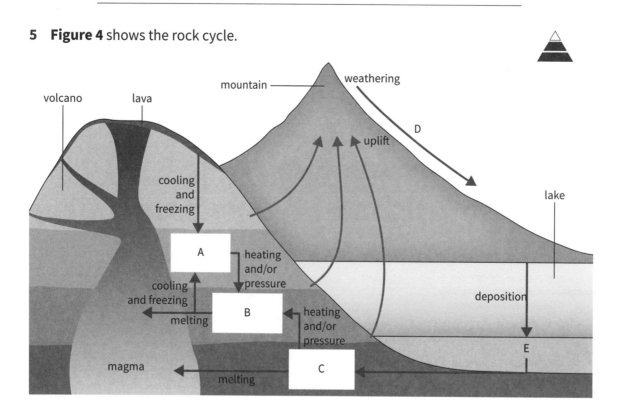

Figure 4

a   Name the types of rock represented by labels A, B, and C.   **[3 marks]**

A _____

B _____

C _____

b   Sedimentary rocks are formed through four main processes:

weathering → D → deposition → E

Name processes D and E.   **[2 marks]**

D _____

E _____

c   Give **one** piece of evidence for uplift.   **[1 mark]**

_____

6   **Figure 5** shows the composition of Earth's crust.

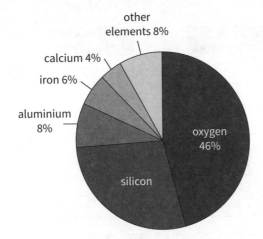

Figure 5

a   Name the most abundant element in Earth's crust.   **[1 mark]**

_____

b   Calculate the percentage of silicon in Earth's crust.   **[2 marks]**

EXAM TIP

Remember pie charts need to add up to 100.

_____ %

c   Name the layer of Earth found beneath the crust.   **[1 mark]**

_____

d   Earth has an outer core and an inner core.

Name the state of matter of:

i   the outer core   **[1 mark]**

EXAM TIP

Are they solid, liquid, or gas?

_____

ii   the inner core   **[1 mark]**

_____

7   **Figure 6** represents the greenhouse effect.

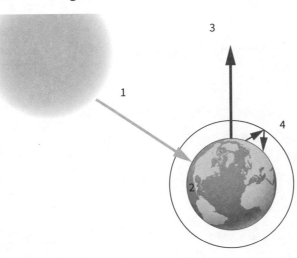

Figure 6

a Match each statement to the correct process by drawing lines. **[3 marks]**

EXAM TIP

Look for key bits of information about where the energy is coming from and going to.

Statement	Process
Earth's surface warms up and emits thermal radiation	1
some thermal radiation is trapped by gases in the atmosphere	2
some thermal radiation is transferred into space	3
energy transferred from the Sun warms Earth's surface	4

b The greenhouse effect is increasing as some gases are released into Earth's atmosphere.

　i Name **one** gas that causes an increase in the greenhouse effect. **[1 mark]**

EXAM TIP

Think about the carbon cycle.

　_____

　ii State **one** source of the gas named in part **b i**. **[1 mark]**

　_____

c An increase to the greenhouse effect is causing global heating, resulting in climate change.

　i Define the term global heating. **[2 marks]**

　_____

　_____

　ii State **two** negative effects of climate change. **[2 marks]**

　_____

　_____

　iii Describe **one** way in which countries are aiming to prevent climate change. **[1 mark]**

　_____

　_____

8 **Figure 7** shows a simplified cross-section of the rocks on a cliff face.

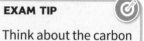

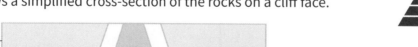

Figure 7

a Select a letter from **Figure 7** that matches each description below. **[4 marks]**

igneous rock _____

sedimentary rock _____

metamorphic rock _____

rock that may contain fossils _____

b State and explain which rock in **Figure 7** is the oldest. **[4 marks]**

_____

_____

_____

_____

c Siltstone is a type of sedimentary rock. Suggest **one** property of siltstone. **[1 mark]**

_____

> **EXAM TIP**
>
> Even if you've never heard of siltstone, you can answer this question by giving properties of any sedimentary rock.

d Slate is a type of metamorphic rock that forms from mudstone.

  i Describe how slate is formed. **[2 marks]**

_____

_____

  ii Explain **one** property of slate that makes it useful for making roof tiles. **[2 marks]**

_____

_____

C6 **9** There are a number of different techniques that can be used to separate mixtures. Match each mixture to the technique that should be used by drawing lines. **[2 marks]**

Mixture
coloured ink in a felt-tip pen
pure water from seawater
sand from sandy water

Technique
filtration
chromatography
distillation

Forces and interactions

A **force** is a **push** or a **pull**. Forces can change the speed, direction, or shape of an object.

All forces arise because objects interact. Forces always occur in pairs. An example of an **interaction pair** is:

- the force of the Earth on you (gravity)
- the force of you on the Earth (also gravity).

Measuring and representing forces

Forces are measured in **newtons (N)** using a **newtonmeter** or spring balance.

You use force arrows to show the size and direction of forces in diagrams.

a ball resting on a table

force exerted by the table on the ball

force exerted by the Earth on the ball (due to gravity)

Squashing and stretching

Two or more forces can **deform** objects, even solids. You can imagine solids as particles connected by bonds that behave like springs. (You use a different version of this model of a solid in chemistry).

For example:

- When you stand on the floor (a solid), the floor pushes up – this is the **reaction** force.
- When you pull a solid, it gets a bit longer – this is a **tension** force.

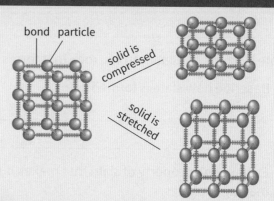

bond   particle

solid is compressed

solid is stretched

bonds are compressed and push back

bonds are stretched and pull back

Springs

Springs are a special case of squashing and stretching. They obey **Hooke's Law**.

- Hooke's Law: The extension of a spring is proportional to the force stretching it, so if you double the force, the **extension** doubles (up to the **elastic limit**).
- A graph of force against extension is a straight line.

Not all objects obey Hooke's Law.

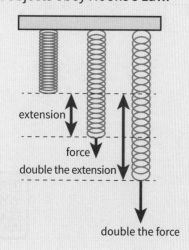

extension

force

double the extension

double the force

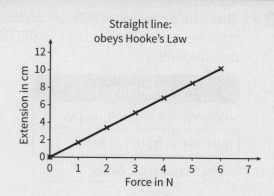

Straight line: obeys Hooke's Law

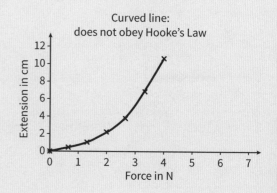

Curved line: does not obey Hooke's Law

Contact and non-contact forces

There are two types of force.

- **Contact forces** act when an object is in contact with the surface of another object, air, or water. For example, tension, reaction, friction, and drag, and **upthrust** (the upwards force of a fluid on an object).

- **Non-contact forces** act if objects are not in contact don't need objects to be physically touching – they act at a distance. For example, gravitational forces, **magnetic forces**, and **electrostatic forces**.

- Masses, magnets, and charges produce **fields**. A field is a region in which an object experiences a force.

Friction

On a microscopic scale, all surfaces are rough. Solid surfaces in contact exert a force on each other called **friction**. **Lubrication** reduces friction.

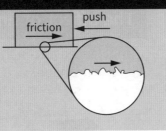

Drag

Particles in fluids (gases or liquids) exert a **drag** force on objects moving through them.

- Moving through a gas: **air resistance**.
- Moving through a liquid: **water resistance**.

Gravity

Every object exerts a gravitational force **(gravity)** on every other object because they have mass.

Mass is the amount of stuff something is made of. It is also a measure of how hard it is to get it to move, or change its motion. It is not a force. Mass is measured in kilograms (kg) or grams (g).

Weight is the force due to gravity that acts on an object. Weight is measured in newtons (N) because it is a force.

You can calculate weight using:

weight (N) = mass (kg) × **gravitational field strength, g (N/kg)**

$$W = mg$$

On Earth, gravitational field strength g is 10 N/kg. It is less on the Moon (1.6 N/kg) because the Moon has less mass than the Earth. This is why things weigh less on the Moon.

g is more than 10 N/kg on planets with more mass.

Gravitational field strength decreases with distance.

Worked example: Calculating weight

Calculate the weight of a book of mass 500 g on Earth.

The mass of the book is 500g. Convert this mass to kilograms by dividing by 1000.

$$\frac{500}{1000} = 0.5 \, kg$$

On Earth, g is 10 N/kg
weight (N) = mass (kg) × gravitational field strength (N/kg)
= 0.5 kg × 10 N/kg
= 5 N

Key terms Make sure you can write a definition for these key terms

air resistance   contact force   deform   drag   elastic limit   electrostatic force   extension
field   force   friction   gravitational field strength   gravity   Hooke's Law   interaction pair
lubrication   magnetic force   mass   newton (N)   newtonmetre   non-contact force
pull   push   reaction   tension   upthrust   water resistance   weight

P1 Forces continued

Balanced, unbalanced, and resultant forces

You add forces together to get the **resultant force**. The size and the direction of each force is taken into account. If forces are in the same direction they add. If they are in opposite directions they subtract.

Forces are **balanced** when:

- equal and opposite forces cancel out (arrows are equal length)
- the resultant force is zero.

Forces are **unbalanced** when:

- equal and opposite forces do not cancel out
- the resultant force is not zero.

The effect of balanced forces

When the forces acting on an object are balanced, the object is in **equilibrium**.

Balanced forces do *not* change an object's motion, or its size or shape.

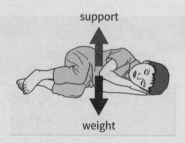

support

weight

Stationary objects stay still.

Moving objects continue to move at a steady speed and in the same direction.

air resistance | The push from the engine is the *same size* as the resistive forces acting on the car. The speed of the car *stays the same*. | thrust due to the engine

The effect of unbalanced forces

Unbalanced forces change an object's motion, or its size or shape.

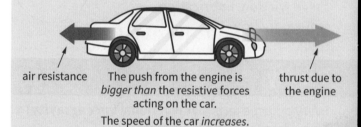

air resistance | The push from the engine is *bigger than* the resistive forces acting on the car. The speed of the car *increases*. | thrust due to the engine

Moving objects **accelerate** (speed up, slow down, change direction).

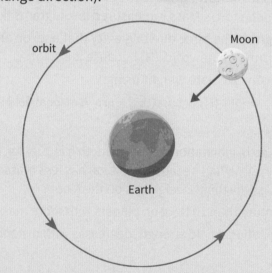

orbit

Moon

Earth

For objects moving in a circle, like the Moon in orbit around the Earth, the direction of motion changes, but the speed does not.

Key terms

Make sure you can write a definition for these key terms

accelerate   balanced   equilibrium   resultant force   unbalanced

Retrieval

Learn the answers to the questions below and test yourself.

P1 Questions

Answers

Forces

1	What is the unit of force?		newton (N)
2	Name the measuring instrument used to measure force.		newtonmeter/spring balance
3	What do force arrows show?		size and direction of force
4	Name **five** types of contact force.		air resistance, friction, upthrust, tension, reaction
5	Name **three** types of non-contact force.		gravity/gravitational, magnetic, electrostatic
6	What is a field (physics)?		a region where something feels a force

Hooke's Law

7	What do the bonds between the particles of a solid behave like?		springs
8	State Hooke's Law.		extension is proportional to force
9	What is a reaction force?		the force of a solid on an object (a support force)

Friction and drag

10	What is friction?		the force between two solid surfaces in contact
11	How do you reduce friction between surfaces?		use lubrication
12	What is drag?		the force of the air or water on a moving object/air resistance or water resistance

Gravity

13	What is weight?		the force due to gravity that acts on an object
14	What is mass?		the amount of matter (stuff) a thing is made up of
15	Give the equation to calculate weight.		weight = mass × gravitational field strength
16	What is the gravitational field strength on Earth?		10 N/kg

Resultant forces

17	How can you work out a resultant force?		add all the forces acting on an object, taking account of direction
18	What happens to an object with zero resultant force?		it is stationary or travels at constant speed/ steady speed in the same direction
19	What happens to a moving object when the forces on an object are *not* balanced?		the object will slow down, accelerate, or change direction

(Put paper here)

✎ Practice

Practice questions

1 **Figure 1** shows a force diagram for a stationary boat.

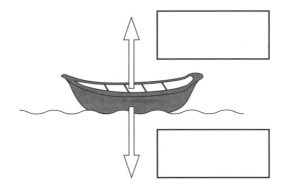

Figure 1

EXAM TIP

Be clear in the wording you use to describe the forces.

a Label the force arrows in **Figure 1**. Choose answers from the box. **[2 marks]**

> reaction   weight   upthrust   drag

b Name **two** contact forces. Choose answers from the box in part a. **[2 marks]**

i _____

ii _____

EXAM TIP

The unit of force is an uppercase letter – the lowercase letter is wrong.

c Give the unit of force. **[1 mark]**

_____

2 Forces can deform objects. Objects can be compressed or stretched.

a Identify whether the object in each situation is being compressed or stretched. Tick the correct box in **Table 1**. **[4 marks]**

Table 1

Situation	Compressed?	Stretched?
when you are sitting on a chair, the chair is		
when a tennis ball hits the racquet, the strings are		
when you put a book on a table, the table is		
when you are standing on the floor, the floor is		

b Complete the sentences by choosing the correct words in bold.

[2 marks]

Hooke's Law says that, if you double the force you apply to a spring, the extension will **double / halve**.

The graph of force against extension for a spring is a **curved / straight** line.

3 When objects move through the air and through water, forces act on them.

Complete the sentences. Choose answers from the box. Each answer may be used once, more than once, or not at all. **[5 marks]**

> bigger   particles   air resistance   smaller   further apart
> closer together   water resistance

EXAM TIP

Don't worry about not using all of the words in the box.

When a stone moves through the air, it collides with _____

in the air. This produces a force called _____. When the stone

moves through water, there is a force called _____ acting

on it. The force of the water is _____ than the force of the air

because the particles are _____.

4 There is a gravitational field around Earth.

a Which is the correct definition of gravitational field?
Tick **one** box. **[1 mark]**

the region where an object has mass ☐

the region where there is a balanced force on an object ☐

the region where a force acts on a mass ☐

b **Figure 2** shows two people standing on the surface of Earth.

Draw arrows on **Figure 2** to show the direction of the gravitational force acting on the people. **[2 marks]**

EXAM TIP

Do you fall off the Earth?

Figure 2

c You are standing on Earth and there is a gravitational force on you. Complete the sentence about forces on the Earth and the Moon. **[1 mark]**

The Moon is less massive than the Earth. If you were standing on the

Moon, the gravitational force on you would be _____

than the gravitational force acting on you on Earth.

5 The forces acting on an object can be balanced or unbalanced.

a Complete the sentences. Choose answers from the box.   **[3 marks]**

balanced   unbalanced

When a car is accelerating, the forces acting on it are

_____.

When a skateboarder is travelling at a steady speed, the forces

acting on her are _____.

When a cyclist is stationary, the forces acting on him

are _____.

EXAM TIP

You will need to use some words more than once.

b Objects can be in equilibrium. **Figure 3** shows the forces acting on a block.

5 N

A

5 N   5 N

B

5 N   2 N

C

Figure 3

EXAM TIP

If the arrows pointing left are negative and the arrows pointing right are positive, which box adds to zero?

i In which diagram, A, B, or C, is the block in equilibrium?   **[1 mark]**

_____

ii Select **two** reasons for your answer. Tick **two** boxes.   **[2 marks]**

the forces are the same magnitude (size)   ☐

the forces are not the same magnitude (size)   ☐

the forces are acting in the same direction   ☐

the forces are acting in opposite directions   ☐

6 A student is investigating friction. They put a box on a ramp and lift the ramp until the box starts to move. They want to find out how the type of surface affects the height they have to lift the ramp to make the box move.

ramp   box   box

a Name the independent variable.   **[1 mark]**

_____

b Name the dependent variable. [1 mark]

_____

c Suggest **one** control variable. [1 mark]

_____

d **Table 2** shows the results of the experiment.

Table 2

Surface	Height ramp is lifted in cm
wood	15
paper	17
carpet	25

Suggest an explanation for the results. Use the terms friction and gravitational force in your answer. [2 marks]

_____

_____

7 A student is standing on the floor. They are not moving. With reference to forces, explain why they remain stationary. Use ideas about particles and bonds in your answer.

[4 marks]

_____

_____

_____

_____

_____

8 A student wants to find the weight of their pencil case.

a Name the measuring instrument they would use to measure it.

[1 mark]

_____

b Another student says that they think it weighs about 100 g. Explain why this statement is incorrect. [1 mark]

_____

_____

c The mass of the pencil case is 0.1 kg. Calculate the weight of the pencil case. Show your working. (Gravitational field strength, $g = 10$ N/kg) [3 marks]

_____ N

9   A student watches a video of a person skydiving. Put the statements
    in order to describe and explain what the student observes.
    The first and last letters have been done for you.   **[5 marks]**

    A   When the air resistance is equal to the weight, the parachutist
         travels at a steady speed, called the terminal velocity.

EXAM TIP

Work out a rough
answer before adding
the letters into the
boxes.

    B   The parachutist is travelling slowly so they can land safely.

    C   The air resistance increases as they accelerate.

    D   The parachutist opens their parachute.

    E   The air resistance suddenly increases, so the parachutist suddenly slows
         down.

    F   The air resistance increases until it equals the weight of the
         parachutist, and they reach a lower terminal velocity than before.

    G   As the parachutist jumps out of the plane, they accelerate.

    G → ☐ → ☐ → ☐ → ☐ → ☐ → B

10 A student throws a ball upwards. The ball moves upwards,
    slowing down. It stops momentarily and speeds up as it comes
    back down. The student catches the ball.

    a   Draw force diagrams in the boxes for:

         •   the ball as it is moving upwards

         •   the ball when it stops momentarily.

         Ignore air resistance. Label the arrows.   **[4 marks]**

EXAM TIP

The ball stops briefly
when it gets to the top
of the throw before
it starts coming back
down again.

ball when it is moving upwards	ball when it has stopped momentarily

    b   Use your diagrams to explain the motion of the ball from
         the moment it leaves the student's hand until they catch
         it again.   **[3 marks]**

    _____

    _____

    _____

    _____

    _____

11 A student is watching a video of astronauts travelling into space.

a   Describe and explain, in terms of gravitational field strength, what happens to the weight of an astronaut as they move away from Earth.   **[2 marks]**

_____

_____

_____

b   The gravitational field strength on a planet is 2.5 N/kg. Calculate the mass of an astronaut with a weight of 200 N. Show your working.   **[4 marks]**

EXAM TIP

Look back at Analysing and evaluating data to see how to change the subject of an equation.

_____

12 a   A student is watching a game of football. A player kicks a ball. The ball rolls along the ground from left to right, slowing down as it does so.

i   Draw a diagram showing the forces on the ball as it rolls from left to right.   **[3 marks]**

ii   State the other force in each interaction pair of forces acting on the ball and its direction.   **[3 marks]**

_____

_____

_____

_____

b   An astronaut outside a spacecraft throws a spanner. As they throw the spanner, they move backwards. Explain why.   **[2 marks]**

EXAM TIP

Think about what is missing in space.

_____

_____

c   Compare the moving football and the moving astronaut (once they have thrown the spanner) in terms of forces.   **[4 marks]**

_____

_____

_____

_____

_____

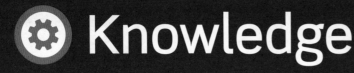
P2 Sound

Waves

A wave is an **oscillation** or a **vibration** that transfers **energy** or information from a source to a detector *without* transferring matter.

Water waves are **transverse** – the direction of movement of the water is *perpendicular* (at 90°) to the wave direction.

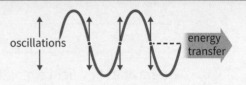

Transverse wave:
oscillations at right angles to energy transfer

Reflection and superposition

All waves can bounce off surfaces. This is called **reflection**.

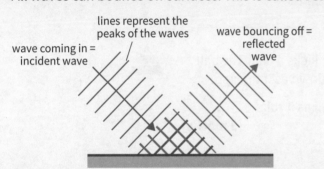

lines represent the peaks of the waves

wave coming in = incident wave

wave bouncing off = reflected wave

All waves can add up or cancel out. This is called **superposition**.

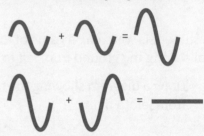

Making sounds and sound waves

Sound is produced by any object that vibrates. Sound waves are **longitudinal** – the direction of vibration is *parallel* to the wave direction.

A sound wave is a variation of **pressure**.

rarefactions = regions of low pressure

oscillations

energy transfer

Longitudinal wave: oscillations are parallel to the direction of energy transfer

compressions = regions of high pressure

Travelling sound waves

Sound waves need a **medium** (substance) to travel through. Sound waves:

- travel fastest in solids (particles are closest together)
- travel slowest in gases (particles are furthest apart) – speed in air is 340 m/s
- cannot travel through a **vacuum** (no particles)
- travel a million times slower than light.

 Key terms Make sure you can write a definition for these key terms

amplitude   auditory nerve   cochlea   compression   decibel (dB)   diaphragm
eardrum   energy   frequency   hertz (Hz)   longitudinal   loudness

Wave features

All waves have three features – **frequency**, **amplitude**, and **wavelength**.

The frequency is the number of waves that pass a fixed point per second. Frequency is measured in **hertz (Hz)**.

You can represent a longitudinal sound wave with a transverse wave diagram that relates to pressure.

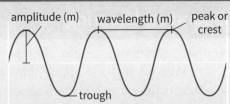

Detecting sound

Sound waves can be detected by your ears or a **microphone**.

Both produce a changing electrical signal, which transfers information.

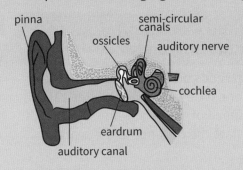

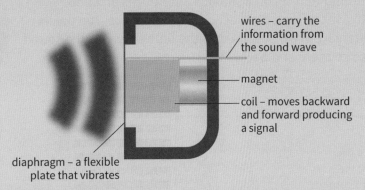

Sound waves make the **eardrum** vibrate causing bones (**ossicles**) and fluid in the **cochlea** in your ear to vibrate, sending a signal down the **auditory nerve**.

In a microphone, a **diaphragm** vibrates when a sound wave hits it. The diaphragm is like your eardrum.

Pitch and loudness

An **oscilloscope** can be used to display a wave on a screen. The wave displayed on the screen is a transverse representation of the longitudinal sound wave. The grid helps to compare the frequency and amplitude of different sound waves.

Pitch depends on frequency:

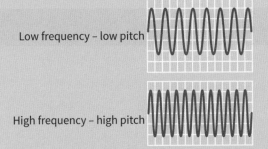

Loudness depends on amplitude:

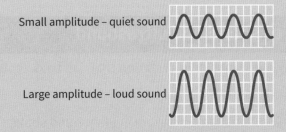

Loudness is measured in **decibels (dB)**.

Key terms

Make sure you can write a definition for these key terms

medium   microphone   oscillation   ossicles   pitch   pressure   rarefaction
reflection   superposition   transverse   undulation   vacuum   vibration   wavelength

Sound and hearing

Humans can hear a range of frequencies between 20 Hz and 20 000 Hz. This is called the **audible range**. Different animals have different hearing ranges. Dogs and bats hear much higher frequencies, whilst elephants hear much lower frequencies.

Ultrasound is sound which has a frequency greater than 20 000 Hz.

Absorption of sound and echoes

Sound is **absorbed** by materials, especially soft materials like curtains.

When sound reflects off a surface, it produces an **echo**. You can use the time of an echo to find distance. You divide the distance by two because it is the time taken for the sound wave to go there and back.

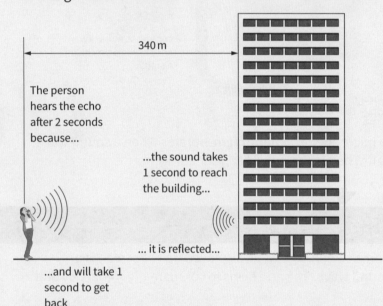

The person hears the echo after 2 seconds because...

...the sound takes 1 second to reach the building...

... it is reflected...

...and will take 1 second to get back

340 m

Worked example: Calculating distance

A ship sends out a sound wave to the seafloor. It detects an echo after 4 seconds. The speed of sound in water is 1500 m/s. Calculate the distance to the seafloor.

$$\text{distance} = \text{speed} \times \text{time}$$
$$= 1500 \text{ m/s} \times 4 \text{ s}$$
$$= 6000 \text{ m} \rightarrow$$ This is the distance the sound wave travels in total – there and back. You need to divide this by 2 to get the distance to the seafloor.
$$= 3000 \text{ m}$$

 Ⓛ

Uses of sound and ultrasound

Sound waves transfer information that can be detected by microphones and ears.

Ultrasound is used for:

- cleaning – changing pressure in ultrasound shakes off dirt
- physiotherapy – ultrasound transfers energy that heats human tissue
- imaging – the reflection of ultrasound enables doctors to see inside the human body.

Key terms

Make sure you can write a definition for these key terms

absorb   audible range   echo   ultrasound

Learn the answers to the questions below and test yourself.

P2 Questions | Answers

	#	Question	Answer
Waves	1	What do waves transfer?	energy or information
	2	In which direction do the vibrations in transverse waves move?	perpendicular/at right angles to the direction the wave travels
	3	Name the three properties of a wave.	frequency, amplitude, wavelength
Sound	4	In which direction do the vibrations in longitudinal waves move?	parallel to the direction the wave travels
	5	In which type of medium do sound waves travel fastest?	solid
	6	What can sound *not* travel through?	a vacuum
Detecting sound	7	What does an ear convert a sound wave into?	an electrical signal
	8	What does a wave with a high frequency sound like?	high pitched
	9	What is the audible range of a human?	20 Hz to 20 000 Hz
Echoes	10	What is an echo?	a reflection of sound
	11	What is ultrasound?	sound with a frequency at or above 20 000 Hz

Put paper here

Previous questions | Answers

#	Question	Answer
1	Give the unit of force.	newton (N)
2	Name a contact force.	air resistance/friction/upthrust/tension/reaction
3	What is drag?	the force of the air or water on a moving object/air resistance or water resistance
4	What is weight?	the force of Earth on an object due to its mass

Put paper here

Practice

Practice questions

1 Waves have different features.

a Match each feature of a wave to its definition by drawing lines.

[2 marks]

Feature
wavelength
amplitude
frequency

Definition
number of waves per second
distance from one point on a wave to the same point on the next wave
distance from the middle to the top of a wave

EXAM TIP

These are really important definitions to learn.

b Waves can be reflected from a surface. Identify the diagram, **A**, **B**, or **C**, in **Figure 1** that correctly shows the reflection of a wave. **[1 mark]**

EXAM TIP

Think about the angles.

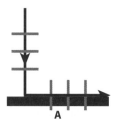 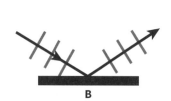 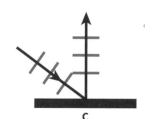

A   B   C

Figure 1

_____

2 Sound can travel through solids, liquids, and gases.

a Describe an everyday situation that shows that sound can travel through solids. **[1 mark]**

_____

_____

b Sound moves away from a source and can be detected. Complete the sentences by choosing the correct words in bold. **[4 marks]**

A source of sound waves is something that is **moving / vibrating**. A sound wave transfers **energy / movement** without transferring **energy / matter**. Sound can be detected by **loudspeakers / microphones**.

3 Your ears detect sound. The parts of the ear are shown in **Figure 2**.

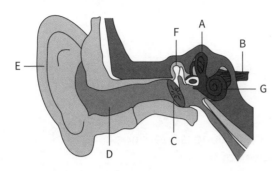

Figure 2

Give the letter of:

a the part of the ear that transfers an electrical signal to the brain

[1 mark]

_____

b the part of the ear that is the first thing that vibrates when you hear a sound [1 mark]

_____

c the part of the ear made of bones, which can shatter if the sound is too loud. [1 mark]

_____

4 **Figure 3** shows three sound waves on an oscilloscope.

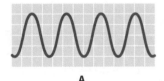 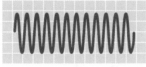 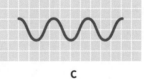

A B C

Figure 3

a Give the letters of the two waves with the same loudness. [1 mark]

_____

b Give the letter of the wave with the highest pitch. [1 mark]

_____

c Give the letter of the quietest sound. [1 mark]

_____

5 A fishing boat transmits a pulse of ultrasound from the bottom of the boat.

   a Which is the frequency of ultrasound? Choose the answer from the box. **[1 mark]**

> 50 Hz   500 Hz   5000 Hz   50 000 Hz

The sound reflects from the seabed.

   b Give the name of the reflection of sound. **[1 mark]**

   c The time for the boat to receive the reflected sound is 6 seconds. Calculate the depth of the water if the speed of sound in water is 1500 m/s. **[3 marks]**

> **EXAM TIP**
>
> Look back at the Knowledge section to see a worked example for calculating distance.

_____ m

   d Give another use of ultrasound, apart from measuring distance. **[1 mark]**

6 **Figure 4** shows the speed of sound in three different materials, A, B, and C.

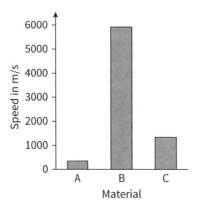

Figure 4

> **EXAM TIP**
>
> Sound needs particles to travel.

   a Give the letter of the material that is in the gas state. **[1 mark]**

   b Suggest and explain which of the materials is a solid. **[2 marks]**

7 A student makes a sound by holding one end of a ruler on the desk, pulling down the other end, and letting go.

Figure 5

a Describe what the ruler is doing to the air to make a sound wave.

[2 marks]

_____

_____

b **Figure 6** shows the sound wave produced by the ruler. The student pulls the ruler down *further* and lets it go. Draw the wave that would be produced on **Figure 6**. [2 marks]

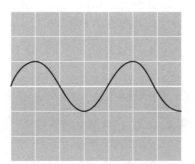

Figure 6

EXAM TIP

Draw carefully using the gridlines to show how the amplitude and the wavelength have changed.

c Explain the wave you have drawn in part b. Use the words amplitude and frequency in your answer. [2 marks]

_____

_____

8 **Table 1** shows data for two ships that have sunk.

Table 1

Name	Date lost	Where	Depth in m
HMS *Titanic* (British passenger ship)	1912	North Atlantic	3800
MV *Bukoba* (Tanzanian ferry)	1996	Lake Victoria	25

Objects in an ocean or lake can be located by sending out sound waves and measuring the time it takes to detect the reflection. The speed of sound in water is 1500 m/s.

a Calculate the time it would take a sound wave to be detected if it was reflected from HMS *Titanic* on the seafloor. Round your answer to the nearest 0.1 s. Show your working. **[4 marks]**

EXAM TIP

Look back at Analysing and evaluating data to see how to change the subject of an equation.

_____ s

b Suggest **one** problem with using this method to locate MV *Bukoba*. **[2 marks]**

_____

_____

c Suggest how you could produce an accurate measurement of the depth of the seafloor. **[2 marks]**

_____

_____

9 A teacher sets up an experiment with two loudspeakers at a distance apart. The loudspeakers produce sound of the *same* pitch and amplitude. They set it up so there is an area where the waves superpose, as shown in **Figure 7**.

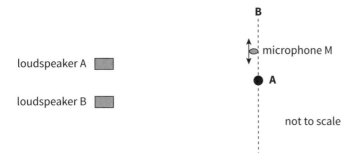

Figure 7

a Define superposition of waves. **[1 mark]**

_____

_____

b Point A is the same distance from both speakers. The waves join together and add up. Describe what the microphone detects. **[1 mark]**

EXAM TIP

Think in terms of waves.

_____

_____

c The microphone detects a loud sound, then a quiet sound, then a loud sound as it moves from A to B. Explain what that tells you about the way the waves superpose. **[2 marks]**

_____

_____

d Explain why the microphone does not detect any silences (absence of sound). **[2 marks]**

_____

_____

P1 **10** A student is investigating springs. They hang a weight on a spring, as shown in **Figure 8.**

The student decides to investigate how the weight affects the extension of the spring. Here is a list of variables:

A extension of spring

B type of spring

C weight

D temperature of laboratory

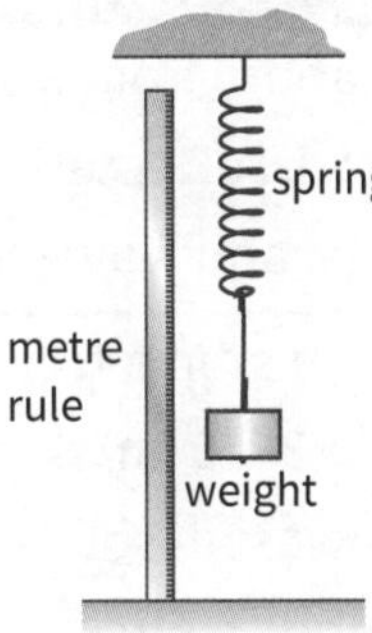

spring

metre rule

weight

Figure 8

a Give the letter of the independent variable. **[1 mark]**

_____

b Give the letter of the dependent variable. **[1 mark]**

_____

c Give the letter of a control variable. **[1 mark]**

_____

d Complete the sentence by choosing the correct words in bold. **[2 marks]**

_____

The student should plot a **bar chart / line graph** because the data are **categoric / continuous**.

P1 **11** A student finds a website that shows how much you would weigh on different planets in the Solar System. The website uses a person with a mass of 100 kg.

a The weight of that person on Earth is 1000 N. Describe the difference between weight and mass. **[2 marks]**

_____

_____

b Explain how you know, from the data, that the gravitational field strength on Earth is 10 N/kg. **[2 marks]**

_____

_____

⚙ Knowledge

P3 Light

Light waves and waves in matter

	Light waves	Waves in matter
Similarities	• Transfers energy (or information) from a **source** to a **detector** without transferring matter. • Can be **emitted**, **transmitted**, **reflected**, and **absorbed**. • Have a frequency, amplitude, and wavelength.	
Differences	• Can travel through a vacuum or in air. • Travel at 300 million m/s (or 3×10^8 m/s). • Travel fastest in air and slowest in solids. • Can be emitted by a **luminous** source. • Can be reflected by non-luminous objects.	• Need a **medium** (solid, liquid, or gas) to travel through. • Sound travels at 340 m/s in air. • Travel slowest in air and fastest in solids. • Can be reflected at the boundary between two media.

The ray model

You draw **rays** to represent beams of light. The ray model helps to explain **pinhole cameras**, reflection, and refraction. It also helps to explain how images are formed in your eyes, and how lenses work.

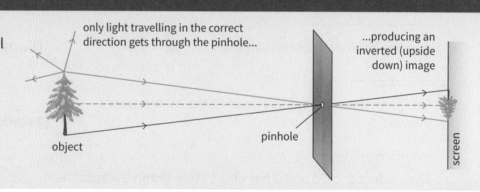

only light travelling in the correct direction gets through the pinhole...

...producing an inverted (upside down) image

object

pinhole

screen

Light transmission and reflection

Materials can be:

• **transparent** – they transmit light so you can see through them

• **translucent** – they transmit light, but it is scattered so that you cannot see clearly through them

• **opaque** – they do not transmit light.

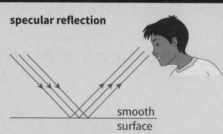

specular reflection

smooth surface

Specular reflection occurs from smooth surfaces.

diffuse scattering

rough surface

Diffuse scattering occurs from rough surfaces.

Key terms

Make sure you can write a definition for these key terms

absorb   angle of incidence   angle of reflection   camera
charge-coupled device (CCD)   convex (converging) lens   detector   diffuse scattering
emit   focal length   focus (focal point)   law of reflection   luminous   medium

Reflection

When light is reflected from a very smooth surface, such as a mirror, the **angle of incidence** is equal to the **angle of reflection**. This is the **law of reflection**. Angles are measured from a line at 90° to the surface called the normal.

angle of incidence = angle of reflection

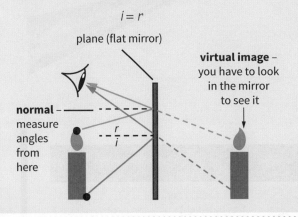

$i = r$

plane (flat mirror)

virtual image – you have to look in the mirror to see it

normal – measure angles from here

r
i

Refraction

Light changes direction when it goes between different materials, like air and water. This is **refraction**.

Refraction happens when light slows down or speeds up. It slows down when it goes into a denser medium.

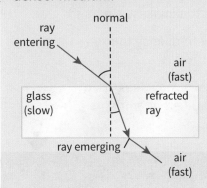

normal
ray entering
air (fast)
glass (slow)
refracted ray
ray emerging
air (fast)

Light bends towards the normal when it slows down

Light bends away from the normal when it speeds up

Lenses and the eye

The lenses in your eyes are **convex (converging) lenses**. They focus the light and allow you to see. The light is refracted at the cornea and lens, producing images on the **retina**. An image on your retina, or that you can put on a screen is a **real image**.

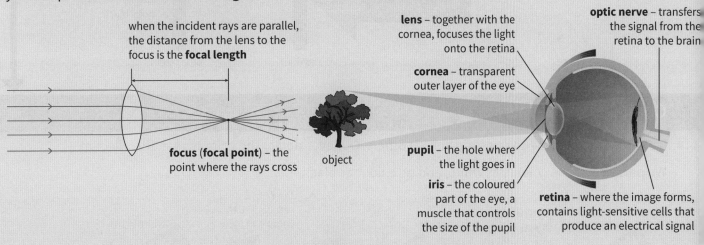

when the incident rays are parallel, the distance from the lens to the focus is the **focal length**

focus (focal point) – the point where the rays cross

object

lens – together with the cornea, focuses the light onto the retina

cornea – transparent outer layer of the eye

pupil – the hole where the light goes in

iris – the coloured part of the eye, a muscle that controls the size of the pupil

optic nerve – transfers the signal from the retina to the brain

retina – where the image forms, contains light-sensitive cells that produce an electrical signal

Cameras

Cameras work in a similar way to the eye, using a lens to form an image.

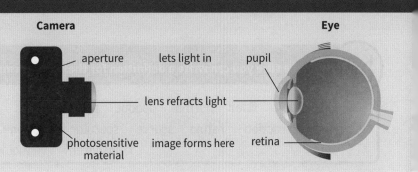

Camera

aperture   lets light in

lens refracts light

photosensitive material   image forms here

Eye

pupil

retina

Colour and prisms

You can use a **prism** to split white light into a continuous **spectrum**. This is **dispersion**.

White light is made up of seven bands of colour. When we say 'blue' we mean a range of frequencies that makes up a band.

Red light has a lower frequency than blue light.

Different frequencies, or wavelengths, of light are refracted in different amounts.

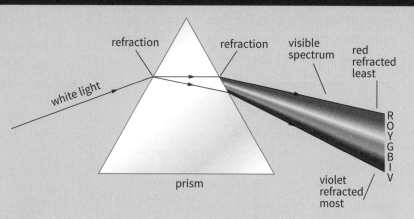

Filters

Filters absorb some colours, but not others.

The colour of a filter tells you the colour that it transmits. All the other colours are absorbed.

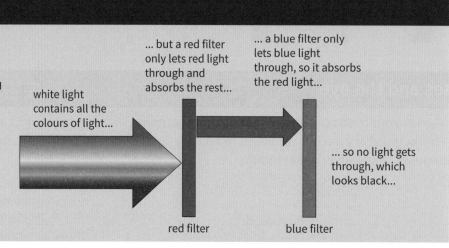

Coloured materials

Materials reflect some colours and absorb others. Our eyes detect the colours that are reflected.

We perceive all the colours as white, and no colour as black.

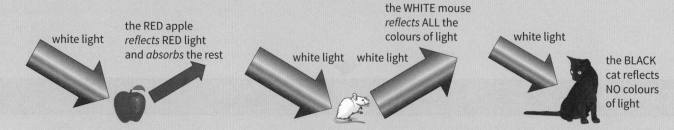

Key terms — Make sure you can write a definition for these key terms

dispersion   filter   normal   opaque   photosensitive   pinhole camera   prism   ray   reflect
refraction   retina   source   specular reflection   spectrum   translucent   transmit
transparent   virtual image

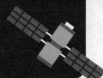
Learn the answers to the questions below and test yourself.

	P3 Questions		Answers
Light and matter	1 What is a luminous source?	Put paper here	an object that emits light
	2 What is a transparent object?		an object that transmits light so you can see through it
	3 What type of reflection happens from a smooth surface?		specular reflection
	4 What type of reflection happens from a rough surface?		diffuse scattering
Reflection and refraction	5 State the law of reflection.	Put paper here	the angle of incidence equals the angle of reflection ($i = r$)
	6 What happens to light when it is refracted?		it changes speed and direction
	7 What does a convex lens do to light?		refracts it to a focus/focal point
	8 On which part of the eye is an image formed?		the retina
	9 Which part of a camera is equivalent to the retina of the eye?		photosensitive material
Prisms and colour	10 What can you use to make a continuous spectrum of white light?	Put paper here	prism
	11 What does a red filter do to white light?		transmits red, absorbs all the other colours
	12 What does a blue book do to white light		reflects blue, absorbs all the other colours

	Previous questions		Answers
	1 Name a non-contact force.	Put paper here	gravity/gravitational, magnetic, electrostatic
	2 What is equilibrium?		a situation where there is zero resultant force
	3 In which direction do the vibrations in a longitudinal wave move?		parallel to the direction the wave travels
	4 What does a wave with a high frequency sound like?		high pitched
	5 What is an echo?		a reflection of sound

Practice questions

1 Light is produced by a source, like the Sun, and travels to a detector, like our eyes. In between, it interacts with matter. It takes time to travel.

a Match each key word to its definition by drawing lines. **[3 marks]**

Key word	Definition
luminous	light travels through it, but you cannot see through it
transparent	gives out light
translucent	does not allow light through it
opaque	you can see through it

> **EXAM TIP**
> Use a pencil and a ruler so that you can change your answer if you want.

b The statements in **Table 1** are about light interacting with matter. Are they true or false? Tick the correct boxes.

Table 1

Statement	True?	False?
colourless glass is opaque		
the Moon is luminous		
tissue paper is translucent		

2 Surfaces reflect light.

a Complete the sentences. Choose answers from the box. Each answer may be used once, more than once, or not at all. **[4 marks]**

> **EXAM TIP**
> Read the instructions carefully. This one tells you that you might use some words more than once.

specular   diffuse   paper   mirrors   superposition

There is _____ reflection when light reflects according to the law of reflection. This happens with _____. If light reflects at different angles, we call it _____ scattering. This happens when light reflects from _____.

Figure 1 shows a beam of light reflected from a mirror.

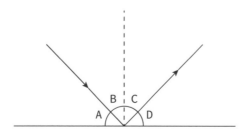

Figure 1

b Give the letter of the angle of incidence. [1 mark]

_____

c Give the letter of the angle of reflection. [1 mark]

_____

d A student says that the angle between the ray coming in and the ray going out is always 90°. Is this statement true or false? [1 mark]

_____

3 Light refracts when it moves from one material to another. **Figure 2** shows light going into a block.

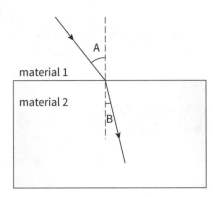

Figure 2

Complete the sentences by choosing the correct words in bold. [4 marks]

In the diagram, the angle of refraction is **angle A / angle B**. The dashed line is called the **normal / reaction**. Material 2 is **less / more** dense than material 1. Light moves fastest in **material 1 / material 2**.

4 You detect light with your eyes. **Figure 3** shows a diagram of the eye.

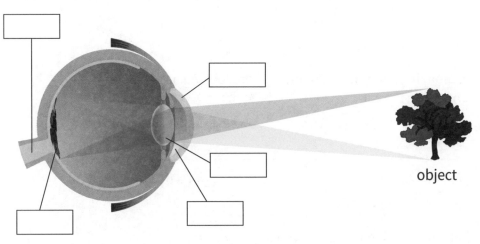

object

Figure 3

a Label the parts of **Figure 3**. Choose answers from the box. **[5 marks]**

optic nerve   cornea   lens   retina   iris

EXAM TIP

Start from the left-hand side – these are the easier ones to work out if you're not sure.

b Describe what the pupil is. **[1 mark]**

_____

c Match each part of the eye with a camera part by drawing lines.

[2 marks]

Part of the eye
pupil
retina
eyelid

Camera part
photosensitive material
aperture
lens cap

5 A prism disperses light.

a The statements in **Table 2** are about dispersion. Are they true or false? Tick the correct boxes. **[3 marks]**

Table 2

Statement	True?	False?
violet light is refracted more than red light		
refraction does not depend on colour		
different colours are slowed down by different amounts		

 EXAM TIP

Only tick true OR false, not both. You won't get any marks if you do that.

b Complete the sentences about coloured materials and filters by drawing lines. **[3 marks]**

A blue filter
A red filter
A green book
A black mat

reflects green light.
transmits blue light.
absorbs all colours of light.
absorbs blue light.

6 You are sitting in a chair in a room in your house at night. You are looking at a cat. There is an electric light above the cat.

a Name the luminous object in this situation. **[1 mark]**

_____

b Name an opaque object in this situation. **[1 mark]**

_____

c Describe the journey that light takes that enables you to see the cat.

[3 marks]

_____

_____

7 **Figure 4** shows the coin in the cup trick. In diagram A, a student looks towards a cup that has a coin in it. They cannot see the coin. In diagram B, they *can* see the coin.

EXAM TIP

When drawing these lines it needs to go to the eye.

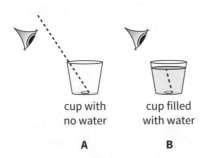

cup with no water

cup filled with water

A

B

Figure 4

a Add another ray to diagram B to show how the coin is now visible.

[2 marks]

b Explain the change in direction of the ray in diagram B as it comes out of the water.

[2 marks]

_____

_____

c Light changes direction as it goes through a convex lens. Which diagram, A, B, or C, in **Figure 5** shows this?

EXAM TIP

The blocks are shown here as rectangles, but in reality are a curved convex lens.

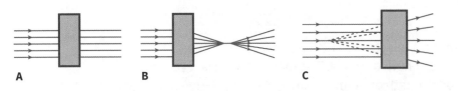

A

B

C

Figure 5

[1 mark]

_____

8 A student wants to answer the following question:

How does the type of material affect the amount of light transmitted through it?

They set up the equipment as shown in **Figure 6**.

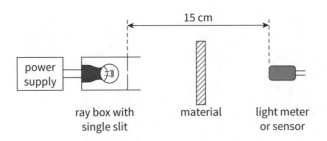

15 cm

power supply

ray box with single slit

material

light meter or sensor

Figure 6

a Give the names of the variables in this experiment. **[2 marks]**

Independent variable _____

Dependent variable _____

b Will they use their data to plot a line graph or a bar chart? **[1 mark]**

_____

c Explain your answer to part **b**. **[1 mark]**

_____

9 Light does not travel instantaneously. It travels fast and takes a very short time to travel distances on Earth. The speed of light is 300 million m/s.

a Suggest why it took a long time for people to realise that light does not travel instantaneously. **[2 marks]**

_____

_____

b It takes light 8 minutes to travel from the Sun to Earth. Earth is 150 million km from the Sun.

It takes light about 40 minutes to travel from the Sun to Jupiter. Use ratios to calculate the distance from the Sun to Jupiter. **[3 marks]**

> **EXAM TIP**
>
> Look back at the Knowledge section for C3 – Chemical reactions – to see a worked example for using ratios.

_____

10 A teacher uses lenses to make a telescope. The lens nearest the object, the objective lens, has a focal length of 50 cm. The lens nearest the eye, the eyepiece lens, has a focal length of 5 cm.

a Define focal length. **[1 mark]**

_____

b In each box, draw a diagram to show light going through the lens to a focus. **[2 marks]**

objective lens	eyepiece lens

> **EXAM TIP**
>
> When drawing ray diagrams, using a ruler is essential.

c Explain your answer. **[3 marks]**

_____

_____

_____

_____

P2 **11** A student plays different notes on a guitar.

   a Using one of the strings, the student makes a high pitch.
Complete the sentences by choosing the correct words in bold.
[3 marks]

EXAM TIP

It might help to sketch out the waves.

     A high-pitched sound has a **high / low** frequency. Frequency is the number of waves per **hour / second**. Frequency is measured in **hertz / metres**.

   b They want to play a louder note of the same pitch. Which is the wave feature that they need to change? Choose the answer from the box.
[1 mark]

frequency   speed   wavelength   amplitude

_____

   c Suggest how the student could make a louder sound with the same string. **[1 mark]**

_____

P1 **12** A student makes a parachute. They attach it to a ball of modelling clay using a piece of string and drop it from the top of some stairs.

   a Name **two** factors that affect the air resistance acting on the moving object. **[2 marks]**

    i _____

   ii _____

     When they first drop the parachute, it accelerates. After a short time, it moves at a steady speed.

   b Explain, in terms of forces, why the parachute accelerates. **[2 marks]**

_____

_____

   c Explain, in terms of forces, why the parachute moves at a steady speed. **[1 mark]**

_____

_____

   d Suggest what would happen to the time the parachute takes to reach a steady speed if the student increased the mass of modelling clay attached to the parachute. Explain your answer. **[2 marks]**

_____

_____

⚙ Knowledge

The Universe

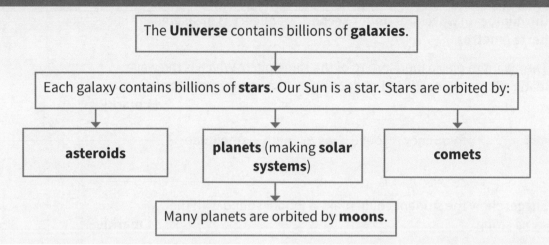

The **Universe** contains billions of **galaxies**.

↓

Each galaxy contains billions of **stars**. Our Sun is a star. Stars are orbited by:

| **asteroids** | **planets** (making **solar systems**) | **comets** |

Many planets are orbited by **moons**.

Earth, satellites, and meteors

Satellites orbit planets. **Moons** are **natural satellites**. Earth is also orbited by:

- **artificial satellites** – they are used to collect weather data and for communication
- space stations – where astronauts live and conduct science experiments.

Meteors are bits of dust or rock that burn up as they move through Earth's atmosphere and produce streaks of light.

Light-time

Astronomers use **light-time** (light-years, light-hours, light-seconds) for measuring *distances* in space (not time). A light-year is the distance that light travels in one year.

Our galaxy (the Milky Way) is 100 000 light-years across.

View of the Milky Way galaxy

From above

Sun

Side on

100 000 light-years

How did our Solar System form?

Scientists think that gravity pulled gas, rocks, and dust together to form the Sun about 5 billion years ago. They think planets formed from a disc of gas and dust surrounding the Sun.

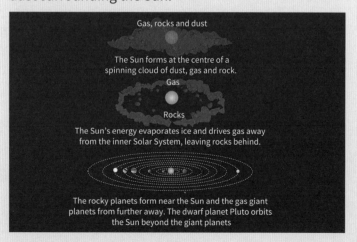

Gas, rocks and dust

The Sun forms at the centre of a spinning cloud of dust, gas and rock.

Gas

Rocks

The Sun's energy evaporates ice and drives gas away from the inner Solar System, leaving rocks behind.

The rocky planets form near the Sun and the gas giant planets from further away. The dwarf planet Pluto orbits the Sun beyond the giant planets

Our Solar System

Our Solar System contains four inner planets (rocky/**terrestrial**), four outer planets (**ice giants** and **gas giants**), and an **asteroid belt** between Mars and Jupiter.

You can see five planets without the use of a telescope – Mercury, Venus, Mars, Jupiter, and Saturn.

Planets orbit (travel around) the Sun because of gravity, and so do comets. Earth takes 365 days to complete one full orbit of the Sun. Meteors and **meteoroids** do not orbit the Sun.

Gravitational field strength, g, varies with the mass of the planet.

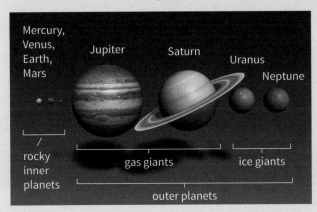

Earth, day, seasons

Earth spins, which explains day and night, and the apparent movement of the Sun and the stars. It takes 24 hours for Earth to complete one full spin. Earth is spinning steadily. It takes 24 hours to complete one spin. This explains:

- day and night; on the side of the Earth that is facing towards the Sun it is daytime. On the side that is facing away from the Sun it is nighttime.
- the apparent movement of the Sun and the stars. To us on the Earth it looks like the Sun and the stars are moving but it is actually the Earth that is spinning.

Earth orbits the Sun with a tilted **axis**, which explains:

- seasons
- why seasons are different in different **hemispheres**.

When the axis is tilted towards the Sun:

- there are more hours of daylight
- the Sun's rays are concentrated over a smaller area.

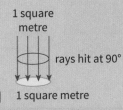

When the axis is tilted away from the Sun:

- there are fewer hours of daylight
- the Sun's rays spread over a larger area.

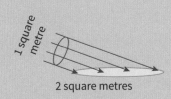

Key terms   **Make sure you can write a definition for these key terms**

artificial satellite   asteroid   asteroid belt   astronomer   axis   comet   galaxy   gas giant

P4 Space continued

Phases of the Moon

The Moon orbits Earth due to gravity. The Moon completes one full orbit in 27.3 days.

Half the Moon is lit at all times. The **phase of the Moon** we see depends on where the Moon is in its orbit.

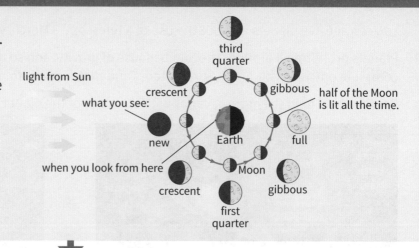

Solar eclipse

During a **solar eclipse**, Earth is in the Moon's shadow. Since the Moon's orbit is tilted, we do not get total eclipses every month.

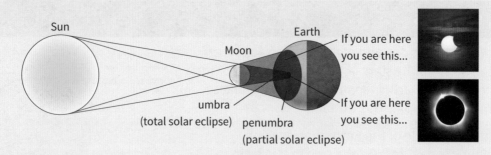

Lunar eclipse

During a **lunar eclipse**, the Moon is in Earth's shadow.

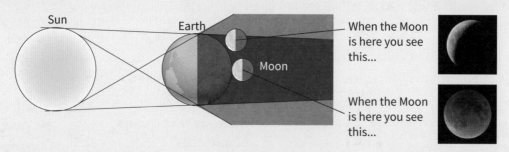

Key terms
Make sure you can write a definition for these key terms

hemisphere   ice giant   light-time   lunar eclipse   meteor   meteoroid   moon   natural satellite
planet   phase of the Moon   solar eclipse   solar system   star   terrestrial   Universe

Learn the answers to the questions below and test yourself.

P4 Questions / Answers

Our Universe

	Question	Answer
1	What is the Universe?	all the stars, planets, and other objects that are there/everything that exists
2	What is a galaxy?	stars and the solar systems around them
3	What is a solar system?	a star and the planets, moons, and asteroids orbiting it
4	What is a satellite?	an object that orbits a planet
5	What is a light-year?	the distance that light travels in a year

The Solar System

	Question	Answer
6	How did our Solar System form?	gravity pulled gas, rocks, and dust together to form the Sun and then the planets
7	Where is the asteroid belt?	between Mars and Jupiter
8	Name the force that makes objects move in orbits.	gravity/gravitational force
9	How long does it take the Earth to a) orbit the Sun b) spin once?	a) 365 days b) 24 hours

The Moon

	Question	Answer
10	How much of the Moon is lit up at any time?	half
11	How long does it take for the Moon to orbit Earth?	27.3 days
12	What is a full moon?	when the Moon is on the far side of Earth to the Sun, fully lit
13	What is a solar eclipse?	when the Moon is between Earth and the Sun, leaving a shadow on Earth

Put paper here

Previous questions / Answers

	Question	Answer
1	Give the equation to calculate weight.	weight = mass × gravitational field strength
2	In which direction do the vibrations in transverse waves move?	perpendicular/at right angles to the direction the wave travels
3	Name the group of bones in the ear.	ossicles
4	What happens to light when it is refracted?	it changes speed and bends
5	What does a red filter do to white light?	transmits red, absorbs all the other colours

Put paper here

Practice questions

1 There are many objects visible in the night sky.

a Which objects can you see without needing to use a telescope? Choose answers from the box. **[1 mark]**

the Moon   Venus   Neptune   Jupiter

_____

b Match each object to its definition by drawing lines. **[3 marks]**

Object
moon
solar system
galaxy
Universe

Definition
collection of stars and solar systems
all the galaxies, stars, moons, and other celestial objects
collection of planets and moons in orbit around a star
natural object in orbit around a planet

> **EXAM TIP**
> Start with the ones you are confident about and then see which ones are left at the end.

2 **Figure 1** shows the orbit of Earth around the Sun.

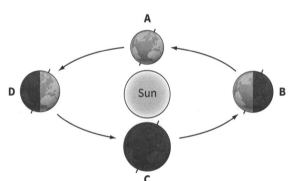

Figure 1

a Give the letter of the position on the Earth when it is winter in the northern hemisphere. **[1 mark]**

_____

> **EXAM TIP**
> It might help you work it out if you know that the UK is in the northern part of the Earth and it is winter when the axis in that hemisphere is pointing away from the Sun.

b Identify the **two** main reasons why it is hotter in the summer than in the winter. Tick **two** boxes. **[2 marks]**

Earth is closer to the Sun ☐

the axis of Earth is tilted away from the Sun ☐

the axis of Earth is tilted towards the Sun ☐

the Sun is in the sky for longer during the day ☐

> **EXAM TIP**
> Never leave these blank – tick two boxes even if you're not sure of the answer.

3 **Figure 2** shows an eclipse.

Figure 2

a Label Figure 2. Choose answers from the box. **[5 marks]**

Earth   Moon   umbra   penumbra   Sun

b Complete the sentence. **[1 mark]**

This is a diagram of a _____ eclipse.

4 Earth is part of the Solar System. Complete the sentences. Choose answers from the box. Each answer may be used once, more than once, or not at all.
[5 marks]

Mercury   Mars   Jupiter   Sun   Moon

The four inner planets include _____ and
_____.

The asteroid belt is between _____ and _____.

There is only one star in our Solar System, called the _____.

EXAM TIP

You don't need to list all four inner planets.

5 There are many objects that can be observed in the night sky. Five of them are listed below.

A   planet   D   asteroid

B   the Moon   E   space station

C   comet

Complete **Figure 3** by adding the letters to the Venn diagram. **[3 marks]**

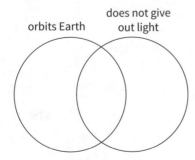

Figure 3

EXAM TIP

Just add the letters – don't try to squeeze the words in here.

P4 Practice   179

6 Compare the inner and outer planets of the Solar System in terms of:

a what they are made of [2 marks]

_____

_____

b the reason they orbit the Sun. [1 mark]

_____

_____

EXAM TIP

Compare questions need things that are the same and things that are different. The number of points will tell you how many things to write.

7 It is hotter on Earth in the summer than in the winter.

A student sets up an experiment to model the way light from the Sun hits Earth in summer and winter. They use two lamps, two trays of sand, and two thermometers, as shown in **Figure 4**.

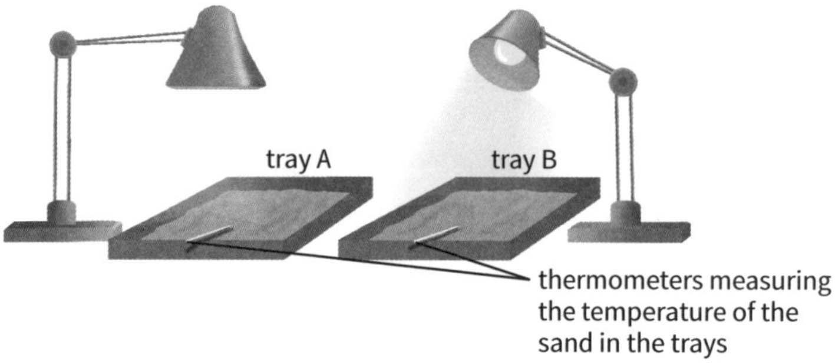

tray A   tray B

thermometers measuring the temperature of the sand in the trays

Figure 4

The student is investigating the effect of the angle of the rays on the temperature of the sand.

a Suggest **two** control variables in this investigation. [2 marks]

i _____

ii _____

b Suggest how the temperature in tray A will be different from the temperature in tray B. Explain your answer. [2 marks]

_____

_____

c Explain why the angle of the rays of light from the Sun onto Earth changes during the year. [2 marks]

_____

_____

8 Distances in space are often measured in light-time rather than metres or kilometres.

a Explain why light-time is a measure of distance and not time. [1 mark]

_____

_____

b The Sun, our nearest star, is 8 light-minutes away. The Moon is 1.4 light-seconds. It took the *Apollo 11* astronauts three days to get to the Moon.

Use ratios to estimate how many years it would take astronauts to get to the Sun (if they could do so safely). Use calculations to support your answer. **[5 marks]**

EXAM TIP

Look back at the Knowledge section for C3 – Chemical reactions – to see a worked example for using ratios.

_____ years

9 Galileo was an astronomer who observed phases of the planet Venus from Earth using his telescope.

Use your knowledge of the phases of the Moon to suggest whether phases of Earth would be visible from Venus. **[4 marks]**

EXAM TIP

This is a tricky question because we have not been to Venus to observe this, but we can make a good suggestion based on what we know from Earth.

_____

_____

_____

_____

P3 **10** A student uses a ray diagram to explain how a reflected image is formed in a shop window. **Figure 5** shows their diagram.

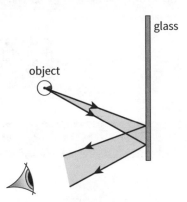

Figure 5

a Complete Figure 5 to show the location of the image. **[2 marks]**

b Explain why the image is a virtual image. **[1 mark]**

_____

c Sometimes you can see the image and the object behind the glass. Explain why, in terms of how light interacts with glass. **[2 marks]**

_____

_____

P5 Electricity and magnetism

Electrostatics

You can charge **insulators** by rubbing them on other insulators. This transfers **electrons**.

Atoms contain electrons, which have a **negative charge**. If you remove electrons from an object, it will have a **positive charge**.

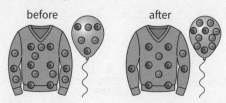

Like charges **repel**, and unlike charges **attract**.

Electric fields

Electric fields are regions around **electric charges** where a force acts on any charged object.

Electric fields:

- produce non-contact forces
- are represented by field lines
- are similar to gravitational and magnetic fields
- are strong where field lines are close together

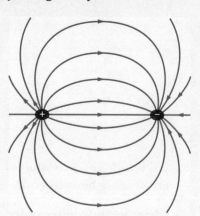

Electric current

Current is the flow of charge per second. It is measured in **amps (A)** using an **ammeter**. The symbol for electric current is *I*.

In metals, the charges are electrons. When you connect a **battery** or **cell** to a metal wire to create a circuit, the electrons move. This is because the battery produces a field in the wire that produces a *force* on the charges.

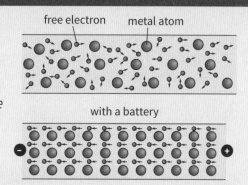

Circuit symbols

You represent components in a circuit with **circuit symbols**.

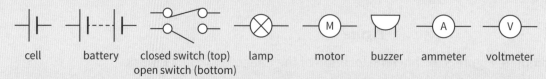

| cell | battery | closed switch (top) open switch (bottom) | lamp | motor | buzzer | ammeter | voltmeter |

Key terms

Make sure you can write a definition for these key terms

ammeter   amp (A)   atom   attract   battery   cell   circuit symbol
conductor   current   electric charge   electric field   electron   insulator
negative charge   ohm (Ω)   positive charge   potential difference (p.d.)
rating   repel   resistance   voltmeter   volt (V)

Potential difference

Potential difference (p.d.) is the energy transferred to the charges by the battery or power supply, or by the charges to the components. It is measured in **volts (V)** with a **voltmeter**. The symbol for p.d. is *V*.

On the cell circuit symbol, the long line is positive and the short line is negative.

A higher p.d. means a bigger current. A bigger current means more energy is transferred.

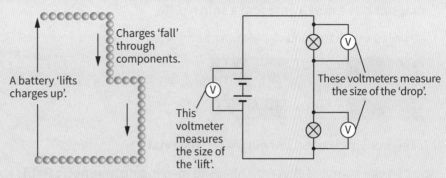

A battery 'lifts charges up'.

Charges 'fall' through components.

This voltmeter measures the size of the 'lift'.

These voltmeters measure the size of the 'drop'.

You can measure the p.d. of a cell, battery, or electrical component by connecting a voltmeter across it. This measures its **rating** – the change in energy transferred *to* (lift) or *from* (drop) charges.

Resistance

Resistance is a measure of how difficult it is for the current to flow. It is measured in **ohms (Ω)**. The symbol for resistance is *R*.

To find the resistance of a component, you measure the p.d. across it and the current through it.

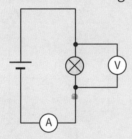

You then use this equation:

$$\text{resistence } (\Omega) = \frac{p.d.(V)}{current\ (A)}$$

$$R = \frac{V}{I}$$

Worked example: Calculating resistance

Calculate the resistance of a lamp with a current of 3 A through it and a p.d. of 12 V across it.

$$R = \frac{V}{I}$$

$$= \frac{12\ V}{3\ A}$$

$$= 4\ \Omega$$

You rearrange $R = \frac{V}{I}$ to

get $I = \frac{V}{R}$ and $V = IR$

Small and big numbers

1 A = 1000 mA (milliamps)   1000 Ω = 1 kΩ (kilohms)

$$1\ mA = \frac{1\ A}{1000}$$ $$1\ \Omega = \frac{1\ k\Omega}{1000}$$

$$= 0.001\ A$$ $$= 0.001\ k\Omega$$

Insulators have a large resistance and **conductors** have a small resistance.

Everything conducts if the p.d. is high enough, even the air.

Magnets and magnetic fields

A **magnet** has a **north pole** and a **south pole**.

Like poles repel and unlike poles attract.

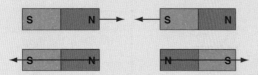

Nickel, iron, and cobalt are **magnetic materials**.

You can use compasses or iron filings to investigate **magnetic fields**. These are regions where magnetic materials experience a force.

small compasses

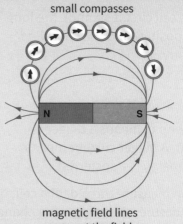

magnetic field lines represent the field

Series circuits

Series circuits have one loop. If one component breaks, nothing else works.

In series circuits, the current is the *same* everywhere.

The p.d. across each component *adds up* to the p.d. across the battery.

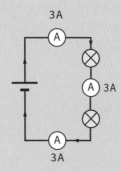

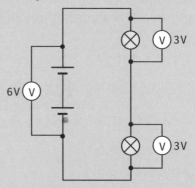

Parallel circuits

Parallel circuits have more than one loop (sometimes called branching circuits). If one component breaks, the other components continue to work.

In parallel circuits, the current in the branches *adds up* to the *total* current.

The p.d. across each component is the *same*.

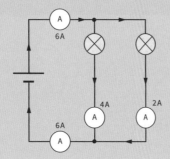

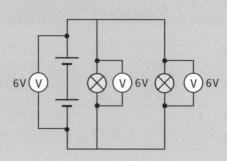

P5

Earth's magnetic field

Currents in the centre of the Earth produce a magnetic field around it. The Earth behaves as if there is a big bar magnet at its centre.

Compasses point north, so Earth's magnet has a magnetic north pole near the geographic North Pole.

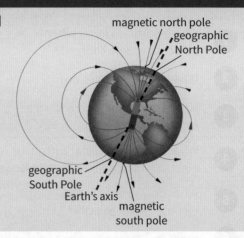

Electromagnets

There is a magnetic field around a current-carrying wire. The field gets weaker as you move away from the wire.

A coil of wire carrying a current is an **electromagnet**. It produces a magnetic field like that of a bar magnet.

You make the electromagnet stronger by:

- having more turns on the coil
- increasing the current
- using a core of magnetic material.

You can turn an electromagnet on and off. They are stronger than permanent magnets.

Electromagnets are used for lifting cars and trains, or in starter motors in cars.

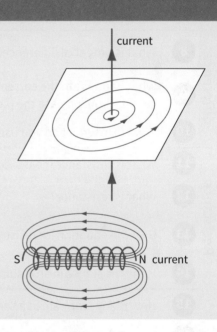

Motors

Motors spin because the magnetic fields of the coil and permanent magnet interact.

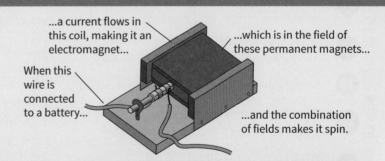

...a current flows in this coil, making it an electromagnet...

...which is in the field of these permanent magnets...

When this wire is connected to a battery...

...and the combination of fields makes it spin.

Key terms

Make sure you can write a definition for these key terms

electromagnet　magnet　magnetic field　magnetic material　motor
north pole　parallel　series　south pole

Learn the answers to the questions below and test yourself.

	P5 Questions		Answers
Charges	**1** Which particles move when objects become charged?	Put paper here	electrons
	2 What do like charges do?		repel
	3 Name the region where charges experience a force.		electric field
Electric current	**4** What moves in a metal wire in an electric circuit when a current flows?	Put paper here	electrons
	5 What do you need for an electric circuit to work?		a complete circuit, a battery
	6 What is current?		the amount of charge moving per second
	7 What instrument do you use to measure current?		an ammeter
Potential difference	**8** What is potential difference (p.d.)?	Put paper here	the size of the push on the charges from the cell or battery, the energy transferred to or by charges
	9 What happens to the current in a circuit if you increase the p.d.?		it increases
	10 What instrument do you use to measure p.d.?		a voltmeter
Resistance	**11** What is resistance measured in?	Put paper here	ohms (Ω)
	12 What is resistance?		the opposition to the flow of current in a circuit
	13 Give the equation for resistance.		$resistance = \dfrac{p.d.}{current}$
	14 Is the resistance in an insulator high or low?		high
Series and parallel circuits	**15** How many loops are in a series circuit?	Put paper here	one
	16 How many loops are in a parallel circuit?		more than one
	17 What can you say about the current at different points of a series circuit?		it is the same
	18 What happens to the brightness of bulbs in a series circuit if you add more bulbs.		the bulbs get dimmer/the brightness reduces
	19 What is the total current in a parallel circuit?		the sum of the currents in each loop
	20 What happens to the brightness of bulbs in a parallel circuit if you add more bulbs?		the brightness stays the same
	21 What can you say about the p.d.s across components in series?		they add up to the p.d. of the battery
	22 What can you say about the p.d.s across components in parallel?		the p.d. across each loop is the same as the p.d. of the battery

23	What is a magnetic field?		a region where a magnetic material feels a force
24	Name **three** magnetic materials.		nickel, cobalt, iron/steel
25	Name **two** ways to investigate a magnetic field.	Put paper here	iron filings, compasses
26	What shape is the magnetic field around a current carrying wire?		circular
27	What shape is the magnetic field around Earth?	Put paper here	same as a bar magnet
28	How do you make a simple electromagnet?		wind a wire around an iron core/nail, connect the wire to a battery
29	How do you make an electromagnet stronger?	Put paper here	more turns on the coil, bigger current, magnetic core
30	What is in a simple motor?		a current carrying coil in a magnetic field that can spin

(side labels: magnetic fields / Electromagnets)

Previous questions | Answers

1	What do waves transfer?		energy or information
2	What is a transparent object?		an object that transmits light (so you can see through it)
3	What happens to light when it goes from air to water?	Put paper here	it bends towards the normal/slows down
4	What is a light-year?		the distance light travels in a year
5	Why do we have seasons on Earth?		because Earth's axis is tilted

Practice questions

1 Particles can be charged. They can have a positive charge or a negative charge. If they have no charge, they are neutral.

a Complete the sentences about particles with charge by drawing lines. **[3 marks]**

Two positive charges will		a negative charge.
A positive and a negative charge will		repel.
Electrons have		attract.
Neutral means		no charge.

b Which is the correct definition of electric field? Tick **one** box. **[1 mark]**

the region where an object has charge ☐

the region where there is a balanced force on an object ☐

the region where a force acts on a charge ☐

2 Circuit components can be connected in series or parallel.

a Write the name of the component under the circuit symbol or picture in **Figure 1**. Choose answers from the box. **[5 marks]**

lamp   cell   voltmeter   motor   ammeter   wire

_____ _____ _____ _____ _____

Figure 1

> **EXAM TIP**
>
> What we think of as a battery is actually called a cell. A battery is really lots of cells all together.

Figure 2 shows four circuits.

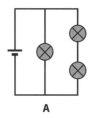 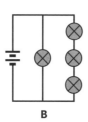 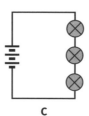 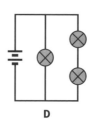

    A   **B**   **C**   **D**

Figure 2

b Give the letters of the parallel circuits shown in **Figure 2**. **[1 mark]**

_____

c Give the letter of the circuit where the current is the same everywhere. **[1 mark]**

_____

> **EXAM TIP**
>
> Parallel circuits are like ladders.

d In circuit C, the potential difference (p.d.) of the battery is 9 V. Identify the p.d. across each of the bulbs. Choose the answer from the box. **[1 mark]**

> 1.5 V   3 V   9 V

_____

3 Some materials are magnetic and can be used to make a magnet.

a Which of these metals is magnetic? Choose answers from the box. **[1 mark]**

> nickel   copper   iron   aluminium

_____

b Name a piece of equipment you would need to investigate the magnetic field around a magnet. **[1 mark]**

_____

c **Figure 3** shows the magnetic field between two arrangements of magnets. Write the label N or S in each of the four boxes in Figure 3. **[2 marks]**

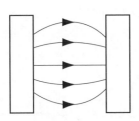 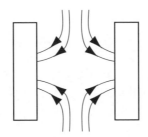

Figure 3

4 You can calculate the resistance of a component using this equation:

$$resistance = \frac{p.d.}{current}$$

A lamp has a current of 2 A flowing in it when the p.d. is 12 V.

a Complete the calculation. Choose the correct unit of resistance from the box. **[3 marks]**

> V   A   Ω

$$resistance = \frac{12\,V}{\rule{3cm}{0.4pt}}$$

= _____ unit _____

b Complete the sentences about conductors and insulators by choosing the correct words in bold. **[3 marks]**

Materials that are good conductors have a very **high / low** resistance. Materials such as **metal / plastic** are insulators and **do / do not** conduct well.

5 A student rubs a rod with a cloth so that both the rod and the cloth become charged.

a Explain why the rod and the cloth have opposite charges. **[1 mark]**

_____

b Use ideas about atoms to explain where the charge has come from. **[2 marks]**

_____

_____

c The student hangs up the rod by a piece of string. They charge another rod and bring it close to the first one. Suggest and explain what will happen. **[2 marks]**

_____

_____

6 A student makes an electromagnet. They wind a piece of wire around a nail and connect the ends of the wire to a battery.

a Suggest **one** statement they should include in their risk assessment. **[1 mark]**

_____

They change the number of turns on the wire around the nail and count the number of paperclips that the electromagnet can pick up each time.

b Name the independent variable. **[1 mark]**

_____

c Name the dependent variable. **[1 mark]**

_____

d Suggest **one** control variable. **[1 mark]**

_____

e Explain why they need to plot a bar chart and not a line graph. **[1 mark]**

_____

> **EXAM TIP**
>
> There are lots of ways to remember the differences – for example, 'I change the independent variable'.

> **EXAM TIP**
>
> Think about the type of data produced.

7 Electromagnets can have many uses, such as picking up cars in scrapyards. They can be much stronger than permanent magnets.

a Describe another difference between electromagnets and permanent magnets that would be useful in a scrapyard. **[1 mark]**

_____

Another use of an electromagnetic is in a window alarm, as shown in **Figure 4**.

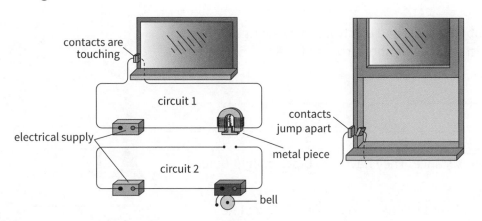

Figure 4

b Explain why the bell rings when the window is opened. **[4 marks]**

_____

_____

_____

_____

EXAM TIP

What will happen to the circuit when the window is opened?

8 A student wants to find the resistance of a motor. They connect the circuit, as shown in **Figure 5**.

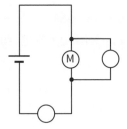

Figure 5

a Write V or A in the circles in **Figure 5** to show the correct meters. **[1 mark]**

b The motor has a current of 0.5 A flowing through it when the p.d. is 10 V. Calculate the resistance of the motor. Show your working. **[3 marks]**

EXAM TIP

Look back at the Knowledge section to see a worked example for calculating resistance.

_____

c Change the subject of this equation to give an equation for current. [3 marks]

EXAM TIP

Look back at Analysing and evaluating data to see how to change the subject of an equation.

_____

d Use the equation for current to explain the link between current and resistance. [2 marks]

_____

_____

e Explain, using ideas about atoms and electrons, why a longer wire has a higher resistance than a shorter wire of the same material. [2 marks]

_____

_____

9 A student is investigating resistance. They have two types of light bulb, A and B.

a When the p.d. across bulb A is 8 V the current is 4 mA. Calculate the resistance of the bulb. Show your working. [4 marks]

EXAM TIP

Look back at the Knowledge section to see a worked example for calculating resistance.

_____

b Bulb B has a current of 2 mA through it when the p.d. across it is 8 V. Use ratios to work out the resistance of bulb B. Do not do a calculation. Show your reasoning. [2 marks]

EXAM TIP

Look back at the Knowledge section for C3 – Chemical reactions – to see a worked example for using ratios.

_____

_____

c The student connects up bulb A and bulb B in parallel with the battery that has a p.d. of 8 V.

i Draw a circuit diagram showing this arrangement. [2 marks]

EXAM TIP

Always use a ruler when drawing circuit diagrams.

ii Write down the p.d. across each bulb. [1 mark]

_____

d Calculate the total current in the battery. [2 marks]

_____

e Explain why the total resistance of the circuit is less than the resistance of bulb A or bulb B. **[2 marks]**

_____

_____

10 A current flowing in a wire produces a magnetic field.

a Describe the shape of the magnetic field around the wire. **[1 mark]**

b Describe how the magnetic field strength changes as you move away from the wire. **[1 mark]**

_____

_____

P4 11 A student sees that the Moon seems to change over time. They see the Moon is completely lit.

a How long will it be before the student sees the Moon like that again? Circle the answer in the box. **[1 mark]**

day   week   month   year

EXAM TIP

You can go back to previous chapters to look up the answers.

b Name the force keeping the Moon in orbit around Earth. **[1 mark]**

_____

P3 12 A student investigates light. First, they use white light and a prism to produce a spectrum.

a Explain why a prism produces a spectrum. **[2 marks]**

_____

_____

Next, they shine light onto different materials and observe what happens. Three of their experiments are shown in **Figure 6**.

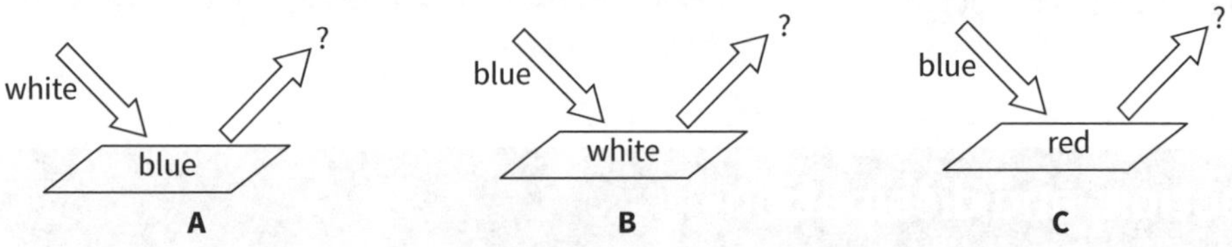

Figure 6

b Compare and explain what is observed in the three experiments. **[2 marks]**

_____

_____

c Describe, in terms of frequency, how blue light differs from red. **[1 mark]**

_____

Knowledge

P6 Energy

Energy and units

An energy store is a way of thinking about how much energy something has. It helps us to do calculations involving energy.

Energy is measured in joules. There are 1000 joules in 1 kilojoule (kJ).

Energy stores

kinetic	energy an object has because it is moving
gravitational potential	energy an object has because of its height above the ground
elastic potential	energy an elastic object has when it is stretched or compressed
thermal	energy an object has because of its temperature (the total kinetic and potential energy of the particles in the object)
chemical	energy that can be transferred by chemical reactions involving foods, fuels, and the chemicals in batteries
nuclear	energy stored in the nucleus of an atom
magnetic	energy a magnetic object has when it is near a magnet or in a magnetic field
electrostatic	energy a charged object has when near another charged object

Energy transfers

Energy can be transferred between stores by:

Heating
Energy is transferred from one object to another object with a lower temperature.

Waves
Waves (e.g., light and sound waves) can transfer energy by radiation.

Electricity
When an electric current flows it can transfer energy.

Forces
Energy is transferred when a force moves or changes the shape of an object.

Law of conservation of energy: Energy cannot be created or destroyed, only transferred between stores.

Conduction, convection, and dissipation

Temperature in Celsius (°C) or Kelvin (K) is a measure of the average *speed* of the particles. Energy in a thermal store is the total energy of all the particles.

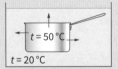

$t = 50\,°C$
$t = 20\,°C$

Temperature difference: energy transfer by heating

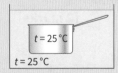

$t = 25\,°C$
$t = 25\,°C$

No temperature difference: **equilibrium**

Energy transfer to the surroundings: **dissipation**. Dissipation can be reduced by **insulation** or **lubrication**.

cooler liquid

Heating by particles
- in liquids and gases: **convection**
- in solids: **conduction**

warm liquid

Moving fluids produce **convection currents**

Start: Ball stationary at top of hill

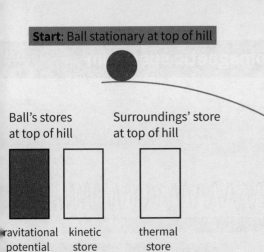

Ball's stores at top of hill

Surroundings' store at top of hill

gravitational potential store   kinetic store

thermal store

You can show how energy is transferred using a diagram. Define the start and end points of the transfer. Show which stores the energy is in before and after the transfer.

Transfer: Ball rolling down hill

Forces act on the ball, transferring energy between stores

End: Ball rolling at bottom of hill

Ball's stores at bottom of hill

Surroundings' store at bottom of hill

gravitational potential store   kinetic store

thermal store

Energy resources

Energy resource	Produces CO_2	Renewable	Reliable
Fossil fuels	✓		✓
Geothermal		✓	
Solar		✓	
Wind		✓	
Wave		✓	
Nuclear			✓

Power stations

Thermal power stations use fossil fuels, such as coal, oil, gas, or biofuels, such as wood. **Nuclear power stations** use uranium.

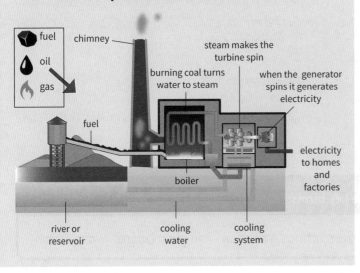

fuel
oil
gas

chimney

steam makes the turbine spin

burning coal turns water to steam

when the generator spins it generates electricity

fuel

boiler

electricity to homes and factories

river or reservoir

cooling water

cooling system

Key terms

Make sure you can write a definition for these key terms

chemical store   conduction   convection
convection current   dissipation
elastic potential   electromagnetic
electrostatic   energy resource   energy store
equilibrium   fossil fuel   gravitational potential
insulation   joule   kilojoule   kinetic
law of conservation of energy   lubrication
magnetic   non-renewable   nuclear
nuclear power station   renewable
thermal power station   non-renewable
nuclear   nuclear power station

Knowledge

P6 Energy continued

Radiation

- All objects emit infrared **radiation**.
- Hotter objects emit more.
- Heating by radiation transfers energy to a thermal store.
- Unlike conduction and convection, radiation transfers energy through a vacuum (space).
- All energy reaching Earth from the Sun is transferred by radiation.

The electromagnetic spectrum

| radio waves | microwaves | infrared (IR) | visible light | ultraviolet (UV) | X-rays | gamma rays |

increasing energy →

long wavelength over 10 000 m

short wavelength 0.000 000 000 000 01

← increasing wavelength

increasing frequency →

Work

$$\text{Work (J or Nm)} = \text{force (N)} \times \text{distance (in the direction of the force) (m)}$$

Work is done against a force, usually gravity or friction. The units of work are Joules (J) or Newton-metres (Nm).

Simple machines like **levers** and **ramps** reduce the force needed.

You can lift a box vertically upwards...

...it takes a force of **80N**...

...so you transfer 80J if you lift it up **1m**

Alternatively, you can push it up a ramp, and use a force of **20N**...

...but you have to move it a bigger distance...

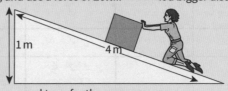

1 m   4 m

...and transfer the **same** energy because **20N × 4m = 80J**

Worked example: Work

A force of 20 N acts over 3 m. Calculate the work done.

Write the equation	work done = force x distance
Add the numbers	= 20 N x 3 m
Answer, with units	= 60 J or 60 Nm

Worked example: Work with changing units

A force of 20 N acts over 3 cm. Calculate the work done.

Write the equation	work done = force x distance
Add the numbers, remembering to convert to standard units, so 3 cm = 0.03 m	= 20 N x 0.03 m
Answer, with units	= 0.6 J or 0.6 Nm

Key terms

Make sure you can write a definition for these key terms

kilowatt   kilowatt hour   lever   ramp   power   power rating   radiation   simple machine   watt   work

Energy and power

Power is the energy transferred (or work done) per second.

$$\text{Power (W)} = \frac{\text{energy transferred (J)}}{\text{time (s)}} \quad \text{or} \quad \frac{\text{work done (J)}}{\text{time (s)}}$$

So: energy transferred (J) = power (W) x time (s)

Electrical appliances such as ovens and showers have **power ratings** of many **watts** or **kilowatts**, where 1kW = 1000W.

Worked example: Power

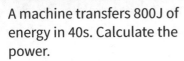

A machine transfers 800J of energy in 40s. Calculate the power.

$$Power = \frac{energy\ transferred}{time}$$

$$= \frac{800\ J}{40\ s}$$

$$= 20\ W$$

Worked example: Power with changing units

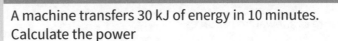

A machine transfers 30 kJ of energy in 10 minutes. Calculate the power

First change the units:

$$30\ kJ = 30\ 000\ J$$
$$10\ minutes = 10 \times 60\ s = 600\ s$$
$$power = \frac{energy\ transferred}{time}$$
$$= \frac{30\ 000\ J}{600\ s}$$
$$= 50\ W$$

Electricity companies calculate the energy people use by multiplying the power in kW by the time in hours to find energy in kilowatt hours (kWh):

$$\text{energy transferred (kWh)} = \text{power (kW) x time (h)}$$

You can reduce costs and save fuel by:

* reducing dissipation
* using lower power devices for less time.

Worked example: Power calculating cost

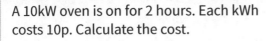

A 10kW oven is on for 2 hours. Each kWh costs 10p. Calculate the cost.

First, calculate the number of kWh.
$$Number\ of\ kWh = 10\ kW \times 2\ h$$
$$= 20\ kWh$$
$$Cost = number\ of\ kWh \times$$
$$cost\ per\ kWH$$
$$= 20\ kWh \times 10\ p$$
$$= 200\ p\ or\ £2.00$$

Worked example: (changing units) Power calculating cost

A 100 W light bulb is on for 15 minutes. Calculate the cost.

First calculate the number of kWh. Remember there are 1000 W in 1 kW, so 10 W = 0.01 kW. 15 minutes = 0.25 hours.

$$Number\ of\ kWh = 0.01\ kW \times 0.25\ h$$
$$= 0.0025\ kWh$$
$$cost = number\ of\ kWh \times cost\ per\ kWh$$
$$= 0.0025\ kWh \times 10\ p$$
$$= 0.025\ p$$

Learn the answers to the questions below and test yourself.

	P6 Questions		Answers
Energy stores and resources			
1	What is the unit of energy?		joule (J)
2	How many joules are there in a kilojoule?		1000 (one thousand)
3	Name the **seven** main energy stores.		thermal, nuclear, elastic, kinetic, gravity, electrostatic or magnetic, chemical
4	What is the law of the conservation of energy?		energy cannot be created or destroyed, only transferred between stores
5	What do we use fossil fuels for?		making electricity, transportation, and heating
6	What does non-renewable mean?		it will run out/cannot be made again
7	What happens if adults take in more energy from foods than they use?		it is stored as fat
8	Name **three** renewable resources.		any three from: solar, wind, tidal, wave, biofuels, falling water/hydroelectricity, hot rocks/geothermal
9	What does a thermal power station do?		burns fossil fuels to drive a generator to produce electricity
10	What is the main gas created from burning fossil fuels?		carbon dioxide
11	What happens when using a hydroelectric energy resource?		water falls down through turbines in a dam, spinning a generator
12	How can you use biomass to make energy?		burn it
13	Name **three** fossil fuels.		coal, gas, oil
Transferring energy			
14	What are the **two** ways energy is transferred by particles?		conduction, convection
15	How is energy transferred through a vacuum?		radiation
16	What **two** ways of transferring energy do not involve heating?		forces, electric current
17	What is dissipation?		transferring energy in a way we do not want or to a store we do not need
18	Energy is dissipated in any energy transfer process. Give **two** ways.		any two from: friction, air resistance, electrical resistance, heating the surroundings by hot objects
19	Name **two** ways to reduce dissipation.		lubrication, insulation
20	What, in terms of temperature, is equilibrium?		objects at the same temperature
21	What **two** units of temperature are used in science?		degrees Celsius and Kelvin
22	What does it mean if something is energy efficient?		less energy is wasted
23	What is the equation for work?		force × distance
24	What is the unit of work?		newton-metre (Nm) or joule (J)
25	Name **two** simple machines.		ramp, lever
26	Name **two** forces you can do work against.		friction, gravity

Put paper here

Energy and power

27	Write the equation for power (use energy and time).		$\text{power (W)} = \dfrac{\text{energy (J)}}{\text{time (s)}}$
28	How many watts are in a kilowatt?		1000
29	Write the equation to calculate the cost of energy transferred in a home.		cost = power (kW) × time (h) × price per kWh
30	Name **two** ways to reduce the cost of using appliances.		less powerful device, use it for less time

Put paper here

Previous questions | Answers

1	What do like charges do?		repel
2	What is a magnetic field?		a region where a magnetic material feels a force
3	What type of reflection happens from a rough surface?		diffuse scattering
4	What is weight?		the force of Earth on an object due to its mass
5	What does a blue book do to white light?		reflects blue, absorbs all the other colours

Put paper here

Exam-style questions

1 Quantities like energy and power have different units.

a Complete the sentences. Choose answers from the box.
Each answer may be used once, more than once, or not at all.

[4 marks]

1000	joule	100	10	watt	1 newton

> **EXAM TIP**
>
> Kilo is 1000, which is the same whatever the base unit is.

The unit of energy is the _____.

The unit of power is the _____.

There are _____ J in one kilojoule (kJ).

There are _____ W in 1 kilowatt.

b Complete this sentence. **[3 marks]**

The law of conservation of energy says:

Energy cannot be _____ or _____

only _____ between stores.

2 There are different types of energy resources.

a Which resources are non-renewable? **[2 marks]**

Tick **two** boxes.

> **EXAM TIP**
>
> Non-renewable types are the ones we burn.

water ☐

coal ☐

oil ☐

wind ☐

b Match the energy resource to its definition by drawing lines.

[3 marks]

Energy resource	Definition
hydroelectricity	movement of water through turbines twice a day
biofuels	water falling through turbines
geothermal	water pumped underground to produce steam from hot rocks
tidal	wood and other fuels that can be grown

c Name **one** other energy resource that uses water. **[1 mark]**

_____

3 Energy can be transferred between stores.

a Complete the sentences. Choose answers from the box. **[4 marks]**

> an electric current   forces
> heating by particles   heating by radiation

When you use a bicycle, energy is transferred by _____.

When you use an electric kettle, energy is transferred to the kettle by

_____. Inside the kettle, energy is transferred by

convection, which is _____. Energy is transferred from

the outside of the kettle by infrared, which is _____.

EXAM TIP

The last sentence is the easiest one to start with.

b Define dissipation. **[1 mark]**

_____

c You can reduce dissipation using insulation. Name another method of reducing dissipation. **[1 mark]**

_____

4 A person pulls a sled. They use a force of 20 N. The sled moves a distance of 4 m in the direction of the force.

work done = force × distance (in the direction of the force)

EXAM TIP

Look back at the Knowledge section to see a worked example for calculating work done.

a Which method of calculating the work done is correct?
Tick **one** box. **[1 mark]**

$\text{work} = \dfrac{20\,N}{4\,m}$ ☐

$\text{work} = 20\,N \times 4\,m$ ☐

b Complete the sentence. Choose the answer from the box. **[1 mark]**

> friction   less   gravity   more

When the person pulls the sled, they do work against

_____.

c Another student transfers 200 joules of energy in 10 seconds. Calculate the power by completing the calculation. **[3 marks]**

$\text{power} = \dfrac{\text{energy transferred}}{\text{time}}$

$= \dfrac{200\,J}{\underline{\hspace{1cm}}\,s} = \underline{\hspace{2cm}}$ unit _____

EXAM TIP

Look back at the Knowledge section to see a worked example for calculating power.

5 Energy can be transferred by conduction, convection, and radiation.

a Which statements are true?

Tick **two** boxes. **[2 marks]**

liquids are good conductors ☐

radiation is given out by all objects ☐

convection only happens in gases ☐

solids are good conductors ☐

EXAM TIP

Only tick two – any more and you'll not get any marks.

b Complete the sentences. Choose answers from the box.

Each word may be used once, more than once, or not at all. **[3 marks]**

> the same   dissipation   equilibrium   different

Energy is transferred between two objects that are at

_____ temperatures.

Energy will be transferred until the objects are at

_____ temperature. When this happens, we say

the objects are in _____.

c Describe the difference between a hot liquid and a cold liquid in terms of particles. **[2 marks]**

_____

_____

_____

_____

EXAM TIP

'Describe' questions want to know why something is the way it is.

6 A family is using coal to heat a room in their house. They use an electric cooker for cooking.

a Complete the sentences. **[4 marks]**

There is more energy in the _____ store of

the coal before they light the fire. When the fire has gone

out, there is less energy in the _____ of the coal

and more energy in the _____ of the

surroundings.

Energy is transferred by _____, and radiation.

EXAM TIP

You don't need to answer questions in order. Start with the line you find easiest.

b The electricity that the oven needs is generated in a power station.

Name these parts of a thermal power station: **[3 marks]**

i where water is converted to steam.

_____

ii where a potential difference is produced

_____

iii object that spins when steam moves through it

_____

c Describe **one** environmental impact of generating electricity using fossil fuels. Explain why fossil fuels produce this effect.

[2 marks]

_____

_____

> **EXAM TIP**
>
> Only one is needed here – any more will just waste time.

7 A student wants to investigate which colour can emit the most infrared radiation. They get identical cans and paint them different colours. They decide to pour boiling water at 100 °C into the cans and measure the time it takes the boiling water to cool to 50 °C. Answer the following questions about this investigation.

a Name the independent variable. **[1 mark]**

_____

b Name the dependent variable. **[1 mark]**

_____

c Name a control variable. **[1 mark]**

_____

d Describe **one** statement the student will need to include in their risk assessment. **[1 mark]**

_____

> **EXAM TIP**
>
> For a risk assessment, think about WHAT can hurt you; HOW it can hurt you; and what you can do to PREVENT it hurting you.

8 Foods contain different amounts of energy, and activities transfer different amounts of energy, as shown in **Table 1** and **Table 2**.

Table 1

Type of food	Energy content in J/g
pizza	11 000
chips	15 000

Table 2

Type of activity	Energy transferred in J/min
running	20 000
walking	5000

a Show that the total energy in 20 g of pizza and 20 g of chips is 520 000 J. Show your working. **[2 marks]**

> **EXAM TIP**
>
> Always show your working in case you make a mistake. You might get error-carried-forward marks.

b Calculate the number of minutes you would need to run to transfer 520 000 J. Show your working. **[2 marks]**

EXAM TIP

Look back at the Knowledge section to see a worked example for calculating energy transfer.

c Do you need to walk for a longer or a shorter time to transfer 520 000 J? Explain your answer. **[2 marks]**

9 **Table 3** shows the energy transferred by two kettles in one minute, which is 60 seconds.

Table 3

Kettle	Energy transferred in 1 minute	Power in W	Power in kW	Time to boil kettle in min
A	42 000			4
B	60 000			3

EXAM TIP

There are 1000 W in 1 kW.

a Complete Table 3 by calculating the power of each kettle in watts (W) and kW (kW). **[4 marks]**

b Use your answer to part a to explain why kettle B takes a shorter time to boil the water. **[1 mark]**

_____

_____

c Calculate the cost of boiling the water using kettle B. Start by calculating the number of kWh.

3 minutes = 0.01 hours, 1kWh costs 10p **[3 marks]**

EXAM TIP

Look back at the Knowledge section to see a worked example for calculating cost.

_____

_____

_____

10 Look at circuits A, B, and C (**Figure 1**).

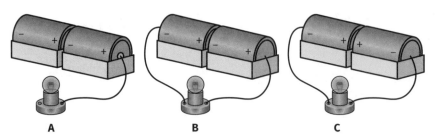

Figure 1

a State the letter of the circuit in which the bulb is lit. **[1 mark]**

_____

EXAM TIP

Look at the charges on the cells.

b Complete the sentences to describe what you could do to make the bulb light in the other two circuits.   **[2 marks]**

In circuit _____, you could _____

_____

In circuit _____, you could _____

_____

c Complete the sentences.   **[2 marks]**

A student adds a bulb to one of the working circuits.
The current in the circuit _____ because the resistance _____.

P1 **11** A cyclist is sitting on their bicycle at the start of a race. The dot represents the cyclist.

a Draw arrows to show two forces acting on the cyclist.

Label the arrows.   **[2 marks]**

●

b Describe the **two** interaction pairs that are producing the forces in part a.   **[2 marks]**

_____

_____

_____

c The cyclist rides at a steady speed for a section of the race.

Complete the sentence by choosing the correct word in bold and writing an explanation.   **[2 marks]**

We know that the forces acting on the cyclist are **balanced / unbalanced** because _____

_____

_____

P7 Motion and pressure

Speed

Speed is the distance an object travels in a given time. In science, speed is measured in **metres per second (m/s)**. You may also see speed represented in miles per hour (mph) and kilometres per hour (km/h).

You calculate speed using:

(L)
$$speed\,(m/s) = \frac{distance\,(m)}{time\,(s)}$$

In any journey, your **instantaneous speed** changes. So, we usually work out the **average speed**.

(L)
$$average\,speed\,(m/s) = \frac{total\,distance\,(m)}{total\,time\,(s)}$$

Typical speeds:

- humans walking: 1 m/s
- humans running: 3 m/s
- sound: 340 m/s

Worked example: Calculating average speed

Calculate the average speed of a cat that travels 20 m in 10 s.

$$average\,speed\,(m/s) = \frac{total\,distance\,(m)}{total\,time\,(s)}$$
$$= \frac{20\,m}{10\,s}$$
$$= 2\,m/s$$

Distance–time graphs

On a **distance–time graph**, the slope (gradient) of the line is the speed:

A horizontal line shows zero speed – the object is stationary.

A steep line shows a faster speed than a shallow line.

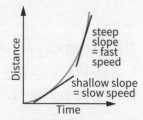

If the slope increases, the object is **accelerating**.

Worked example: Calculating speed

You can calculate speed from a distance–time graph. Calculate the fast speed in the final section of the graph.

$$speed\,(m/s) = \frac{distance\,(m)}{time\,(s)}$$
$$= \frac{30\,m - 10\,m}{14\,s - 9\,s}$$
$$= \frac{20\,m}{5\,s}$$
$$= 4\,m/s$$

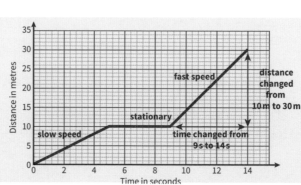

Relative motion

All speeds are relative (there is **relative motion**). Usually, speed is relative to the ground (which is not moving).

You can calculate your speed relative to a moving object:

- If you are travelling at the same speed and in the same direction as the moving object, your relative speed is zero.
- If the object is moving away from you, your relative speed is smaller than if the object is moving towards you.

Car B is moving at 10 km/h relative to Car A...

...but is moving at 110 km/h relative to Car C.

Pressure in gases

Gas particles collide with the walls of a container, producing **gas pressure**.

Pressure is bigger if:

- the temperature is higher
- the volume is smaller
- the **density** is greater.

Hot gas
Faster molecules
More collisions
Higher pressure

Cold gas
Slower molecules
Fewer collisions
Lower pressure

Large volume
Fewer collisions
Smaller pressure

Smaller volume
More collisions
Bigger pressure

Atmospheric pressure

Atmospheric pressure is the pressure exerted by the air.

It decreases with height because:

- there is less weight of air above it
- the air is less dense as you go upwards.

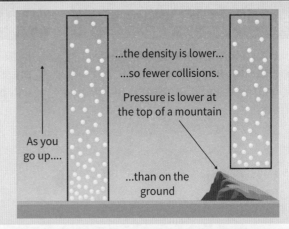

As you go up....

...the density is lower...

...so fewer collisions.

Pressure is lower at the top of a mountain

...than on the ground

Key terms

Make sure you can write a definition for these key terms

acceleration   atmospheric pressure   average speed   density   distance–time graph
gas pressure   instantaneous speed   metres per second (m/s)   relative motion   speed

P7 Motion and pressure continued

Pressure on solids

Pressure acts at 90° (normal) to any surface.

Pressure depends on the force and the area over which it acts.
The pressure will be large if a force acts over a small area.

You can reduce pressure by increasing the area.

Studs have a small area...

... which produces a BIG PRESSURE, so you sink into the ground.

Snowshoes have a BIG AREA...

...which produces a small pressure, so you DON'T sink into the ground.

Calculating pressure

You calculate pressure using:

$$\text{pressure (N/m}^2) = \frac{\text{force (N)}}{\text{area (m}^2)}$$

$$P = \frac{F}{A}$$

The unit for pressure is newtons per metre squared (N/m²) or pascals (Pa).

1 N/m² = 1 pascal (Pa). You can also use N and cm² to give pressure in N/cm².

Worked example: Calculating pressure

Calculate the pressure exerted on a desk by a 10 N block of area 0.2 m².

$$P = \frac{F}{A}$$

$$= \frac{10\,N}{0.2\,m^2}$$

$$= 50\,N/m^2 \text{ or } 50\,Pa$$

Pressure in liquids

Liquids are virtually **incompressible**. They exert a **liquid pressure** in all directions that is at 90° (normal) to the surface.

Upthrust

Liquid pressure explains **upthrust**. If there is a bigger pressure at the bottom of the object than at the top, there will be a net upwards force.

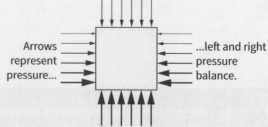

A smaller pressure above produces a smaller force...

Arrows represent pressure...

...left and right pressure balance.

... than the force from below, where the pressure is bigger.

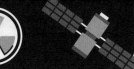
Turning forces or moments

A **moment** is a force that acts at a distance from a **pivot**. A moment has a turning effect.

You calculate a moment using:

moment (Nm) = force (N) × distance (m)

The unit of a moment is the **newton-metre (Nm)**.

If the clockwise moments are equal to the anticlockwise moments, the system will be balanced. This is the **law of moments**.

Worked example: Calculating moment

Calculate the moment of a 10 N force acting at 0.4 m from a pivot.

moment = force × distance
= 10 N × 0.4 m
= 4 Nm

Balanced systems

The seesaw is balanced because:

600 N × 0.5 m = 200 N × 1.5 m

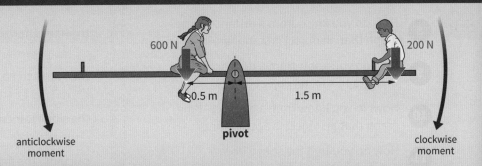

anticlockwise moment

600 N   0.5 m   **pivot**   1.5 m   200 N

clockwise moment

Worked example: Calculating balance

Work out if this seesaw is balanced.

clockwise moment:
500 N × 1.5 m = 750 Nm
anticlockwise moment:
400 N × 2 m = 800 Nm
No, this seesaw is not balanced. It will turn anticlockwise.

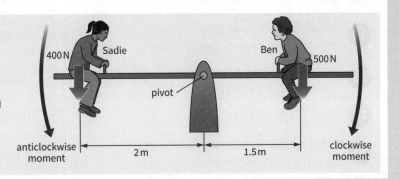

400 N   Sadie   Ben   500 N

pivot

anticlockwise moment   2 m   1.5 m   clockwise moment

Key terms   **Make sure you can write a definition for these key terms**

incompressible   law of moments   liquid pressure   moment
newtonmetre (Nm)   pivot   pressure   upthrust

Learn the answers to the questions below and test yourself.

	P7 Questions	Answers
Speed		
1	Give the equation for calculating speed.	$speed = \dfrac{distance}{time}$
2	What are the scientific units of distance and time?	metre, second
3	What is the scientific unit of speed?	metres per second (m/s)
4	Give the equation for average speed.	$average\,speed = \dfrac{total\,distance}{total\,time}$
5	What is instantaneous speed?	speed at a particular time
6	How do we describe an object that is speeding up?	it is accelerating
7	What is a typical walking speed for humans?	1 m/s
8	How do you know from a distance–time graph that an object is stationary?	the line is horizontal
9	How do you know from a distance–time graph that an object is fast?	the line is steep
10	How do you know from a distance–time graph that an object is accelerating?	the slope is increasing
11	How do you find the speed from a distance–time graph?	calculate the gradient/slope of the line
12	What is speed usually relative to?	the ground
Pressure in a gas		
13	Why do gases exert pressure?	particles collide with a surface
14	What effect does an increase in temperature have on gas pressure?	pressure increases
15	What effect does a decrease in volume have on gas pressure?	pressure increases
16	What is atmospheric pressure?	the pressure exerted by the air
17	What happens to atmospheric pressure as you go up a mountain?	it decreases
Pressure in a liquid		
18	Can you compress a liquid?	no, hardly at all
19	In which direction does water pressure act?	in all directions
20	What happens to liquid pressure as you go deeper in water?	it increases
21	Name the force exerted by a liquid on a floating object.	upthrust
22	When does an object float on a liquid?	when the upthrust is equal to the weight.
23	State the angle between a surface and the pressure exerted by a fluid.	90°

Put paper here

Calculating pressure	24	What is 1 pascal equal to?	$1\,N/m^2$
	25	Give the equation for calculating pressure.	$pressure = \dfrac{force}{area}$
	26	Name a situation where you want pressure to be big.	using a knife, studs on football boots
Moments	27	How do you calculate the moment of a force?	$moment = force \times distance$ (from a pivot)
	28	What is the law of moments?	if the clockwise moments equal the anticlockwise moments, the system is balanced
	29	What effect does a moment have on an object?	causes it to rotate or turn

Put paper here

Previous questions   Answers

1	How long does it take Earth to orbit the Sun?		one year/365 days
2	What do like charges do?		repel
3	What instrument do you use to measure p.d.?		a voltmeter
4	What is the main gas created from burning fossil fuels?		carbon dioxide
5	Name **two** simple machines.		ramp, lever

Put paper here

Practice questions

1 You can calculate the speed of an object. Complete these sentences about speed by drawing lines. **[4 marks]**

Average speed	m and km.
Instantaneous speed	is the speed at a particular moment.
The units of speed are	is the total distance over the total time.
The units of distance are	s and h.
The units of time are	m/s and km/h.

2 Complete the sentences about gas pressure. Choose answers from the box.

> higher   lower

[2 marks]

If the temperature is higher, then the gas pressure is _____.

If the volume of a gas is smaller, then the gas pressure is

_____.

3 Identify the everyday situations where the pressure on solids needs to be low. Tick the correct boxes in **Table 1**. **[2 marks]**

Table 1

Situation	Low pressure needed?
using football boots with studs	
using skis or snowshoes	
using a backpack with shoulder straps	
using a knife to cut vegetables	

4 **Figure 1** shows the journey of a car.

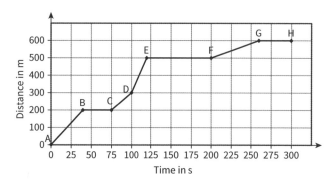

Figure 1

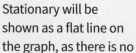
EXAM TIP

Stationary will be shown as a flat line on the graph, as there is no increase in distance.

a Give the letter(s) of the section(s) of the graph where the car is stationary. **[1 mark]**

_____

b Give the letter of the section of the graph where the car is fastest. Explain your answer. **[2 marks]**

_____

_____

c Calculate the speed of the car in section CD. Show your working. **[3 marks]**

_____ m/s

d Calculate the average speed of the car for the whole journey. Show your working. **[3 marks]**

_____ m/s

5 Forces applied to objects can make them turn.

a Complete the sentences by choosing the correct words in bold. **[8 marks]**

A **balanced / turning** force is called a moment, which you calculate by multiplying **force / mass** and **distance / time** from a **centre / pivot**. The unit of a moment is the **newton / newton metre**.

A seesaw will be balanced if the **anticlockwise / upwards** moments are equal to the **clockwise / sideways** moments. This is the **law / theory** of moments

Figure 3 shows a seesaw.

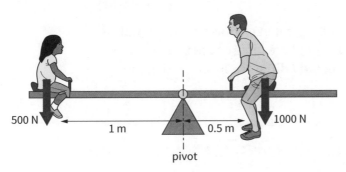

Figure 3

b Determine whether the seesaw is balanced. Show your working. **[4 marks]**

6 When people go up mountains, they can have problems because of the change in atmospheric pressure.

    a Describe how pressure changes as you go up a mountain. **[1 mark]**

    _____

    b Explain why the pressure changes. **[1 mark]**

    _____

7 A person is on a train travelling at 30 m/s. They observe a person on a platform walking towards them at 2 m/s.

    a Calculate the speed of the person on the train relative to the person on the platform. **[2 marks]**

EXAM TIP

Look back at the Knowledge section to see an illustration of relative motion.

    _____

    b Give the speed of the train relative to the person on the train. **[1 mark]**

    _____

P1 8 Two students are in a boat. The boat is floating on a lake.

    a One of the forces acting on the boat is the force of the students on the boat. There are two other forces acting on the boat. Complete the statements. Choose answers from the box. **[2 marks]**

water air Earth ground

    the force of _____ on the boat (gravitational force)

    the force of _____ on the boat (upthrust)

    b Complete the sentences about the force of the students on the boat. Choose the correct words in bold. **[4 marks]**

    Forces arise from **interactions / pulling** between objects. An example is the force of the students on the boat and the force of **the boat / Earth** on the students. These forces are **equal / different** in size and in the **same / opposite** direction.

P5 **9** A student sets up an experiment with an electromagnet. They plot the graph shown in **Figure 4**.

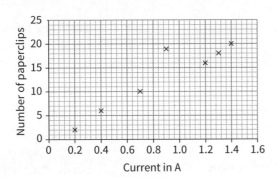

Figure 4

a Draw a line of best fit on the graph in **Figure 4**. [1 mark]

b Circle any anomalies, or write *none*. [1 mark]

_____

c Suggest **two** things the student did to get repeatable data. [2 marks]

_____

_____

d Write a conclusion for this experiment. [1 mark]

_____

e Suggest why the student should have plotted a bar chart not a line graph. [1 mark]

_____

> **EXAM TIP**
>
> Your line of best fit needs to go through most but not all of the points. This is not a dot-to-dot.

Glossary

absorb   Take into a material.

accelerate   When an object's speed changes.

acceleration   The amount by which speed increases in one second.

accurate   Data that is close to the true value of what you are measuring.

acid   An acid is a solution with a pH less than 7.

adaptation   Characteristic that helps an organism to survive in its environment.

adaptation (cell)   The structure and features of a cell that make it suited to carrying out a particular job.

addiction   A need to keep taking a drug to feel normal.

adolescence   The period of time when a child changes into an adult.

aerobic respiration   Chemical reaction where glucose reacts with oxygen to release energy, carbon dioxide, and water.

air resistance   The force on an object moving through the air that causes it to slow down (also known as drag).

alkali   An alkali is a soluble base.

alkali metals   Another name for the Group 1 elements.

alveolus   A structure inside the lungs where gas exchange takes place with the blood.

ammeter   A device for measuring electric current in a circuit.

amp (A)   Unit of measurement of electric current, symbol A.

amplitude   The distance from the middle to the top or bottom of a wave.

anaerobic respiration   Chemical reaction that takes place without oxygen. Glucose is converted into lactic acid and energy is released.

angle of incidence   The angle between the incident ray and the normal line.

angle of reflection   The angle between the reflected ray and the normal line.

anomalous result   A result that is very different from the other repeats of that measurement.

antagonistic muscles   A pair of muscles that work together to control movement at a joint – as one muscle contracts, the other relaxes.

anther   The part of a flower that produces pollen.

artificial satellite   A human-made spacecraft.

asteroid   Lumps of rock orbiting the Sun left over from when the Solar System formed.

asteroid belt   A region of space filled with asteroids.

astronomer   A scientist who studies space.

atmosphere   The mixture of gases surrounding Earth.

atmospheric pressure   Pressure caused by the collision of air particles that produce a force on an area.

atom   The smallest part of an element that can exist.

attract   Be pulled together, for example, opposite poles of a magnet attract, and positive and negative charges attract.

audible range   The range of frequencies that you can hear.

auditory nerve   An electrical signal travels along the auditory nerve to the brain.

average speed   The total distance travelled in the total time taken for a complete journey.

axis   The imaginary line that Earth spins around.

balanced (forces)   Forces acting on an object that are the same size but act in opposite directions.

balanced diet   Eating food containing the right nutrients in the correct amounts.

balanced formula equation   In a balanced formula equation, chemical formulae represent the reactants and products. The equation shows how atoms are rearranged, and gives the relative amounts of reactants and products.

bar chart   A way of presenting data when one variable is discrete or categoric and the other is continuous.

base   A base is a substance that neutralises an acid.

battery   Two or more electrical cells joined together.

bias   A preference for something or someone.

bile   Substance that breaks fat into small droplets.

bioaccumulation   The build-up of toxic chemicals inside organisms in a food chain.

biodiversity   The variety of organisms living in an area.

boiling   The change of state from liquid to gas that occurs when bubbles of the substance in its gas state form throughout the liquid.

boiling point The temperature at which a substance boils.

bone A tissue that forms a hard structure, used to protect organs and for movement.

bone marrow A soft tissue found inside bones that makes red and white blood cells.

camera A device that produces an image.

carpel The female reproductive part of the flower.

carbohydrase Enzyme that breaks down carbohydrates into sugar molecules.

carbohydrate Nutrient that provides energy.

carbon cycle The carbon cycle shows stores of carbon, and summarises how carbon and its compounds enter and leave these stores.

carbon store A place where carbon and its compounds may remain for a long time. Carbon stores include the atmosphere, oceans, sedimentary rocks, fossil fuels, the soil, and living organisms.

carnivore Animal that eats other animals.

cartilage The strong, smooth tissue that covers the end of bones to prevent them rubbing together.

catalyst Substance that speeds up a reaction without being used up.

categorical A variable that has values that are words.

cell The smallest functional unit in an organism – the building block of life.

cell (electrical) An electrical component that uses chemicals to produce a potential difference.

cell membrane The cell component that controls which substances can move into and out of the cell.

cell wall The plant cell component that surrounds the cell, providing support.

cementation The glueing together of sediments by different chemicals to make sedimentary rocks.

ceramic A non-metallic hard, brittle, heat-resistant material.

cervix The ring of muscle at the entrance to the uterus. It keeps the baby in place whilst the woman is pregnant.

change of state The process by which a substance changes from one state to another.

charge-coupled device (CCD) A grid of pixels at the back of a digital camera that absorbs light and produces an image.

chemical formula A formula that shows the relative number of atoms of each element in a compound.

chemical property How a substance behaves in its chemical reactions.

chemical reaction A change in which atoms are rearranged to create new substances.

chemical (store) Energy stored in food and fuels.

chemical symbol A one-letter or two-letter code for an element that is used by scientists in all countries.

chloroplast The plant cell component where photosynthesis takes place.

chromatogram An image obtained from chromatography.

chromatography A technique to separate mixtures of liquids that are soluble in the same solvent.

chromosome Long strand of DNA that contains many genes.

circuit symbol A simple diagram to show different components in circuits.

climate change A long-term change in weather patterns.

cochlea Snail-shaped tube in the inner ear with the sensory cells that detect sound.

combustion A burning reaction, in which a substance reacts quickly with oxygen and gives out light and heats the surroundings.

combustion reaction A chemical reaction in which a substance reacts quickly with oxygen and gives out light and heat.

comet Dust particles frozen in ice that orbit the Sun.

community The collection of the different types of organism present in an ecosystem.

compaction The process of squashing sediments together to make new rocks by the weight of layers above.

competition This happens when there are not enough resources available.

composite A mixture of materials with properties that are a combination of those of the materials in it.

compound A substance made up of atoms of two or more elements, joined together strongly.

compression The part of a longitudinal wave where the air particles are close together.

concentration A measure of the number of particles of a substance in a given volume.

condenser An apparatus where a gas changes state to a liquid

condensing Changing state from gas to liquid.

conduction A way in which energy is transferred through solids, and to a much lesser extent in liquids and gases.

conductor A material that conducts charge or energy well, such as a metal or graphite.

conservation of mass In a chemical reaction, the total mass of the reactants is equal to the total mass of the products. This is conservation of mass. Mass is conserved in chemical reactions and in physical changes.

conserved In a chemical reaction, the total mass of the reactants is equal to the total mass of the products. This is conservation of mass. Mass is conserved in chemical reactions and in physical changes.

consumer Organism that eats other organisms as food.

contact force A force that acts when an object is in contact with a surface, air, or water.

continuous A variable that has values that can be any number.

continuous variation Characteristic that can take any value within a range of values.

contraception A method of preventing pregnancy.

control measure Something you put in place to reduce the risk of a hazard causing harm.

control variable A variable that you have to keep the same in an investigation.

convection The transfer of energy by the movement of gases or liquids.

convection current The movement of heated liquids or gases.

convex (converging) lens A lens that produces converging rays of light (rays of light that come together).

corrosive A substance is corrosive if it can burn your skin or eyes.

crust The rocky outer layer of Earth.

current The flow of electrical charge (electrons) around a complete circuit per second.

cytoplasm A jelly-like substance found in cells, where all the chemical reactions take place.

DNA Chemical that contains all the information needed to make an organism.

data Words or numbers that you obtain when you make observations or measurements.

decibel (dB) A commonly used unit of sound intensity or loudness, symbol dB.

decomposer Organism that breaks down dead plant and animal material, returning nutrients to the soil or water.

decomposition reaction A chemical reaction in which a compound breaks down to form simpler compounds and/or elements.

deficiency A lack of vitamins or minerals, which can cause disease or poor growth.

deforestation The cutting down or burning of trees in forests.

deform To change shape.

density The mass per unit volume – how heavy something is for its size.

dependent variable A variable that changes when you change the independent variable.

deposition The settling of sediments that have moved away from their original rock.

depressant A drug that slows down the body's reactions by slowing down the nervous system.

detector A device used to receive and measure light.

diaphragm A large dome-shaped muscle that contracts and relaxes when breathing in and out.

diffuse scattering Reflection from a rough surface.

diffusion The movement of liquid particles or gas particles from a place of high concentration to a place of low concentration.

digestion Process where large molecules are broken down into small molecules.

digestive system Group of organs that work together to break down food.

directly proportional relationship A relationship where doubling the independent variable causes a doubling of the dependent variable.

discontinuous variation Characteristic that can only be a certain value.

discrete A variable that can have whole-number values only.

dispersion The splitting up of a ray of light of mixed wavelengths by refraction into its components.

displacement reaction   In a displacement reaction, a more reactive metal displaces, or pushes out, a less reactive metal from its compound.

dissipation   Energy that is spread out or 'wasted' by heating the environment.

dissolve   The mixing of a substance (the solute) with a liquid (the solvent) to make a solution.

distance–time graph   A graph that shows how far an object moves each second.

distillation   A technique that uses evaporation and condensation to obtain a solvent from a solution.

drag   The force acting on an object moving through air or water that causes it to slow down.

drug   Chemical substance that affects the way your body works.

durable   A property of a material meaning that it is difficult to damage.

eardrum   A membrane that transmits sound vibrations from the outer ear to the middle ear.

echo   A reflection of a sound wave by an object.

ecosystem   The name given to the interaction between plants, animals, and their habitat in a particular location.

egg cell   A cell containing female genetic material.

ejaculation   When semen is released from the penis.

elastic potential (store)   Energy stored when objects change shape

elastic limit   The point beyond which a spring will not return to its original length when the force is removed.

electric charge   A property of a material or particle that can be positive or negative.

electric field   A region where a charged material or particle experiences a force.

electromagnet   A temporary magnet produced using an electric current.

electromagnetic   The electrical and magnetic forces or effects produced by an electric current.

electromagnetic spectrum   The range of all types of electromagnetic radiation.

electron   A negatively charged particle found in atoms. Electrons flow through a wire when a current flows.

electrostatic force   The force acting between two charged objects.

electrostatic (store)   A store associated with the arrangement of charged particles.

element   A substance that cannot be broken down into other substances.

embryo   A ball of cells that forms when the fertilised egg divides.

emit   To give out.

endangered   When a population is small and at risk of extinction.

endothermic change   An endothermic change transfers energy from the surroundings.

energy   Energy is needed to make things happen.

energy resources   Materials or mechanisms for heating or generating electricity.

energy store   Something such as a food or hot object that enables you to account for the energy at the start and end of a transfer.

environment   The conditions found in a habitat.

environmental variation   The variation in characteristics caused by your surroundings and life experiences.

enzyme   Special protein that can break large molecules into small molecules.

equilibrium   Balanced.

equilibrium (thermal)   Objects are at thermal equilibrium when they are at the same temperature.

erosion   The breaking of a rock into sediments, and their movement away from the original rock.

ethanol   The drug found in alcoholic drinks.

evaporation   The change of state from liquid to gas that occurs when particles leave the surface of a liquid. It can happen at any temperature.

evolution   Development of a species over time

exhale   Breathing out, to remove carbon dioxide.

exothermic change   An exothermic change transfers energy to the surroundings.

extension   The amount by which an object gets longer when a force is applied.

extinct   When no more individuals of a species are left anywhere in the world.

fermentation   Chemical reaction used by microorganisms to convert glucose into ethanol, carbon dioxide, and energy.

fertilisation   The process where the nucleus of a sperm cell joins with the nucleus of an egg cell.

fertiliser   Chemical containing minerals, normally applied to soil.

fibre   Provides bulk to food to keep it moving through the digestive system.

field   A region in which an object experiences a force.

filament   The part of a flower that holds up the anther.

filter   A piece of material that allows some radiation (colours) through but absorbs the rest.

filtrate   The liquid or solution that collects in the container after the mixture has passed through the filter paper.

filtration   A way of separating pieces of solid that are mixed with a liquid or solution by pouring through filter paper.

fluid sac   Contains fluid. This acts as a shock absorber, protecting the foetus from bumps.

focal length   The distance from the lens to the focus (or focal point).

focus (focal point)   The point at which the rays refracted by a convex lens cross over.

foetus   The name given to an unborn baby from eight weeks of development.

food chain   A diagram that shows the transfer of energy between organisms.

food test   Chemical test to detect the presence of a particular nutrient in a food.

food web   A diagram showing a set of linked food chains.

force   A push or pull that can change the shape or movement of an object.

formula equation   A formula that shows the relative number of atoms of each element in a compound.

fossil   The remains of plants and animals that have turned to stone.

fossil fuel   Coal, oil, and gas made from the remains of trees and sea creatures over millions of years.

freezing   The change of state from liquid to solid.

freezing point   The temperature at which a substances freezes.

frequency   The number of complete waves or vibrations produced in one second.

friction   The force that resists movement because of contact between surfaces.

fruit   The part of a plant that contains seeds.

fuel   A material that burns to transfer useful energy.

galaxy   A number of stars and the solar systems around them grouped together.

gametes   Reproductive cells. The male gamete is a sperm cell and the female gamete is an egg cell.

gas   In the gas state, a substance can flow and can also be compressed.

gas giant   An outer planet in the Solar System made mainly from gas.

gas pressure   The force exerted by air particles when they collide with a surface.

gene   Section of DNA that contains the information for a characteristic.

germination   The period of time when a seed starts to grow.

gestation   The time from fertilisation until birth.

global heating   The gradual increase in Earth's mean air temperature.

gravitational field strength   The force of gravity that acts on each kilogram of mass.

gravitational potential (store)   Energy due to the position of an object in a gravitational field.

gravity   A non-contact force that acts between two masses.

greenhouse effect   The absorbing of energy by gases in the atmosphere, such as carbon dioxide.

greenhouse gas   A gas that contributes to climate change, such as carbon dioxide.

group   A vertical column of the Periodic Table. The elements in a group have similar properties.

guard cells   Cells that open and close the stomata.

habitat   The area in which an organism lives.

halogens   Another name for the Group 7 elements.

hazard   Something that could hurt you or someone else.

hemisphere   Half of Earth – either from the equator to the North Pole or from the equator to the South Pole.

herbivore   Organism that feeds on plants.

hertz (Hz)   The unit of frequency, symbol Hz.

hibernation   When animals sleep through winter in order to survive.

histogram   A way of presenting frequency data.

Hooke's Law   A law that says that if you double the force on an object, the extension will double.

hypothesis   What you think will happen in an investigation, with reasons using scientific knowledge.

ice giant   An outer planet in the Solar System made mainly of elements heavier than hydrogen and helium.

igneous   Rock made when liquid rock (magma or lava) cools and freezes.

implantation   The process where an embryo attaches to the lining of the uterus.

impure substance   A substance is impure if it has different substances mixed with it.

incompressible   Cannot be compressed (squashed)

independent variable   A variable you change that changes the dependent variable.

indicator   A substance that changes colour to show whether a solution is acidic or alkaline.

infrared radiation   Radiation given off by the Sun and other objects that brings about energy transfer.

inhale   Breathing in, to take in oxygen.

inherited variation   The variation in characteristics inherited from biological parents.

inner core   The solid iron and nickel at the centre of Earth.

insecticide   Chemical used to kill insects.

insoluble   A substance that cannot dissolve in a certain solvent is insoluble in that solvent.

instantaneous speed   The speed at a particular moment.

insulation   Materials that do not conduct electricity or transfer energy well.

insulator   A material that does not conduct electricity or transfer energy well.

interaction pair   When two objects interact there is a force on each one that is the same size but in opposing directions.

interdependence   The way in which living organisms depend on each other to survive, grow, and reproduce.

joint   Point where two or more bones meet.

joule (J)   The unit of energy, symbol J.

kilojoule (kJ)   A unit of energy, symbol kJ – 1 kilojoule = 1000 J

kilowatt (kW)   A unit of power, symbol kW – 1 kilowatt = 1000 W

kilowatt hour (kWh)   The unit of energy used by electricity companies, symbol kWh.

kinetic (store)   Energy of moving objects.

labia   Folds of skin around the opening to the vagina.

large intestine   Organ where water passes back into the body, leaving a solid waste of undigested food called faeces.

lava   Liquid rock that is above Earth's surface.

law of conservation of energy   Energy cannot be created or destroyed, only transferred between stores.

law of moments   An object is in equilibrium if the clockwise moments equal the anticlockwise moments.

law of reflection   The angle of incidence is equal to the angle of reflection.

leaf cell   The plant cells that contain chloroplasts, where photosynthesis takes place.

lever   A simple machine that multiplies the force.

ligament   Joins two bones together.

light-time   Distance measured in terms of how far light travels in a given time.

linear relationship   A relationship where increasing the independent variable causes an increase in the dependent variable. This is shown as a straight-line graph.

line graph   A way of presenting results when there are two numerical variables.

line of best fit   A smooth line on a graph that travels through, or very close to, as many of the points plotted as possible.

lipase   Enzyme that breaks down lipids into fatty acids and glycerol.

lipids   Nutrients that provide a store of energy and insulate the body.

liquid   In the liquid state, a substance can flow but cannot be compressed.

liquid pressure   The pressure produced by collisions of particles in a liquid.

longitudinal   A wave where the vibrations are in the same direction as the direction the wave moves.

loudness   How loud you perceive a sound of a certain intensity to be.

lubrication   A substance that reduces friction between surfaces when they rub together.

luminous   Gives out light.

lunar eclipse   An eclipse that happens when Earth comes between the Sun and the Moon.

lung volume   The volume of air your lungs can hold.

magma   Liquid rock that is below Earth's surface.

magnesium   A mineral needed by plants for making chlorophyll.

magnet   A material with a north and south pole that has its own magnetic field.

magnetic field   A region where there is a force on a magnet or magnetic material.

magnetic force   The force between two magnets, or between a magnet and a magnetic material.

magnetic material   A material that is attracted to a magnet, such as iron, steel, nickel, and cobalt.

magnetic (store)   A store associated with the arrangement of magnets.

mantle   The layer of Earth that is below the crust. It is solid but can flow very slowly.

mass   The amount of matter (stuff) a thing is made up of.

medicinal drug   Drug that has a medical benefit to your health.

median   The middle value, when the data are placed in numerical order.

medium   The material that affects light or sound by slowing it down or transferring the wave.

melting   The change of state from solid to liquid.

melting point   The temperature at which a substance melts.

menstrual cycle   The monthly cycle during which the uterus lining thickens, and then breaks down and leaves the body if an egg is not fertilised.

metal   Elements on the left of the stepped line of the Periodic Table. Most elements are metals. They are good conductors of energy and electricity.

metalloid   Elements near the stepped line of the Periodic Table are metalloids.

metamorphic   Rock formed by the action of heating and/or pressure on the sedimentary or igneous rock.

meteor   A piece of rock or dust that makes a streak of light in the night sky.

meteoroid   A small rocky or metallic body in outer space.

metres per second (m/s)   A unit of speed, symbol m/s.

microphone   A device for converting sound into an electrical signal.

microscope   An optical instrument used to magnify objects, so small details can be seen clearly.

migration   When animals move somewhere warmer or with more food.

mineral   Essential nutrient needed in small amounts to keep you healthy.

mitochondria   The cell component where respiration takes place.

mixture   A mixture is made up of substances that are not joined together chemically.

mode   The most common value or group in the data.

molecule   A group of two or more atoms, joined together strongly.

moment   A measure of the ability of a force to rotate an object about a pivot.

moon   A rocky body orbiting a planet – it is a natural satellite.

motor   A component or machine that spins when a current flows through it.

multicellular   An organism made up of many cells.

muscular skeletal system   A system of organs and tissues that allow animals to move.

muscle   Tissue that contracts to cause movement.

natural polymer   Polymers made by plants and animals, including wool, cotton, and rubber.

natural satellite   A moon in orbit around a planet.

natural selection   Process by which the organisms with the characteristics that are most suited to the environment survive and reproduce, passing on their genes.

negative charge   The charge on an electron, or on an object that has had electrons transferred to it.

nerve cell   An animal cell that transmits electrical impulses around the body.

neutral   A solution that is neither alkaline nor acidic. Its pH is 7.

neutralisation reaction   In a neutralisation reaction, an acid cancels out a base or a base cancels out an acid.

newton (N)   The unit of force, symbol N.

newtonmeter   A piece of equipment used to measure weight in newtons.

newton-metre (Nm)   The unit of moment, symbol Nm.

niche A particular place or role that an organism has in an ecosystem.

nitrates Minerals containing nitrogen for healthy growth.

noble gases Another name for the Group 0 elements.

non-contact force A magnetic, electrostatic, or gravitational force that acts between objects not in contact.

non-metal Elements on the right of the stepped line of the Periodic Table. They are poor conductors of energy and electricity.

non-renewable Some fuels are non-renewable. They form over millions of years and will one day run out.

normal An imaginary line at right angles to a surface where a light ray strikes it.

north pole The pole of a magnet that points towards the north.

nuclear (store) Relating to fuels such as uranium.

nuclear power station A power station that uses uranium as a fuel.

nucleus The cell component that controls the cell and contains genetic material.

obese Extremely overweight.

observation Looking carefully at an object or process.

ohm (Ω) The unit of resistance, symbol Ω.

opaque Objects that absorb, scatter, or reflect light and do not allow any light to pass through.

ore A rock that you can extract a metal from.

organ A group of tissues working together to perform a function.

organism A living thing.

organ system A group of organs working together to perform a function.

oscillation Something that moves backwards and forwards.

ossicles The small bones of the middle ear (hammer, anvil, and stirrup) that transfer vibrations from the eardrum to the oval window.

outer core The liquid iron and nickel between the Earth's mantle and inner core.

ovary (human) Contains egg cells.

ovary (plant) The part of a flower that contains ovules.

oviduct Tube that carries an egg to the uterus.

ovulation The release of an egg from an ovary.

ovule The female gamete of a plant.

oxidation reaction A chemical reaction in which substances react with oxygen to form oxides.

oxide A compound that contains at least one oxygen atom and one other element.

oxygen debt Extra oxygen required after anaerobic respiration to break down lactic acid.

pH scale The pH scale shows whether a substance is acidic, alkaline, or neutral. An acid has a pH below 7. An alkaline solution has a pH above 7. A solution of pH 7 is neutral.

parallel A circuit in which there are two or more paths or branches for the current.

particle The tiny things that materials are made from.

particle model A way to describe the movement and arrangement of particles in a substance.

pattern (trend) When the results follow a predictable direction.

peer review A process where the editor of a journal sends research to other scientists working in the field so they can judge whether the work is correct.

penis The structure that caries sperm and semen out of the body.

period (menstruation) Loss of uterus lining through the vagina.

period A horizontal row of the Periodic Table. There are trends in the properties of the elements across a period.

Periodic Table A table of all the elements in which elements with similar properties are grouped together.

phase of the Moon Shape of the Moon as we see it from Earth.

photosensitive A material that reacts when exposed to light.

phosphates Minerals containing phosphorus for healthy roots.

photosynthesis The process plants use to make their own food, glucose. In photosynthesis, carbon dioxide and water react together to make glucose and oxygen.

physical change A change that is reversible in which new substances are not made. Examples of physical changes include changes of state, and dissolving.

physical property A property of a material that you can observe or measure.

pie chart A way of presenting data when one variable is discrete or categoric and the other is continuous.

pinhole camera A model of a camera.

pitch A property of sound determined by its frequency.

pivot The point about which an object can turn or rotate.

placenta The organ where substances pass between the mother's blood and the foetus's blood. It acts as a barrier, stopping infections and harmful substances reaching the foetus.

planet A large natural satellite of a star.

plasma The liquid part of blood, which carries carbon dioxide to the lungs where it is exhaled.

pollen The male gamete of a plant.

pollination The transfer of pollen from the anther to the stigma.

polymer A substance made up of very long molecules.

population The number of plants or animals of the same type that live in the same area.

porous A porous material has small gaps that may contain substances in their liquid or gas states. Water can soak into a porous material.

positive charge The charge on a proton, or on an object that has had electrons transferred from it.

potential difference (p.d.) A measure of the push of a cell or battery, or the energy that the cell or battery can supply.

power The energy transferred (or work done) per second.

power rating The number in watts or kilowatts that tells you the rate at which an appliance transfers energy.

precise This describes a set of repeat measurements that are close together.

predator An animal that eats other animals.

prediction A statement that says what you think will happen.

pressure A force exerted on a certain area.

prey An animal that is eaten by another animal.

prism A triangular-shaped piece of glass used to produce a spectrum of light.

producer Organism that makes its own food using photosynthesis.

product A substance that is made in a chemical reaction.

property A quality of a substance or material that describes its appearance, or how it behaves.

protease Enzyme that breaks down proteins into amino acids.

protein Nutrient used for growth and repair.

puberty The physical changes that take place during adolescence.

pull A type of force.

pure substance A substance is pure if it has no other substances mixed with it.

push A type of force.

quadrat A square made of wire.

radiation The transfer of energy as a wave.

ramp A simple machine that reduces the force needed to lift an object by a certain height.

random error Errors that vary between one result and another.

range The difference between the biggest and smallest values.

rarefaction The part of a longitudinal wave where the air particles are spread out.

rating The value of potential difference at which a cell or bulb operates.

ratio A number that shows how many times bigger one quantity is than another.

ray A line used to model a beam of light.

reactant A starting substance in a chemical reaction.

reaction (force) The support force provided by a solid surface like a floor.

reactive A substance is reactive if it reacts vigorously with substances such as dilute acids and water.

reactivity series A list of metals in order of how vigorously they react.

recreational drug Drug that is taken for enjoyment.

recycling Collecting and processing materials that have been used, to make new objects.

red blood cell An animal cell that transports oxygen around the body.

reflect Bounce off.

reflection The change in direction of a ray or wave after it hits a surface and bounces off.

refraction The change in direction of a ray or wave as a result of its change in speed.

relative motion The difference between the speeds of two moving objects, or between the speeds of a moving object and a stationary object.

relative number The number of atoms of one type compared with the number of atoms of another type in an element or compound.

renewable Energy resource whose supply will not run out.

repeatable When you repeat measurements in an investigation and get similar results, they are repeatable.

repel Be pushed away from each other, for example, like magnetic poles repel, and like electrical charges repel.

reproducible When other people carry out an investigation and get similar results to the original investigation, the results are reproducible.

residue The solid that collects in the filter paper.

resistance How difficult it is for current to flow through a component in a circuit.

respiration A chemical reaction where food and oxygen are converted into energy, water, and carbon dioxide.

resultant force The single force that can replace all the forces, and which will have the same effect.

retina The layer of light sensitive cells at the back of the eye.

reversible A chemical reaction or physical change that can be reversed (changed back).

risk How you could hurt yourself.

risk assessment The process of identifying hazards and working out how to reduce the risks from these hazards.

rock cycle The rock cycle explains how rocks change and are recycled into new rocks over millions of years.

root hair cell A plant cell that takes in water and minerals from the soil.

salt A compound in which the hydrogen atoms of an acid are replaced by atoms of a metal element.

saturated solution A solution in which no more solute will dissolve.

scrotum The bag of skin that holds the testes.

secondary data Graphs or data that someone else has collected.

sedimentary Rock made from sediments.

seed The structure that develops into a new plant.

seed dispersal The movement of seeds away from the parent plant.

semen Fluid containing sperm.

series A circuit in which components are joined in a single loop.

sex hormone Chemical messenger that travels in the blood and causes the changes that take place during puberty and reproduction.

simple machine Lever or gear that reduces the force required to do something, but increases the distance.

skeleton All the bones in an organism.

small intestine Organ where small digested molecules are absorbed into the bloodstream.

solar eclipse An eclipse where all or part of the Sun is covered by the Moon.

solar system A star (for example, the Sun) and the planets and other bodies in orbit around it.

solid In the solid state, a substance cannot be compressed and it cannot flow.

solubility The solubility of a substance is the mass that dissolves in 100 g of water.

soluble A substance that can dissolve in a certain solvent, often water, is soluble in that solvent.

solute The solid or gas that dissolves in a liquid.

solution A mixture of a liquid with a solid or a gas. All parts of the mixture are the same.

solvent The liquid in which a solid or gas dissolves.

source Things that emit (give out) light or sound.

south pole The pole of a magnet that points towards the south.

specialised cell A cell whose shape and structure enable it to perform a particular function.

species Organisms that have lots of characteristics in common and can mate to produce fertile offspring.

spectrum A band of colours produced when light is spread out by a prism.

specular reflection Reflection from a smooth surface.

speed A measure of how far something travels in a given time.

sperm cell A cell containing male genetic material.

sperm duct Tube that carries sperm from the testes to the penis.

spread The difference between the highest and lowest measurements of a set of repeat measurements.

stamen The male reproductive part of the flower.

star A body in space that gives out its own light.

starvation Extreme case of not eating enough food.

states of matter The three forms in which a substance can exist – solid, liquid, and gas.

stigma The part of a flower that is sticky to catch grains of pollen.

stimulant A drug that speeds up the body's reactions by speeding up the nervous system.

stomach Organ where food is churned with digestive juices and acids.

stomata Holes found on the bottom of the leaf that allow gases to diffuse in and out of the leaf.

style The part of a flower that holds up the stigma.

sublimation The change of state from solid to gas.

substance A material that is not a mixture. It has the same properties all the way through.

superpose When waves join together so that they add up or cancel out.

synthetic polymer A substance made up of very long molecules that does not occur naturally.

systematic error A consistent set of errors in data.

temperature A measure of how hot or cold something is, measured in degrees Celsius or kelvin.

tendon Joins a muscle to a bone.

tension A stretching force.

terrestrial Made of rock.

testes Produce sperm and the male sex hormones.

thermal (store) Energy in objects as a result of the motion of their particles.

thermal decomposition A chemical reaction in which a compound breaks down when heated to form simpler compounds and/or elements.

thermal power station A power station that uses fossil fuels to generate electricity.

tissue A group of similar cells working together to perform a function.

trachea A large tube running down the throat and connecting the mouth and nose to the lungs.

translucent Objects that transmit light but diffuse (scatter) the light as it passes through.

transmit When light or other radiation passes through an object.

transparent Objects that transmit light and you can see through them.

transport Movement of sediments far from their original rock.

transverse The vibrations are at right angles to the direction the wave moves.

troposphere The part of the atmosphere nearest Earth.

ultrasound Sound at a frequency greater than 20 000 Hz, beyond the range of human hearing.

umbilical cord Connects the foetus to the placenta.

unbalanced (forces) Opposing forces on an object that are unequal.

undulation A smooth up and down movement.

unicellular Consisting of just one cell.

universal indicator An indicator that changes colour to show the pH of a solution. It is a mixture of dyes.

Universe Everything that exists.

unreactive Elements that take part in only a few chemical reactions are unreactive.

uplift Uplift happens when huge forces from inside Earth push rocks upwards.

upthrust An upwards force caused by the difference in air or pressure between the top and bottom of an object.

urethra Tube that carries urine or sperm out of the body.

uterus Where a baby develops until its birth.

vacuole The plant cell component that contains cell sap and helps to keep the cell firm.

vacuum A space in which there is no matter.

vagina Receives sperm during sexual intercourse. This is where the male's penis enters the female's body.

variation Differences in characteristics within a species.

vibration Backwards and forwards motion of the parts of a liquid or solid.

villi Tiny projections in the small intestine wall that increase the area of absorption.

virtual image An image that cannot be focused onto a screen.

vitamin Essential nutrient needed in small amounts to keep you healthy.

voltmeter A device for measuring voltage.

volt (V) Unit of measurement of voltage, symbol V.

volume The amount of space an object takes up.

vulva External parts of the female reproductive system.

water resistance The force on an object moving through water that causes it to slow down (also known as drag).

watt (W) The unit of power, symbol W.

wavelength The distance from the peak on one wave to the peak on the next wave.

weathering Weathering breaks up all types of rock into smaller pieces, called sediments.

weight The force of Earth on an object due to its mass.

withdrawal symptom Unpleasant symptom a person with a drug addiction suffers from when they stop taking the drug.

word equation A method of showing a reaction in a simple way. Reactants are on the left of the arrow and products on the right. The arrow means *reacts to make*.

work A way of transferring energy that does not involve heating.

Index

Group

Key

| Alkali metals | Halogens |
| Noble gases |

relative atomic mass
chemical symbol
name
atomic (proton) number

1.0
H
hydrogen
1

Period	1	2	3	4	5	6	7						3	4	5	6	7	0/8
1																		4 **He** helium 2
2	7 **Li** lithium 3	9 **Be** beryllium 4											11 **B** boron 5	12 **C** carbon 6	14 **N** nitrogen 7	16 **O** oxygen 8	19 **F** fluorine 9	20 **Ne** neon 10
3	23 **Na** sodium 11	24 **Mg** magnesium 12											27 **Al** aluminium 13	28 **Si** silicon 14	31 **P** phosphorus 15	32 **S** sulfur 16	35.5 **Cl** chlorine 17	40 **Ar** argon 18
4	39 **K** potassium 19	40 **Ca** calcium 20	45 **Sc** scandium 21	48 **Ti** titanium 22	51 **V** vanadium 23	52 **Cr** chromium 24	55 **Mn** manganese 25	56 **Fe** iron 26	59 **Co** cobalt 27	59 **Ni** nickel 28	63.5 **Cu** copper 29	65 **Zn** zinc 30	70 **Ga** gallium 31	73 **Ge** germanium 32	75 **As** arsenic 33	79 **Se** selenium 34	80 **Br** bromine 35	84 **Kr** krypton 36
5	85.5 **Rb** rubidium 37	88 **Sr** strontium 38	89 **Y** yttrium 39	91 **Zr** zirconium 40	93 **Nb** niobium 41	96 **Mo** molybdenum 42	(98) **Tc** technetium 43	101 **Ru** ruthenium 44	103 **Rh** rhodium 45	106 **Pd** palladium 46	108 **Ag** silver 47	112 **Cd** cadmium 48	115 **In** indium 49	119 **Sn** tin 50	122 **Sb** antimony 51	128 **Te** tellurium 52	127 **I** iodine 53	131 **Xe** xenon 54
6	133 **Cs** caesium 55	137 **Ba** barium 56	139 **La** lanthanum 57 *	178.5 **Hf** hafnium 72	181 **Ta** tantalum 73	184 **W** tungsten 74	186 **Re** rhenium 75	190 **Os** osmium 76	192 **Ir** iridium 77	195 **Pt** platinum 78	197 **Au** gold 79	201 **Hg** mercury 80	204 **Tl** thallium 81	207 **Pb** lead 82	209 **Bi** bismuth 83	210 **Po** polonium 84	(210) **At** astatine 85	222 **Rn** radon 86
7	(223) **Fr** francium 87	(226) **Ra** radium 88	(227) **Ac** actinium 89 #	(261) **Rf** rutherfordium 104	(262) **Db** dubnium 105	(266) **Sg** seaborgium 106	(264) **Bh** bohrium 107	(277) **Hs** hassium 108	(268) **Mt** meitnerium 109	(271) **Ds** darmstadtium 110	(272) **Rg** roentgenium 111	(285) **Cn** copernicium 112	(286) **Nh** nihonium 113	(289) **Fl** flerovium 114	(289) **Mc** moscovium 115	(293) **Lv** livermorium 116	(294) **Ts** tennessine 117	(294) **Og** oganesson 118

*58–71 Lanthanides

140 **Ce** cerium 58	141 **Pr** praseodymium 59	144 **Nd** neodymium 60	(145) **Pm** promethium 61	150 **Sm** samarium 62	152 **Eu** europium 63	157 **Gd** gadolinium 64	159 **Tb** terbium 65	163 **Dy** dysprosium 66	165 **Ho** holmium 67	167 **Er** erbium 68	169 **Tm** thulium 69	173 **Yb** ytterbium 70	175 **Lu** lutetium 71

#90–103 Actinides

232 **Th** thorium 90	231 **Pa** protactinium 91	238 **U** uranium 92	237 **Np** neptunium 93	239 **Pu** plutonium 94	243 **Am** americium 95	247 **Cm** curium 96	247 **Bk** berkelium 97	252 **Cf** californium 98	(252) **Es** einsteinium 99	(257) **Fm** fermium 100	(258) **Md** mendelevium 101	(259) **No** nobelium 102	(260) **Lr** lawrencium 103

OXFORD
UNIVERSITY PRESS

Great Clarendon Street, Oxford, OX2 6DP, United Kingdom

Oxford University Press is a department of the University of Oxford. It furthers the University's objective of excellence in research, scholarship, and education by publishing worldwide. Oxford is a registered trade mark of Oxford University Press in the UK and in certain other countries.

British Library Cataloguing in Publication Data

Data available

9781382040457

10 9 8 7 6 5 4 3

The manufacturing process conforms to the environmental regulations of the country of origin.

Printed in the United Kingdom by Bell & Bain Ltd, Glasgow.

Acknowledgements
The authors would like to thank the following:

Jo Locke would like to thank to Dave, Emily, and Hermione for all their support. Thank you also to Helen Reynolds whom it is always a pleasure to write with; I couldn't have done it without you. Finally, a thank you to everyone who has worked on this title and provided helpful ideas and advice.

Helen Reynolds would like to thank Michele, Rob, Lesa, and Bill for their never-ending support and encouragement and for lots of tea and for lovely long hikes in the desert. Many thanks to Jo Locke; it is always such a pleasure to work with you! I would also like to thank OUP for developing such an excellent series of books of which this is part, and to all those at OUP who worked to make this the book it has become.

The publisher and authors would like to thank the following for permission to use photographs and other copyright material:

Although we have made every effort to trace and contact all copyright holders before publication this has not been possible in all cases.
If notified, the publisher will rectify any errors or omissions at the earliest opportunity.

Links to third party websites are provided by Oxford in good faith and for information only. Oxford disclaims any responsibility for the materials contained in any third party website referenced in this work.

Cover: Michal Bednarski. Photos: **p19**: Kallayanee Naloka/Shutterstock; **p30**: T-I/Shutterstock; **p40**: Steve Gschmeissner/Science Photo Library; **p43**: Dr Jeremy Burgess/Science Photo Library; **p44**: Power and Syred/ Science Photo Library; **p54**: Scisetti Alfio/Shutterstock; **p62(t)**: Michael W. Tweedie/Science Photo Library; **p62(b)**: Natursports/Shutterstock; **p65**: Protasov AN/Shutterstock; **p70**: Andrew Mcclenaghan/Science Photo Library; **p91**: Migren art/Shutterstock; **p94**: Andrew Lambert Photography/Science Photo Library; **p102(l)**: Love Silhouette/ Shutterstock; **p102(m)**: Bjoern Wylezich/Shutterstock; **p102(r)**: Sebastian Janicki/Shutterstock; **p113**: Turtle Rock Scientific/Science Source/Science Photo Library; **p124**: M. Unal Ozmen/Shutterstock; **p133(t)**: Nutfield Chase/Shutterstock; **p133(m)**: Virrage Images/Shutterstock; **p133(b)**: Oleh Snitsar/Shutterstock; **p175**: MarcelClemens/Shutterstock; **p176(a)**: Warachai Krengwirat/Shutterstock; **p176(b)**: Elymas/Shutterstock; **p176(c)**: Nedelea Cristian/Shutterstock; **p176(d)**: Chris Harwood/ Shutterstock; **p208(l)**: Racheal Grazias/Shutterstock; **p208(r)**: BIGCHEN / Shutterstock.

Artwork by Michal Bednarski, Q2A Media, Integra Software Services, Aptara Inc., Erwin Haya, Phoenix Photosetting, Barking Dog Art, Tech-Set Ltd., Newgen, Six Red Marbles, Wearset Ltd, Peter Bull Art Studio, HL Studios, James Stayte, Edward Fullick, GreenGate Publishing Services, Thomson Digital, Jeff Bowles, Roger Courthold, Mike Ogden, Jeff Edwards, Russell Walker, Cliver Goodyer, Jamie Sneddon, Trystan Mitchell, Tech Graphics, and Pantek Arts Ltd.

Every effort has been made to contact copyright holders of material reproduced in this book. Any omissions will be rectified in subsequent printings if notice is given to the publisher.

MIX
Paper | Supporting responsible forestry
FSC® C007785